L.C. # 58-5620

1-14-59

THE
PHILOSOPHY AND POLICIES
of
WOODROW WILSON

THE
PHILOSOPHY AND POLICIES
of
WOODROW WILSON

Edited by

EARL LATHAM

for the American Political Science Association

THE UNIVERSITY OF CHICAGO PRESS

Library of Congress Catalog Number: 58-5620

THE UNIVERSITY OF CHICAGO PRESS, CHICAGO 37
Cambridge University Press, London, N.W. 1, England
The University of Toronto Press, Toronto 5, Canada

Preface

The program of the 1956 Annual Meeting of the American Political Science Association was organized around the two notable political events of that year: the election of one President of the United States and the centennial celebration for another. The theme for the celebration of the centennial of the birth of Woodrow Wilson was a new appraisal of his philosophy and policies. Many excellent papers were read. Some provided information about Wilson's work and writings, bringing to the attention of the discipline fresh insights of scholarship into events in which Wilson was a principal actor. Others took the already well-established record and reread it in the light of the dominant trends of the twentieth century in America and abroad, making new evaluations of the familiar. All heightened the appreciation of a famous president.

Some of these papers appear in this volume. Room has been given also to papers of scholars in other fields than political science who in 1956 appraised Wilson's life and works. Wilson wrote important books in political science and was president of the American Political Science Association in 1910, but his contributions to public affairs and their study even then broadly overflowed the banks of his academic specialty. Although political scientists perhaps should feel possessive about the only one of their craft to get to the White House, Wilson is one of the seven greatest American presidents on anybody's list; and a rounded view of his philosophy and policies invites the special contributions of historians, economists, and other writers and speakers. Accordingly, this volume contains a selection from the scores of essays about Wilson that were produced in connection with the centennial of his birth.

Cordial acknowledgment is made to the authors who gave their permission to include their works in this volume: Professor Arthur S. Link, Department of History, Northwestern University; Mr. Raymond B. Fosdick, Undersecretary-General of the League of Nations, 1919–1920;

10181

Preface

Professor A. J. Wann, Institute of Labor and Industrial Relations, University of Illinois; Professor Richard P. Longaker, Department of Political Science, Kenyon College; Dr. John Wells Davidson, Washington, D.C.; Professor Lester V. Chandler, Department of Economics, Princeton University; Professor John Perry Miller, Department of Economics, Yale University; Professor Arthur Macmahon, Department of Public Law and Government, Columbia University; Professor William L. Langer, Department of History, Harvard University; Dr. Charles Seymour, President Emeritus, Yale University; Professor Robert E. Osgood, Department of Political Science, University of Chicago; Professor Roland Young, Department of Political Science, Northwestern University; Dr. George B. Galloway, Legislative Reference Service, Library of Congress; Dr. Marshall Dimock, Scrivelsby, Vermont; and Mr. August Heckscher, president of the Twentieth Century Fund.

Special acknowledgment is due August Heckscher of the Twentieth Century Fund and Mrs. Julie d'Estournelles, executive director of the Woodrow Wilson Foundation, for their interest and help in the publication of this volume; and the Woodrow Wilson Foundation for its grant to the American Political Science Association to aid in the preparation and publication of this book.

There must always be regret when fine articles which deserve to be published cannot be included in a volume where they would be appropriate. Special mention should be made of two which had to be left out of this volume for reasons of space. The first is "Woodrow Wilson and the League of Nations" by Professor Quincy Wright, Department of Political Science, University of Chicago. The second is "The Role of the Preliminary Peace Treaty" by Professor Kurt Wimer, East Stroudsburg State Teachers College, East Stroudsburg, Pennsylvania. Both these papers were scholarly contributions to the meetings of the American Political Science Association in Washington, September, 1956.

Table of Contents

Table of Contents

Introduction

As Charles Seymour reminds us in a quotation from Wilson's address on leaders of men, Wilson gave great weight to the influence of the individual leader upon his times: "Great reformers," said Wilson, "do not, indeed, observe times and circumstances. Theirs is not a service of opportunity. They have no thought for occasion, no capacity for compromise. They are early vehicles of the Spirit of the Age. They are born of the very times that oppose them." This early confidence of Woodrow Wilson was strong and his faith in his mission as a leader heroic in its tendency and amplitude. Others, however, have been more tentative in their judgments about leadership, and the question is still unsettled whether any given social event is produced by a single man or occurs by force of the very circumstances that give him distinction. It is one of the manifold forms of the ancient problem of the one and the many, to whose solution philosophy and history have contributed many contradictory pairs, among them, Plutarch and Buckle, Carlyle and Tolstoi, Nietzsche and Marx.

What if Theodore Roosevelt—or Taft—had won the election of 1912? Would the development of economic controls by new agencies like the Federal Trade Commission and the Federal Reserve Board have taken place? If Wilson had lost the election of 1916, would the United States have gone to war? These questions, so put, imply affirmative answers and perhaps the economic controls would eventually have materialized and the war would have been fought and won, no matter who was in the White House. Lester V. Chandler and John Perry Miller both feel that the economic controls came when they did because Wilson was there, and this is the course of most opinion on the matter.

Egocentric explanations of historical events are not necessarily false just because every event is somehow or other connected subliminally with every other event in series of actions which may or may not be

Introduction

"free." Carlyle said that history is "the essence of innumerable Biographies." If the biographies are really innumerable, of course, one ends with the whole people, and the controversy between the partisans of the one and the partisans of the many is moot. But even if one should reject the view of history as biography, it is clear that biographies are important, and some are more important than others. The biography of Woodrow Wilson is certainly of close relevance to an understanding of America in the twentieth century because of the leverage he had, supported by the reinforcing institutions of law and politics, to press policy upon people and events, whether he, in fact, moved them or not.

One of the distinctive aspects of Wilson's biography is the fact that he was an intellectual in politics, a role to which the American culture has not been particularly hospitable. Arthur Link has suggested that Wilson was not really an intellectual "in the ordinary sense of that word" but that he was "most assuredly a creature of brains," saved from pedantry by "the enormous activity of his mind—the constant play of his imagination and his absorption in ideas that could be put to use in the world of practical affairs." Practical intelligence and intellectuality—perhaps the difference is that the first leaves the study to mix with the crowd while the second stays at home. Marshall Dimock, however, rather implies that cerebration usually involves aloofness from the crowd when he says that "Woodrow Wilson, although an intellectual, understood the minds and aspirations of the common people as few political leaders ever have, before or since." The combination in the same man of enormous mental activity, imagination, and ideas, with an understanding of common people, therefore, may qualify Wilson as an intellectual in an extraordinary sense of that word.

Wilson's novelty was not that he was an intellectual but that he was an intellectual in politics at the time in which he ran for office. Intellectuals—even in Link's "ordinary sense": the writers, poets, essayists, philosophers, and academic scholars—had played important parts in the history of the country before the Civil War, notably during the years of the Revolution, during the controversies over the establishment of a new and enduring republic, and in the years immediately preceding the Civil War. One needs only remember Emerson, Whittier, Thoreau, and Longfellow among the many who were in the thick of the hot and bitter political controversies over slavery.

But the years before the Civil War were "pre-industrial," a time

Introduction

when the dominant ethic, the prevailing social code, had not yet been set by the business community and its leaders, whose vogue as culture heroes was still to come. With the widespread acceptance in America of the values of a business society, the climate for participation in the principal social activities chilled intellectuals, and although they did not default their natural function as critics, few found time for, or even inclination toward, struggle in the market places and the precincts. Some took flight. Henry James preceded T. S. Eliot and many others to England, and the 1920's heard noisy abjurations of the American realm.

But from the 1890's to the Great Depression, most intellectuals remained at home and limited themselves to criticism of the economy and its works—some, like William Dean Howells, without real grasp of the economy but repelled by some of its products, some, like Frank Norris and Upton Sinclair, with a morbid fixation on its verifiable horrors. A few saw society as a Darwinian jungle in which rabbits and tigers could scarcely help their natures, but a Veblen preferred to think that men were less deterministically moved, and he talked of captains and engineers as people, not blind forces. Political involvement among the intellectuals was fairly narrowly confined to literary agitation for farmers and unions in the Populist years and to agitation against business values, municipal corruption, and slums in the terms of Theodore Roosevelt. But intellectuals were not actively *in* politics, and although Edward Bellamy was capable of fashioning a paper utopia, the urge to move in active political affairs was evidently not ungovernable.

It was not until the collapse of the economy in 1929 and the advent of a new social and political spirit in the administrations of Franklin Roosevelt that social intelligence was to become respectable, if not fashionable; or fashionable, if not respectable. For six decades and more, intellectuals had rejected politics, as had many of the populace on whose fringes they lived, as a means of achieving goals of personal aspiration. Americans had hardened the philosophy of individual attainment and personal value into the parody of individualism contained in the mottoes of boosterism. The paradoxical thread of these pronouncements was hostility to political institutions as agencies for the support of individual goals. With the collapse of economic institutions, the use of planned intelligence for social reform and economic betterment received some of the prestige that had been monopolized by industry, and intellectuals found practical uses for their skills.

Introduction

It is too much to say, of course, that Woodrow Wilson brought the intellectual into politics, although his was a spectacular success. Having run for only two offices in his life and been elected to both, first as governor of New Jersey and then as President of the United States, Wilson may fairly be said to have set records for a political career that it will always be hard to beat. But it goes a bit too far to give him credit for leading the intellectual into the political affairs of his society. Although Wilson had a spectacular success in winning high office without the apprenticeship usually thought to be necessary, he did not in fact motivate large numbers to follow his somewhat special example. The interest in politics shown by intellectuals in the 1930's and later can be attributed to other, more obvious reasons than the possible example of a dead President. What Wilson actually did was to symbolize in his career a change in social habit which others did not immediately imitate, which prefigured but did not "cause" later successes, but which represented the addition of certain necessary and desirable accretions of intelligent energy too often alienated by habit and prejudice from the main body of social talent.

This intelligent energy was democratic in its commitment. Wilson in fact strongly mistrusted certain forms of expert intelligence, unleavened by connection with or sympathy for the generality of the people. As John Wells Davidson points out, Wilson denounced as undemocratic the suggestion that experts might govern as experts. In the Labor Day speech in the campaign of 1912, Davidson reports Wilson as saying, "What I fear, therefore, is a government of experts. God forbid that in a democratic country we should resign the task and give the government over to experts. What are we for if we are to be scientifically taken care of by a small number of gentlemen who are the only men who understand the job? Because if we don't understand the job, then we are not a free people."

This point of view is that of the democrat. It is not that of intellectuals who lack democratic dedication—critics for whom there are no heresies and who are capable of talking about and taking seriously, for the time at least, any challenging set of first principles, replacing them at will. Wilson's intellectual perceptions were those of the liberal middle-class citizen; that is, his thinking was informed by a working knowledge of public affairs, unified by a conviction about the interconnections of things, distinguished by the cultivation of individual values, given transcendent meaning by a strong religious dedication. Wilson's vision and his theory were in accord, his vision of society and his role in it, on the one hand, and the philosophical and social theory through which he applied his intellectual energy to its problems, on the other.

This stability of intellectual commitment was fortunate for Wilson's own tranquillity, at least, when one considers the conversions from Stalinism, to Trotskyism, to De Gaullism, to latter-day De Maistrean revelation which characterized the unhinged thought of some in the 1930's and later. Wilson has been called "the conservative as liberal," and it is the combination of Burke and Brandeis in a stable mixture that gave Wilson not only the flair for reform but the footing in reality it needs to be effective. Measured by the pieties of doctrinaires, Wilson's social goals were modest. The intellectualism he represented in politics was neither proletarian, bohemian, nor unbuttoned, but modest, respectable, and moral.

Wilson's program was intervention by government between pluto-crats and people, to curb the excesses of the first and to moderate the discontents of the second. In the detail of this program Wilson was "liberal" in economic matters and "conservative" in moral ones. His campaign against the trusts, the reorganization of the banking system, tariff reform, farm supports, hours statutes, child-labor legislation, the attempted limitation of the use of the injunction in labor disputes—these were liberal middle-class measures designed to inhibit the power of business over the commonwealth and the economy, to succor the small enterpriser, and to save the weak and the poor from the excesses of industrialism. In certain other aspects of policy Wilson would not have qualified as a liberal at all by post–New Deal standards. It was Wilson's Department of Justice that rigorously enforced the Espionage and Sedition Acts of 1917 and 1918. It was Wilson's Postmaster-General who closed the mails to literature that later critics were to say was neither objectionably subversive nor in fact obstructive to the war effort. It was Wilson who, as Laski said to Holmes, aroused "my sense of passionate indignation at his refusal to pardon Debs." It was Wilson, as Arthur Link shows, who allowed his Cabinet members to introduce segregation and defended them from attack.

But although conservative in matters of political morality, Wilson was by no means a Conservative in the European sense, in the line that moves through such anti-Enlightenment spirits as Bonald, De Maistre, Carlyle, and Baudelaire. Only a few in American politics—and Wilson was not among them—have publicly supported a view of life that exalts the irrational, finds security in ultramontane orientations, feels that the cosmic order is fixed, unyielding, and implacable, and sees change only as organic growth, to be neither hurried, helped, nor delayed. This kind of conservatism has never had strong roots in America for the reasons stated by De Tocqueville and repeated frequently thereafter. With no feudal class of landed aristocrats in the colonies, the American was born free; and there is a sense in which all are liberals, occupying the great middle ground of social commitment and crowding out the apocalyptic orators of the left and the radicals of the right.

Woodrow Wilson's career contradicts the assertion that intellectuals have no role to play in American politics on the supposition that American politics is devoid of intellectual content, parties are without ideology, and their programs are indistinguishable. It is sometimes only the "imagination of disaster" which seems vivid enough to preoccupy intellectuals who find American liberal politics dull, with nothing less than catastrophic reconstructions capable of engaging the attention. They may agree to set about the recovery of reason in society by serving as what Charles Frankel calls "the class with the right attitude." Otherwise the political role must be rejected; the speaking part is too small and the stage business is too closely controlled in a script written by the successful experience of a political system which has mediated the tensions of plural culture groups without the mystique of violence cultivated in such centers of messianic politics as Berlin, Rome, and Moscow.

But problems that challenge the best intellects should not lack for attention because they do not lend themselves to universal prescriptions. The view has been expressed in the 1950's that there are no more economic problems to solve—as in the 1930's—and that liberals might turn their attention to the salvage of the liberal spirit from the suffocations of a mass culture. This advice proceeds from a rather narrow assumption about the nature of the liberal mission. However much criticism of the culture may be needed, the liberal concern with the economy is not ended with the enactment of a dollar-an-hour minimum wage. Wilson would not have thought so, and his heirs today abdicate their function by acting as though they did.

In fact, some of the principal issues in the program of Woodrow Wilson, in new forms and fresh guises, await the application of earnest attention by intellectuals either with or without the co-operation of liberal democratic politicians. Wilson attacked corporate collectivism in 1912 in his campaign against the trusts, not only because it contributed to monopoly, but because it was capable of imposing corporate values on all phases of life through extensive programs of welfare. Wilson recognized the "organization man" at least four decades before later writers gave him a name. And in the field of foreign affairs, the range of interest and challenge is quite literally world-wide. Wilson's moral diplomacy, with all its shortcomings, might have important new applications in these years of ideological competition.

Woodrow Wilson, therefore, is not only an exemplar of the intellectual in political life, but he stands also for the best in the American liberal tradition. This tradition rates high the integrity of common men, the improvability of social life, the value of the human personality, and the use of social techniques to promote these ideals. It moves by the patient adjustment of interest upon interest and makes life viable through toleration and compromise, which are not pejorative words except for those who generalize from the immediate and the temporal, and who make absolutes out of accidents. It appeals to the intelligence, to the adjudicative and rational faculties, although it is not the innocent that its traducers make believe it is about the wickedness of the wicked. It is empirical and open, not obscurantist and superstitious. It is humble about the truth and hostile to arrogance, whether born in class spirit or rooted in theological bias. It is more a temper and an attitude than a dogma and a creed. But it does not lack the supreme morality, which is charity through understanding, without patronage or bigotry, with deliberate and condign force to keep open the system through which each finds his own salvation.

E. L.

PART ONE

THE PRESIDENT

AND HIS EDUCATION

CHAPTER ONE

Portrait of the President*

By
Arthur S. Link

What was he like, this man to whom had been intrusted the leadership of the American people during the next four fateful years? Whence did he derive his ideals and purposes? To what degree was he a creature of the intellect; to what degree was he governed by his prejudices and passions? How did he operate in the world of men struggling for place and power?

The man who stood before the Chief Justice and took the oath of office as President on that March morning had changed little physically from the early days of his presidency of Princeton, except that the lines in his face were deeper and his hair was grayer. He was of average build and height, about five feet eleven inches in his shoes, but he possessed an extraordinary physiognomy. A perceptive reporter has described it as follows:

Woodrow Wilson's face is narrow and curiously geometrical. It is a rectangle, one might say, the lines are so regular. His forehead is high and his iron gray hair retreats from it somewhat, which adds to this effect. His face is refined, a face that shows breeding and family in every line, but it is heavy boned. The cheek bones are rather high and the jaw thrusts forward in a challenging way. The mouth is small, sensitive, with full lips, a mouth almost too well shaped for a man, and a woman might envy the arched eyebrows. But the almost brutal strength of the general bony structure of the face, and that aggressive jaw promise an active, iron willed, fighting man. His eyes, blue-gray they looked in that light behind his nose glasses, are very penetrating. They have a way of narrowing when he talks that gives him a stern, almost grim expression.[1]

This look of sternness when he set his jaw was perhaps the most notable feature of Wilson's aspect. There is a portrait of him hanging

* From Arthur S. Link, *Wilson: The New Freedom* (Princeton: Princeton University Press, 1956), pp. 61–85, by permission of the Princeton University Press.

[1] W. S. Couch, in the New York *World,* December 18, 1910.

in the Faculty Room in Nassau Hall at Princeton, which well displays the grimness of character that his long and often somber face could reveal. In this remarkable painting, his eyes flash through the glasses, his lips are tightly compressed, and his jaw juts forward, as if in defiance.

But for all his appearance of resolution and personal strength, there was a frailness in Wilson's physique that proved a serious impediment throughout his adult career and ultimately a disaster. Like Theodore Roosevelt, Wilson had been a frail and sickly child; unlike his great contemporary, Wilson never mastered his physical weaknesses or conditioned his body for the severe strains he put upon it. Driving too hard at Princeton, he had narrowly escaped a breakdown in 1906. He conserved his strength more carefully after that warning, and he contrived to carry the burdens of a strenuous political career and of the Presidency until 1919. But he survived only by refusing to allow himself to become exhausted, and this fact goes far toward explaining many of his deficiencies as administrator, intellectual, and friend.

It is easier to describe Wilson's physical characteristics than to analyze his intellectual interests and processes, for he fits into no simple classification. We might begin by pointing out that he was a person of limited interests and narrow reading. He had little command of foreign languages and almost no interest in political developments abroad before he entered the White House; he was indifferent to the great scientific developments that were transforming the philosophy and technology of his age; he knew virtually nothing about serious art and music. His reading in the field of literature, moreover, was desultory, spasmodic, and erratic. He was passionately fond of Keats, Wordsworth, Browning, Swinburne, Shelley, Tennyson, and Arnold, among the English poets; of Jane Austen, Sir Walter Scott, Stanley Weyman, and Mary N. Murfree, among the novelists; and of Lamb, Bagehot, and G. K. Chesterton among the essayists. Yet he never read widely among these few authors; and he was generally ignorant of much of the world's great literature.[2]

Indeed, even in his own specialties of political science, constitutional law, and English and American history, Wilson was surprisingly poorly

[2] Stockton Axson, notes on various parts of R. S. Baker's MS, in the Ray Stannard Baker Collection, Library of Congress (hereinafter cited as "Baker Collection"); R. S. Baker, memorandum of conversations with Stockton Axson, February 8, 10, and 11, 1925, *ibid.*; Gamaliel Bradford, "Brains Win and Lose," *Atlantic Monthly,* CXLVII (February, 1931), 155.

read. Two of his early scholarly books, *The State* (1889) and *Division and Reunion* (1893), gave evidence of intensive scholarship in comparative government and American history. However, they marked the zenith of his career as a scholar; and afterward, during the 1890's, he turned more and more toward the works of a few great historical masters—Macaulay, Green, and Turner, for example—and toward writing in the field of essays and popular history and biography. Then, after he assumed the presidency of Princeton in 1902, his serious reading virtually ceased. Indeed, he told a reporter in 1916, "I haven't read a serious book through for fourteen years,"[3] and there is no evidence to contradict his assertion. It is little wonder, therefore, that he was often ignorant of the currents of economic, political, and social thought that were revolutionizing scholarship in the social sciences after the 1890's, and that he derived such knowledge as he had of these developments at second hand.

There were, besides, curious limitations in Wilson's intellectual processes. This was true, primarily, because he was interested in ideas chiefly to the degree to which they could be put to practical use and hardly at all for their own sake. Thus, because his thinking was pragmatic rather than philosophical, he had little interest in pure speculation and tended to judge public men, both historical and contemporary, not by their thought but by their actions; he was rarely an original thinker.

Yet if Wilson was not an intellectual in the ordinary sense of that word, he was most assuredly a creature of brains, as one of his most understanding friends has put it. What saved him from pedantry was the enormous activity of his mind—the constant play of his imagination and his absorption in ideas that could be put to use in the world of practical affairs, whether in reconstructing the social life of undergraduates at Princeton or in devising a new political order for the world.[4]

There were, in addition, two other resources of strength in the Wilsonian intellect. One was Wilson's ability to absorb ideas and to assimilate and synthesize them rapidly, which revealed a high degree of intelligence. The other was closely related—his ability to cut through verbiage or a maze of detail and to go to the essentials of any problem.

[3] Ida M. Tarbell, "A Talk with the President of the United States," *Collier's*, LVIII (October 28, 1916), 37.

[4] Bradford, *op. cit.*, pp. 153–61.

The Philosophy and Policies of Woodrow Wilson

As his brother-in-law observed from long acquaintance, Wilson had a swift and intuitive comprehension that led him straight to the heart of a subject.[5] Or, as another friendly contemporary has put it:

I have never talked with any other public man who gave me such an impression of being at every moment in complete command of his entire intellectual equipment, such an impression of alertness, awareness. His face mirrors that eagerness. A new fact, a new aspect of an old situation, a felicitous statement of current opinion, brings to his intent eyes an expression of keen intellectual appetite. He pounces upon ideas half conveyed and consumes them before they are well out of one's mind; and his pounce is sure and accurate. He gets swiftly to your point of view, passes upon the facts that you bring him, and in a few minutes' time has stripped the whole situation to the bare bones of its fundamental aspects, and has rested his conclusions and decisions upon a few simple and elemental principles—and all with an incomparable clearness of statement.[6]

Woodrow Wilson was not only a man of ideas; he was, even more importantly, a citizen of another invisible world, the world of the spirit in which a sovereign God reigned in justice and in love. One cannot understand Wilson without taking into account the religious bases of his life and motivation. Born the son of a Presbyterian minister and a devout mother and reared in the southern Presbyterian church, he absorbed completely his father's and his denomination's belief in the omnipotence of God, the morality of the universe, a system of rewards and punishments, and the supreme revelation of Jesus Christ. Mankind, he felt, lived not only by the providence of God but also under his immutable decrees; and nations as well as men transgressed the divine ordinances at their peril. He shared the Calvinistic belief, held in his day mainly by southern Presbyterians and members of the Reformed churches in Europe, in predestination—the absolute conviction that God had ordered the universe from the beginning, the faith that God used men for his own purposes. From such beliefs came a sure sense of destiny and a feeling of intimate connection with the sources of power.

It was almost as if Wilson had been born with these convictions. He apparently never went through that period of doubt which often secures the faith of intellectuals. He was a loyal member and elder in his church; he read the Scriptures daily; and he found strength and

[5] R. S. Baker, memorandum of conversations with Stockton Axson, March 15–16, 1927, Baker Collection.

[6] R. S. Baker, "Wilson," *Collier's*, LVIII (October 7, 1916), 6.

guidance in prayer. "*My* life would not be worth living," he told a friend, "if it were not for the driving power of religion, for *faith*, pure and simple. I have seen all my life the arguments against it without ever having been moved by them. . . . There are people who *believe* only so far as they *understand*—that seems to me presumptuous and sets their understanding as the standard of the universe. . . . I am sorry for such people."[7]

Faith in God and submission to the Christian ethic underlay most of Wilson's political assumptions and fired his ambition to serve the Almighty by serving his fellow men. "The way to success in America," he once declared, "is to show you are not afraid of anybody except God and His judgment. If I did not believe that I would not believe in democracy. . . . If I did not believe that the moral judgment would be the last and final judgment in the minds of men, as well as at the tribunal of God, I could not believe in popular government."[8]

"There are great problems . . . before the American people," Wilson said on another occasion.

There are problems which will need purity of spirit and an integrity of purpose such as has never been called for before in the history of this country. I should be afraid to go forward if I did not believe that there lay at the foundation of all our schooling and of all our thought this incomparable and unimpeachable Word of God. If we cannot derive our strength thence, there is no source from which we can derive it, and so I would bid you go from this place, if I may, inspired once more with the feeling that the providence of God is the foundation of affairs, and that only those can guide, and only those can follow, who take this providence of God from the sources where it is authentically interpreted. . . . He alone can rule his own spirit who puts himself under the command of the spirit of God, revealed in His Son, Jesus Christ, our Savior. He is the captain of our souls; he is the man from whose suggestions and from whose life comes the light that guideth every man that ever came into the world.[9]

Wilson's high integrity, his sense of justice, his devotion to duty, and much of his general motivation stemmed in large measure from his spiritual resources. As president of Princeton University, for example, he refused to demean the university's academic integrity in order to win favor with the alumni or potential donors. As President

[7] Mrs. Crawford H. Toy, "Second Visit to the White House," diary entry dated January 3, 1915, MS in the Baker Collection.

[8] Speech at Philadelphia, July 4, 1914, *New York Times*, July 5, 1914.

[9] Speech before the Sunday School workers and pupils of Trenton, New Jersey, October 1, 1911, *Trenton True American*, October 2, 1911.

of the United States, he refused to accept expensive gifts, even those offered by persons unknown to him.[10] He refused to allow Harper and Brothers to sell movie rights to his books—"a rather cheap exploitation," he called it.[11] He stood firm against nepotism when his brother sought the post of Secretary of the Senate in 1913. He intervened personally to protect persons in the public service from "malicious injustice."[12] He set a moral tone that permeated his entire administration and enabled it to survive a war and demobilization without a single really important scandal. His sense of duty alone carried him through dark days and made him ready to risk his life for what he thought were noble causes. But his most striking personal attribute was his certain sense of destiny and his conviction that the right cause would ultimately triumph.

As a husband, father, and friend, Wilson had many warm and winning qualities. In his family circle he was unquestionably the lord and master, but he was uncommonly tender and assumed responsibilities far surpassing the ordinary. For example, he spent a good part of his income before 1913 in helping to educate numerous relatives on both sides of the family; for years he supported uncomplainingly an indigent sister and her family. Among his family and friends, Wilson was generous, understanding, and intensely loyal, so long as he thought his friends were loyal to him. Discarding his austere official manner in the intimate group, he could be uproariously funny as a storyteller or mimic, or quickly moved by demonstrations of affection.

Another significant aspect of Wilson's personality was his inheritance of many of his attitudes and especially the romantic quality of his thought from his rearing in the South and his close association with southern people. He was a southerner not merely in the superficial sense—in the soft inflections in his speech, his normal courtesy toward friends and associates, and his liking for fried chicken, rice, and sweet potatoes[13]—but in more essential ways. For one thing, he was southern

---

[10] E.g., Wilson to J. B. Phinney, February 3, 1915, Papers of Woodrow Wilson, Library of Congress (hereinafter cited as "Wilson Papers").

[11] Wilson to F. A. Duneka, August 2, 1915, *ibid.*

[12] E.g., Wilson to W. J. Bryan, December 29, 1913, *ibid.*

[13] "Governor Wilson since his marriage has lived on Southern cooking," Ellen Wilson told a reporter in the autumn of 1912. "You see, we have always had cooks from the South or those who were Southern born, and they know how to cook chicken better than anybody in the world, the Governor thinks. . . .

"The Governor's idea of a fine dinner includes chicken Southern style, rice and candied sweet potatoes, with beans and corn, fruit and a salad. Never do we have a meal without rice." *Trenton Evening True American,* October 30, 1912.

in his deification of women and his strong urge to protect them, and in his belief that women should govern their own sphere and not soil themselves by participation in practical affairs. He inherited and retained the upper-class southern affection for the Negro and the belief that the black man should remain segregated and not aspire toward so-called social equality with the whites. He was southern, above all, in his deep love of community and the land and in his personal identification with the living generations of the dead.[14]

These were some of the sources of Wilson's personal greatness, and all of them had an important impact upon his career as a public man. Superb intelligence and power of penetration, religious conviction and a sense of destiny, integrity, warmth among intimates, and love of community and nation combined with boldness and resolution to make Wilson at times a strong and successful political leader.

But there was a less happy side of Wilson's personality and character. It is not pleasant or easy to describe his personal weaknesses, and yet we cannot know the whole man or understand the ultimately tragic nature of his career if we ignore his unlovely qualities, for they always affected and sometimes controlled his personal and political attitudes and relationships.

To begin with, there is revelation in the nature of his friendships. Few public men have ever craved or needed affection more than did Woodrow Wilson; and in his own way and upon his own terms, he returned the love that he received. Yet he demanded, not forthrightness and a masculine type of give-and-take in his friendships, but a loyalty that never questioned, always understood, and inevitably yielded to his own will. In view of his terms of friendship, it was little wonder that he had few intimates and broke sooner or later with most of them, and that his most enduring friends were admiring, uncritical women, both within and without his household, who always understood and comforted and never questioned.

Other weaknesses were Wilson's egotism and his tendency to exalt intuition over reason. Robert Lansing, Secretary of State from 1915 to 1920, analyzed these defects sharply:

When one comes to consider Mr. Wilson's mental processes, there is the feeling that intuition rather than reason played the chief part in the way in which he reached conclusions and judgments. In fact, arguments, however

[14] For an extended discussion of this point see Arthur S. Link, *Wilson: The Road to the White House* (Princeton: Princeton University Press, 1947), pp. 3–4.

soundly reasoned, did not appeal to him if they were opposed to his feeling of what was the right thing to do. Even established facts were ignored if they did not fit in with this intuitive sense, this semidivine power to select the right. Such an attitude of mind is essentially feminine. In the case of Mr. Wilson, it explains many things in his public career, which are otherwise very perplexing.

In the first place it gave a superior place to his own judgment. With him it was a matter of conviction formed without weighing evidence and without going through the process of rational deduction. His judgments were always right in his own mind, because he knew that they were right. How did he know that they were right? Why he *knew* it, and that was the best reason in the world. No other was necessary. It sounds very much like the "because," which is popularly termed "a woman's reason."

In consequence to the high place which Mr. Wilson gave to his own judgment, he was less susceptible than other men to the force of argument. When reason clashed with his intuition, reason had to give way.[15]

Numerous contemporaries have confirmed Lansing's judgment concerning the importance of Wilson's egotism. Wilson's "overpowering self esteem left no place for common counsel of which he talked so much and in which he did not indulge at all," Lindley M. Garrison, Secretary of War from 1913 to 1916, wrote, for example.[16] "This was his great weakness," William Kent said, "a total inability to rely upon others."[17]

Wilson's supreme confidence in his own judgment came out in blunt assertions of his superior wisdom and virtue. "Wilson was the most self-assured, the most egotistical, and the vainest man I ever knew...," an unfriendly Princeton contemporary has written. "He once said to me, 'I am so sorry for those who disagree with me.' When I asked why, he replied, 'Because I know that they are wrong.' "[18] To cite a second example, there was a time when he fell into a hot argument with a professor at the Princeton Theological Seminary. In order to end the disagreement, the theological professor said, "Well, Dr. Wilson, there are two sides to every question." "Yes," Wilson shot back, "a right side and a wrong side!"[19]

[15] "The Mentality of Woodrow Wilson," Diary of Robert Lansing, November 20, 1921, Library of Congress.

[16] L. M. Garrison to William E. Brooks, July 30, 1929, Papers of William E. Brooks, Library of Congress.

[17] W. Kent to R. S. Baker, May 25, 1925, Baker Collection.

[18] Harold C. Syrett (ed.), *The Gentleman and the Tiger: The Autobiography of George B. McClellan, Jr.* (Philadelphia: J. B. Lippincott Co., 1956), p. 314.

[19] William S. Myers (ed.), *Woodrow Wilson: Some Princeton Memories* (Princeton: Princeton University Press, 1946), p. 43.

Portrait of the President

Wilson had another unfortunate quality that Lansing knew firsthand but did not attempt to describe. The President possessed a turbulent emotional makeup, which was all the more charged because he kept it under severe control. As he once candidly said, "If I were to interpret myself, I would say that my constant embarrassment is to restrain the emotions that are inside of me. You may not believe it, but I sometimes feel like a fire from a far from extinct volcano, and if the lava does not seem to spill over it is because you are not high enough to see into the basin and see the cauldron boil."[20]

Thus Wilson could hate as fiercely as he loved, and over the years he accumulated an astounding array of prejudices—against his old foes at Princeton, for example, or against Republicans who he thought opposed him out of spite and lack of character. As George LaMonte, one of Wilson's associates in New Jersey, put it, "Wilson's mind could not work under opposition, for he felt all opposition to be merely irritation, and that if he needed any human associations they must be with people who either lauded him and made it their business to agree with him on everything, or else with people who were comfortable because they didn't understand what he was talking about or were not particularly interested. This accounted for his fondness for women's society."[21]

The President's few intimate friends have left revealing testimony concerning the depths of his prejudices and personal hatreds. Colonel House advised a British friend on the best method of handling Wilson: "Never begin by arguing. Discover a common hate, exploit it, get the President warmed up and then start on your business."[22] "He likes a few [people] and is very loyal to them," the Colonel observed of the President in 1915, "but his prejudices are many and often unjust. He finds great difficulty in conferring with men against whom, for some reason, he has a prejudice and in whom he can find nothing good."[23] Dr. Cary T. Grayson, the White House physician, thought that Wilson was a "man of unusually narrow prejudices" and "intolerant of advice"; and, he added, "If one urges Wilson to do something contrary

[20] Speech before the National Press Club, March 20, 1914, *New York Times*, March 21, 1914.

[21] George LaMonte, quoted in William Kent to R. S. Baker, May 25, 1925, Baker Collection.

[22] Sir Arthur Willert, *The Road to Safety: A Study in Anglo-American Relations* (London: Derek Verschoyle, 1952), p. 63.

[23] The Diary of Edward M. House, November 2, 1915, Yale University Library (hereinafter cited as "House Diary").

to his own conviction, he ceases to have any liking for that person."[24]

This tendency to equate political opposition with personal antagonism and to doubt the integrity of any man who disagreed was relatively unimportant so long as Wilson controlled secure majorities in Congress. It was a fatal weakness after the Republicans won control of Congress in 1918, especially during the momentous controversy over the ratification of the Versailles Treaty. It was a weakness, moreover, that put a heavy strain upon Wilson's talents as an administrator. Because he often equated loyalty with agreement and welcomed flattery instead of hardheaded frankness, he was sometimes a poor judge of men. As Senator John Sharp Williams of Mississippi once wrote, "He was the best judge of measures and the poorest of men I ever knew."[25] Because he resented criticism, his advisers usually either told him what they thought he wanted to hear or else remained discreetly silent.

Wilson's exaltation of intuition, his egotism, and his indulgence in personal prejudice were at the same time sources of strength and of weakness. Perhaps they help to explain why the American people admired his boldness and thrilled to his noble visions and the cadence of his oratory and yet did not love him as an individual as they loved Lincoln for his compassion and the two Roosevelts for their personal warmth. How can we reconcile the curious contradictions in Woodrow Wilson—his craving for affection and his refusal to give on equal terms, his love of the people en masse and his ordinary disdain for individuals, the warm idealism of his speeches and the coolness of many of his official relationships, the bigness of his political visions and the pettiness of his hatreds? Being neither mind reader nor psychiatrist, the biographer can only agree with Colonel House that Wilson was "one of the most contradictory characters in history" and hope that the man will reveal himself in the pages that follow.

The White House was like a wonderful new world. After a family dinner following the inaugural parade, the Wilsons
found a little time to inspect their new quarters. There was a continual running through the house from one room to another, a shrill screaming to someone else as a new place was discovered. Relatives from the hotels going in and out, visitors and acquaintances seeking admission but added to the turmoil. . . . Along toward midnight the day was considered closed. One by one the family and guests wended their way to their rooms. It was not long

---

[24] *Ibid*, April 2, 1916.

[25] R. S. Baker, interview with J. S. Williams, March 11, 1927, Baker Collection.

after the President had gone upstairs that he rang several bells in the house, not knowing at the time which was which. One of the doorkeepers answered the call and when the President appeared he was clothed in his underwear only. He asked for his trunk, which had gone astray and unfortunately contained his night clothes. Immediate search was made and it was located at the station where an automobile was sent for it; but it did not get to the White House until one o'clock in the morning after the President had already retired.[26]

It was fun to wake up in the White House, to roam through the great rooms and corridors, to eat in the big dining room, which was beautiful in spite of the animal heads placed on the walls by Theodore Roosevelt. It was exciting to have a corps of servants, to be able to buy the clothes one wanted for the first time without worrying about the cost, to be always the guest of honor at parties, to have automobiles after going for years without one. How grand it all seemed to Eleanor Wilson as she looked back upon those first days in the presidential mansion![27]

There were, of course, new social duties and irritations. There were the traditional state dinners for the Cabinet, the Supreme Court, and the diplomatic corps. There was the inevitable loss of privacy and control over personal movement. There were constant crowds streaming into the White House. There was, for Wilson, the anguish of having to yield to a valet and give up his old gray sack suits for dress becoming a President of the United States.

And yet the remarkable thing is how little personal life changed for the Wilsons. The efficient household staff they had inherited from the Roosevelts and Tafts ran the White House with a minimum of worry. Characteristically, Ellen Wilson spurned the company of Washington's social elite and used her free time for humanitarian work. "I wonder how anyone who reaches middle age can bear it," she once remarked, "if she cannot feel, on looking back, that whatever mistakes she may have made, she has on the whole lived for others and not for herself." It was the way she lived in Washington. She visited the crowded alley slums, often with food and clothing in hand, and worked quietly among congressmen for the enactment of a measure to provide decent housing for Negroes. She toured the governmental departments and

[26] Irwin H. Hoover, *Forty-two Years in the White House* (Boston: Houghton Mifflin Co., 1934), pp. 58–59.

[27] Eleanor Wilson McAdoo, *The Woodrow Wilsons* (New York: Macmillan Co., 1937), pp. 212–27.

had restrooms for women workers installed where there were none. And one might have found her any day at a meeting of social workers, as a member of the Board of Associated Charities, listening patiently to a caseworker describe the misfortunes of a needy family.[28] Withal, she found time to receive delegations and preside at innumerable teas at the White House. Bearing her imprint, they were simple affairs, where one talked about good works, art, music, or books.

Wilson's personal life of course changed after March 4, 1913, but not his ingrained habit of living and doing business according to a nearly inflexible routine. He rose every morning at eight, had break-fast—usually two raw eggs in orange juice, oatmeal, and coffee—at eight-thirty, and arrived at his office at nine. He read his mail and dic-tated replies to his stenographer. Then, exactly at ten o'clock, he began receiving callers.

No man, not even a cabinet member, got the President's ear except by an appointment approved by Tumulty; and the late visitor to the Executive Offices, whether congressman or senator, went away with-out seeing Wilson. Except in unusual circumstances, interviews were limited to ten or fifteen minutes. Wilson listened, sometimes nodded or said a few words, and then rose to tell his visitor good-by. In spite of his unvarying courtesy, it was obvious that he resented the needless demands that some of his callers made upon his energies and time.

On the rare occasions when he was ahead of schedule, the President might walk into the outer office and greet the crowd waiting for a glimpse of him. Theodore Roosevelt had always had a warm, special greeting for such strangers; Taft had often stopped to repeat their names and make a joke. In contrast, Wilson would walk briskly down the line shaking the outstretched hands mechanically and silently. One old fellow, however, broke the routine. "Mr. Wilson," he said, "I've known all the Presidents in my time, and I want to say right here that you're the greatest and best of them since Lincoln!" When this com-pliment failed to elicit any response, the old man went on: "And when I add that I'm a high-church Presbyterian like yourself, you'll know I'm not lying." Near the end of the line, Wilson turned and shot back, "Whether we are Presbyterians or not, sir, we ought all to speak the truth!"

The appointments were invariably over by one o'clock, when the

[28] McGregor (A. J. McKelway), "The Social Activities of the White House," *Harper's Weekly*, LVIII (April 25, 1914), 26–27; Mrs. Ernest P. Bicknell, "The Home-Maker of the White House," *Survey*, XXXIII (October 3, 1914), 19–22.

President went to lunch with his family. He returned to his office at two or two-thirty for more appointments until four, when he left for the balance of the afternoon. During late afternoons and weekends he often played golf with Dr. Grayson, the White House physician, a quiet and gentlemanly Virginian whom Wilson had inherited from Taft.

Although the President took up golf for exercise at Grayson's suggestion, he soon became a virtual addict. They played at all the courses about Washington except the Chevy Chase Club, in which Wilson refused membership because of its social exclusiveness. "He would play at all hours, sometimes as early as five in the morning and sometimes late in the afternoon. Good or bad weather was just the same to him. When there was snow on the ground, he would have the balls painted red and find amusement in driving them around on the ice and snow."[29]

Dinner in the White House was at seven o'clock. In contrast to Theodore Roosevelt, who gathered writers, politicians, explorers, and persons from all walks of life at his table, the Wilsons usually dined *en famille* or with relatives and a few intimate friends. After Ellen's death in 1914 and Wilson's marriage to Edith Bolling Galt in 1915, social life at the White House quickened, but Ellen had neither energy for nor interest in extensive entertaining. To forget the cares of state, the President often went with his family to the theater and to vaudeville shows. It mattered little whether the plays or the performances were good or bad; Wilson enjoyed them all. During times of crisis Wilson might work in his study late into the night; on the other hand, there were many quiet evenings, when he relaxed with family and friends. George McLean Harper, professor of English literature at Princeton, remembered one of those evenings:

When we got back to the White House, Mr. Wilson had returned and was evidently very glad to be at home again and at his ease in the midst of his family. We had a quiet familiar hour at dinner, with no other guests and no interruptions. It was just like the old times in Princeton. After dinner we drew up our chairs around a blazing wood fire in the drawing room and talked about books. Mr. Wilson stretched himself out on the hearth rug and recited poetry, as we have often heard him do. . . . Like a happy boy home from school for a holiday the President of the United States rocked back and forth in the firelight, with his knees clasped between his hands, declaiming sonnets, while his face glowed with affection.[30]

[29] Hoover, *op. cit.,* p. 61.

[30] George M. Harper to R. S. Baker, February 11, 1929, Baker Collection. The foregoing account of Wilson's daily routine is based upon R. S. Baker, interview with C. L. Swem, July 16, 1925, *ibid.*; William B. Hale, "Watching President Wilson at

There was another side to the life of the new President, however, during the months following the inauguration. There were, among others, the problems of working out a method of doing business with the cabinet members and of running a great government without becoming overwhelmed by the burden of ordinary administrative routine. In solving these tasks of administration, Wilson further revealed his methods and character as President.

The President and his Cabinet met first informally on March 5, 1913, in the Cabinet Room in the Executive Offices, to "come together and talk about getting started," as Wilson said. They met thereafter on Tuesdays and Fridays until about November 1, 1913, when the President eliminated the Friday meetings and substituted a system of individual conferences.

One member has described Wilson's method in these cabinet meetings:

As President Wilson took his seat at the head of the table, he looked the moderator, fitting into place and power. His plan from the first was to present some matter or matters about which he desired what he was fond of calling "common counsel," and after he had received the reaction of Cabinet members, his practice was to call on each member to present any question that concerned departmental policies, for debate and exchange of news. At one Cabinet meeting he would begin with the Secretary of State, and at the next the Secretary of Labor would be called upon first. . . . He never took a vote, pursuing a course, as he often said, more like a Quaker meeting, in which after full discussion the President would say, "It seems to me the sense of the meeting is so and so," and the policy thus ascertained would be the program of the administration.[31]

Wilson's advisers responded with enthusiasm befitting fellow workers in a noble cause. "It is impossible to meet any member of the Cabinet and talk with him five minutes," one observer wrote soon after the inaugural, "without becoming impressed with the fact that the members of the Cabinet believe in one another and believe in their chief, and feel already the exhilaration of taking part in the bringing about of better days."[32] "The President is the most charming man imaginable to

---

Work," *World's Work*, XXVI (May, 1913), 71–72; Francis E. Leupp, "The President—and Mr. Wilson," *Independent*, LXXVI (November 27, 1913), 392–93; An Onlooker, "Woodrow Wilson the Man," *Harper's Weekly*, LVIII (January 10, 1914), 25–26.

[31] Josephus Daniels, *The Wilson Era: Years of Peace, 1910–1917* (Chapel Hill: University of North Carolina Press, 1944), p. 137.

[32] Ernest H. Abbott, "The New Administration: An Impression," New York *Outlook*, CIII (April 5, 1913), 760.

work with," one cabinet member said. ". . . If we can't mak̲
a success, the Democratic Party is absolutely gone, and entire
less."[33]

Slowly, perhaps inevitably, the original ardor cooled as quarrels and controversies arose. But the development that turned the Cabinet from a genuinely deliberative body into an inconsequential forum was Wilson's discovery that news of the discussions was leaking to reporters. The member responsible was Franklin K. Lane, Secretary of the Interior. Lane was so fond of conversation and so much a gossip that he could not resist the temptation to drop broad hints to his newspaper friends.[34] Precisely when Wilson learned of Lane's weakness, we do not know. In any event, in early September, 1913, at the height of one of the recurrent Mexican crises, the President virtually stopped discussing any important question at cabinet meetings because, as he told his friends, he simply could not trust Lane to keep the secrets of state. The result was that the meetings became for the most part, in Garrison's words, an interesting waste of time.[35]

One unfortunate effect of Wilson's policy of saying nothing important during the cabinet meetings was the resentment that the cabinet members consequently felt. "McReynolds added his complaint to that of the other cabinet officials about the President's reticence with them," Colonel House recorded in his diary in September, 1913. "As far as I can gather, he confers with none of them excepting in matters concerning their particular departments. Not one of them has been able to tell me a single thing regarding what the President has in mind for Mexico, or about anything else not connected with their own departments. I can readily see how embarrassing this is to them, and how it hurts their self esteem."[36] Two months later McAdoo "said the Cabinet were complaining that the President did not consult with them regarding Mexico

[33] F. K. Lane to W H. Page, March 12, 1913, in Anne W. Lane and Louise H. Wall (eds.), *The Letters of Franklin K. Lane, Personal and Political* (Boston: Houghton Mifflin Co., 1922), pp. 133–34.

[34] R. S. Baker and A. H. Meneely, interview with N. D. Baker, April 6, 1928, Baker Collection; R. S. Baker, interview with T. W. Gregory, March 14–15, 1927, *ibid.*; R. S. Baker, interview with D. F. Houston, December 1, 1928, *ibid.*; R. S. Baker, interview with W. B. Wilson, January 12–13, 1928, *ibid.*; and W. G. McAdoo, *Crowded Years: The Reminiscenses of William G. McAdoo* (Boston: Houghton Mifflin Co., 1931), pp. 193–94, all attest to the accuracy of this statement.

[35] R. S. Baker, interview with L. M. Garrison, November 30, 1928, Baker Collection.

[36] House Diary, September 6, 1913.

and there was a general feeling among them that he would like to eliminate Cabinet meetings entirely."[37]

As the months passed and, after 1914, the nation entered a period of uncertain neutrality vis-à-vis the European war, Wilson grew increasingly secretive and the cabinet members almost rebellious. The President, House observed, "never seems to want to discuss things with anyone, as far as I know, excepting me. Even the Cabinet bore him with their importunities, and he often complains of them."[38] In the midst of a crisis that threatened to erupt into war with Germany, House could write: "His immediate entourage, from the Secretary of State down, are having an unhappy time just now. He is consulting none of them and they are as ignorant of his intention as the man in the street."[39] And a few months later McAdoo could remark that his chief had no confidence in the judgment of any of his official advisers,[40] while Walter Page noted the impact of their loss of morale: "The members of the Cabinet do not seem to have the habit of frankness with one another. Each lives and works in a water-tight compartment."[41]

To stop at this point in describing Wilson's relations with his Cabinet, however, would be to draw an incomplete and unfair picture of the President as administrator. Wilson conferred with his advisers frequently, usually by correspondence, about matters relating to their own departments. In personal conference he was invariably courteous and generous. "He was the most satisfactory person to confer with I ever knew," Thomas W. Gregory, Attorney-General from 1914 to 1919, testified. "He was always deferential and sympathetic, but he never failed to express himself and to throw light upon and give help in dealing with, the matter under discussion."[42] "To me and with me he was patient, considerate, approachable, sympathetic and amazingly helpful," Newton D. Baker said. "I took my problems to him and always came away with the feeling that he had sought and considered my views and then exercised his clear and powerful mind to the utmost to help me in their solution."[43]

---

[37] *Ibid.*, November 4, 1913.　　　[38] *Ibid.*, November 14, 1914.

[39] *Ibid.*, April 2, 1916.　　　[40] *Ibid.*, August 27, 1916.

[41] The Diary of Walter H. Page, *ca.* September 1, 1916, Harvard University Library.

[42] T. W. Gregory to Josephus Daniels, February 19, 1924, Papers of Thomas Watt Gregory, Library of Congress.

[43] Quoted in George Barton, "Woodrow Wilson: His Human Side," *Current History*, XXII (April, 1925), 2.

Portrait of the President

Wilson's method of running the executive branch was to give virtually complete freedom to his cabinet members in all routine matters and in the formulation of many important policies, so long as those policies did not conflict with his broad objectives or imperil the administration's standing before Congress and the country. For example, he approved when McAdoo launched the Treasury upon bold financial measures; followed Houston in opposing a bill for the establishment of a federal rural credits system; allowed several cabinet members to institute segregation and defended them when their action provoked the impassioned opposition of northern humanitarians; and supported Garrison in a Philippine policy that partially repudiated Democratic platform pledges. Only in important foreign policies, in issues involving his leadership of Congress, and in the disposition of the patronage did he take a personal interest.

A minor case that arose in the early spring of 1914 illustrated his administrative methods and ideals. He had promised Bryan to appoint one Summervell to a certain post and subsequently discovered that the appointment rested legally with the Secretary of War, who wanted another man. "I could obtain the appointment of Mr. Summervell," Wilson wrote, "only through the courtesy of the Secretary of War in yielding his judgment to my insistence in the matter. I do not feel justified in acting in that way. I have never felt justified in coercing the judgment of a Cabinet colleague."[44] It was true. He rarely overruled a cabinet member, and when he did the matter was so serious that the member's resignation had to follow.[45]

In contrast to the usually genial mediator of the Cabinet was the forbidding commander-in-chief, who dealt sternly with his military and naval advisers when he thought their words or actions raised a threat to civilian supremacy over the military establishment. Wilson's attitude toward the professional military class was conditioned by the fact that, like most other Americans of his time, he had no interest in military and naval strategy, little understanding of the role that force plays in the relations of great powers, and a near contempt for *Realpolitik* and the men who made it. Military men, he thought, should speak only when they were spoken to; and the suggestion that his military advisers might know more about important strategic matters than he was

[44] Wilson to W. J. Bryan, March 25, 1914, Wilson Papers.
[45] As in the case of Bryan and Garrison.

enough to evoke suspicions of a sinister attempt to undermine civilian control.

Some generals like Leonard Wood and admirals like Bradley A. Fiske were unwilling to acknowledge the President's omniscience and fell into official disfavor in consequence. Others, like the sometime chief of staff, Major General Hugh L. Scott, were more fortunate because they submitted to the necessity of getting on with the commander-in-chief.

Scott explained his method in a revealing letter. "Your letter of yesterday received, in which you ask me to urge upon the President the appointment of [Robert] Bacon as Secretary of War," he wrote to a friend soon after Secretary Garrison's resignation. "I know Bacon well and am very fond of him indeed, but I feel that my advocacy of his case would not do him any good as the President would resent my talking to him about any political matter; I have never done so on any occasion as I felt that any such attempt would get me a request to mind my own business."[46]

There was one early incident that further illuminated Wilson's attitude toward the professional military class. The Washington "corral" of the Military Order of the Caraboa,[47] numbering about one hundred army, naval, and marine officers and including a major general and a rear admiral, held its annual dinner on December 11, 1913. These veterans of the Philippine campaign made merry by singing "Damn, Damn, Damn the Insurrectos, Cross-Eyed Kakiack Ladrones" and roared at skits that poked fun at the administration's Philippine policy and at Bryan for drinking grape juice and speaking on the Chautauqua circuit.[48]

It is not difficult to imagine that Wilson's face flushed with anger and that his jaw hardened as he read the newspaper accounts of these hilarities on December 13, 1913. Two days later he ordered Garrison and Daniels to determine whether a court-martial should be held. When the two secretaries recommended a severe reprimand instead, the President replied with a humiliating public rebuke of the officers involved.

"Allow me to thank you for your report on the action of certain of-

[46] H. L. Scott to Edward S. Farrow, February 12, 1916, Papers of Hugh L. Scott, Library of Congress.

[47] The Military Order of the Caraboa was organized in Manila in 1902 and included officers who had served in suppressing the Philippine Insurrection from 1898 to 1902.

[48] New York *World,* December 16, 1913.

ficers of the army and navy at the recent dinner of the 'Military Order of the Caraboa,' " Wilson wrote.

The officers who were responsible for the programme of the evening are certainly deserving of a very serious reprimand, which I hereby request be administered; and I cannot rid myself of a feeling of great disappointment that the general body of officers assembled at the dinner should have greeted the carrying out of such a programme with apparent indifference to the fact that it violated some of the most dignified and sacred traditions of the service.

I have been told that the songs and other amusements of the evening were intended and regarded as "fun." What are we to think of officers of the army and navy of the United States who think it "fun" to bring their official superiors into ridicule and the policies of the government which they are sworn to serve with unquestioning loyalty into contempt? If this is their idea of fun, what is their ideal of duty? If they do not hold their loyalty above all silly effervescences of childish wit, what about their profession do they hold sacred?[49]

Few presidents in American history have better understood the importance of good press relations and failed more miserably to get on with newspapermen than Woodrow Wilson. An advocate of "pitiless publicity" as governor of New Jersey, he had talked much about taking reporters into his confidence and had used the newspapers for frequent direct appeals to the people of his state. And he knew that a friendly press, both in New Jersey and throughout the nation, had been a decisive factor in his rise to national leadership.

One of Wilson's first acts as President, therefore, was to institute a semiweekly news conference in order to regularize his relations with the Washington correspondents. "I sent for you. . . ," he told them at the first press conference on March 15, 1913, "to ask that you go into partnership with me, that you lend me your assistance as nobody else can . . . [in telling people in Washington what the country thinks]. I did want you to feel that I was depending upon you, and from what I can learn of you, I think I have a reason to depend with confidence on you to do this thing, not for me, but for the United States, for the people of the United States, and so bring about a day which will be a little better than the days that have gone before us."[50]

No doubt Wilson meant what he said about welcoming the report-

[49] Wilson to the Secretaries of War and of the Navy, December 22, 1913, Wilson Papers.

[50] Printed in L. Ames Brown, "President Wilson and Publicity," *Harper's Weekly*, LVIII (November 1, 1913), 20.

ers as partners in the task of running the government. Nonetheless, the press conferences, which were unpleasant enough at the beginning, became so intolerable that the President met them only irregularly during 1914 and abandoned them altogether in June, 1915. In spite of all his professions of comradeship, Wilson simply did not like most reporters. They were, he thought, busybodies, who would not leave him or his family alone, and muckrakers, whose chief objectives were to steal state secrets, distort the truth, and make sensational headlines.

"When he came down here I attended the first conference he had with the Washington correspondents," one of his few friends among the newspapermen recalled.

It was appalling. He came into the room, suspicious, reserved, a little resentful—no thought of frankness and open door and cordiality and that sort of thing. In the first place, he was embarrassed. There were about two hundred of the correspondents and it was in the East Room of the White House. It was a silly thing to do. It was a conference with two hundred newspapermen. He could not be as frank as he could have been with one; and he was embarrassed and had this rankling feeling and he utterly failed to get across to those men anything except that this was very distasteful to him; and they, on their part, resented it very, very seriously. They came out of that conference almost cursing, indignant.[51]

Wilson's method in the press conferences was to tell reporters as little as possible about important matters. "The President gave the impression that he was matching his wits against ours," wrote the correspondent for the *New York Times*, "as a sort of mental practice with the object of being able to make responses which seemed to answer the questions, but which imparted little or nothing in the way of information."[52] Wilson, said Arthur Krock, "is the most inaccessible executive of recent times and the weekly conferences with him develop no news whatever as he simply parries all questions."[53]

Because he liked to give the impression of frankness, however, Wilson often resorted to evasion by giving answers that were technically true but actually false—a habit that House once called "grazing the truth." "For this reason, it was impossible to rely on anything he said," one of the best reporters of the time has written. "I do not mean that

[51] R. S. Baker, interview with Oliver P. Newman, January 13, 1928, Baker Collection.

[52] R. V. Oulahan to R. S. Baker, March 15, 1929, *ibid.*

[53] A. Krock to Henry Watterson, April 23, 1915, Papers of Henry Watterson, Library of Congress.

he lied. I mean that he took such an intellectual pleasure in stating a thing so as to give an opposite impression to the fact, though he kept strictly to the truth, that one had to be constantly on the alert to keep from being misled."[54]

Many examples of this method of "grazing the truth" might be cited, but one must suffice. In June, 1913, Attorney-General McReynolds submitted to the Cabinet a plan to hobble the components of the former "Tobacco Trust" by a punitive tax, and Wilson advised him to discuss the matter with the Senate leaders. When correspondents asked the President what he thought of McReynolds' "tobacco tax plan," he replied that, as far as he knew, McReynolds had no "tobacco tax plan." Afterward, Wilson explained that he had regarded McReynolds' proposal as a "suggestion" and not a "plan."[55]

Of course there was often little difference between the half-truth and the lie, and sometimes Wilson resorted to outright prevarication when he thought the public interests demanded dissimulation. "When we reached the apartment and were munching our sandwiches before retiring," House recorded in his diary on February 14, 1913, "we fell to talking about various matters. The Governor said he thought that lying was justified in some instances, particularly where it involved the honor of a woman. I agreed to this. He thought it was also justified where it related to matters of public policy." Or again, House wrote in his diary on November 6, 1914, that the President said he felt entirely justified in lying to reporters when they asked questions about foreign policy. House added that he remained silent, for Wilson knew that he disagreed, and they had discussed the question many times.

These tactics deceived no one and did Wilson immense harm among the newspapermen. Wilson's "failure to give the correspondents that measure of confidence and help that had been usual with previous Administrations," James Kerney writes, "was doubtless very influential in setting the tides of sentiment against him at the time when he needed support most."[56] The President's tactics also help to explain the cold

[54] Charles Willis Thompson, *Presidents I've Known and Two Near Presidents* (Indianapolis: Bobbs-Merrill Co., 1929), p. 297.

[55] Brown, *op. cit.,* pp. 19–20.

[56] James Kerney, *The Political Education of Woodrow Wilson* (New York: Century Co., 1926), p. 345. Oliver P. Newman declared that nine-tenths of the correspondents disliked Wilson in a journalistic sense. Their hostility did not perhaps matter so long as Wilson had control of the political situation, Newman added; but Wilson needed their support after 1918 and did not get it. R. S. Baker, interview with O. P. Newman, January 13, 1928, Baker Collection.

contempt that men like Theodore Roosevelt, Henry Cabot Lodge, Elihu Root, and William H. Taft felt toward him. Lodge, for example, fell victim to one of Wilson's half-truths during the campaign of 1916 and ever afterward was convinced that his earlier doubts as to the Democratic leader's honesty were valid. Taft, who was the least virulent of Wilson's critics, made the most charitable comment: "Perhaps it is too rigorous a view to take that a man in his position should not have to lie at times, but what I object to is his unnecessary lying."[57]

There were times when Wilson's resentment at the reporters flared into open anger. When the correspondent for the New York *Herald* reported in late August, 1915, that Wilson had broken with House over Mexican policy, for example, the President wrote to the editor of the *Herald*, denouncing the story as "an invention out of the whole cloth" and demanding that he withdraw the reporter from service in Washington.[58] But Wilson reserved his warmest anger for those newspapermen who would not leave his family alone. At a news conference on March 19, 1914, he finally exploded:

Gentlemen, I want to say something this afternoon. In the first place, I want to say that I know that in saying this I am dealing here in this room with a group of men who respect and observe the honorable limitations of their own function, but there are some men connected with the newspapers who do not. I am a public character for the time being, but the ladies of my household are not servants of the Government and they are not public characters. I deeply resent the treatment they are receiving at the hands of the newspapers at this time. I am going to be perfectly frank with you. Take the case of my oldest daughter. It is a violation of my own impulses even to speak of these things, but my oldest daughter is constantly represented as being engaged to this, that, or the other man in different parts of the country, in some instances to men she has never even met in her life. It is a constant and intolerable annoyance....

Now, I feel this way, gentlemen: Ever since I can remember I have been taught that the deepest obligation that rested upon me was to defend the women of my household from annoyance. Now I intend to do it, and the only way I can think of is this. It is a way which will impose the penalty in a certain sense upon those whom I believe to be innocent, but I do not see why I should permit representatives of papers who treat the ladies of my household in this way to have personal interviews. . . . My daughters have no brother whom they can depend upon. I am President of the United States; I cannot

[57] W. H. Taft to Gus J. Karger, April 8, 1915, Papers of William Howard Taft, Library of Congress.

[58] Wilson to the editor of the New York *Herald,* September 2, 1915, Wilson Papers. Tumulty saved the reporter from his punishment. See John M. Blum, *Joe Tumulty and the Wilson Era* (Boston: Houghton Mifflin Co., 1951), pp. 63–64.

act altogether as an individual while I occupy this office. But I must do some-thing. The thing is intolerable. Every day I pick up the paper and see some flat lie, some entire invention, things represented as having happened to my daughters where they were not present, and all sorts of insinuations. . . .

Now, if you have ever been in a position like that yourselves—and I hope to God you never will be—you know how I feel, and I must ask you gentle-men to make confidential representations to the several papers which you represent about this matter. . . . Now, put yourselves in my place and give me the best cooperation in this that you can, and then we can dismiss a painful subject and go to our afternoon's business.[59]

Wilson's dislike for reporters must have stemmed in part from his disdain of newspapers as agents both of opinion and of news. How were one's friends to know the simple fact of what was happening to him? he asked. "They certainly cannot know from the newspapers. A few, like the New York World, for example, or the Springfield Repub-lican, give the real facts, in their editorials if not in their news columns; but the rest are a tissue of inventions and speculations and of versions of what they would like to believe to be true. I never imagined any-thing like it. And most of the newspapers are owned or controlled by men who fear and would discredit the present administration."[60] Or again: "The real trouble is that the newspapers get the real facts but do not find them to their taste and do not use them as given them, and in some of the newspaper offices news is deliberately invented. Since I came here I have wondered how it ever happened that the public got a right impression regarding public affairs, particularly foreign affairs."[61]

Actually, Wilson's opinion of the press was intuitive rather than rea-sonable, because he read few newspapers in the White House. It was his habit at breakfast to glance through, but not to read thoroughly, the New York *World*, the *Springfield Republican*, and occasionally a few other friendly newspapers; and he would sometimes read the edi-torials that Tumulty clipped and pasted on long yellow sheets. On the whole, however, he ignored the press, particularly the opposition news-papers, and ascertained public opinion in other ways—through his ad-visers and leaders in Congress and, above all, by the tremendous vol-ume of organized opinion, expressed in letters, petitions, resolutions, and telegrams, which poured daily into the White House.

[59] "CONFIDENTIAL—NOT TO BE PUBLISHED, Newspaper Interview, March 19, 1914," MS in the Wilson Papers.

[60] Wilson to X, July 12, 1914.

[61] Wilson to C. W. Eliot, June 1, 1914, printed in R. S. Baker, *Woodrow Wilson: Life and Letters* (Garden City: Doubleday, 1927–39), IV, 234–35.

Yet Tumulty, who had actual charge of the administration's press relations, managed to salvage some measure of journalistic good will. In contrast to Wilson, Tumulty was warmly affectionate in his relations with newspapermen; they in turn "responded with favorable accounts of Wilson, his program, and his purposes."[62] It was Tumulty who prompted Wilson to send flowers when the wife of the *New York Times* correspondent died, or to write appreciative letters to friendly editors and publishers.[63] It was Tumulty, finally, who persuaded the President, before 1917, to give intimate interviews to a few trusted correspondents, Samuel G. Blythe, Ray Stannard Baker, and Ida M. Tarbell.

These three distinguished writers drew warm and winning word-portraits of the President as he desperately wanted the American people to know him. Wilson, Blythe wrote, was "social, sociable, and sagacious," "a person of convictions who has the courage of them," "affable and agreeable," "entirely democratic and unassuming,"[64] "one of the most kindly, courteous, considerate, genial and companionable of men," "whose passion is the people—the real people," personally lonely but sustained by the love of his fellow men.[65]

Baker portrayed the man of intellect and the calm leader in time of crisis. "Here at the center of things where the spirit of the nation questioned itself," Baker wrote after a visit to the White House in 1916, "was a great quietude, steadiness, confidence. . . . It all came to me that night—the undisturbed home, the peaceful surroundings, the thoughtful man at his desk—curiously but deeply as a symbol of immense strength."[66]

---

[62] Blum, *op. cit.,* p. 64.

[63] "Let me say that every day I open the editorial page of the World expecting to find what I do, a real vision of things as they are," Wilson wrote, for example, to the publisher of the New York *World*. Wilson to Ralph Pulitzer, March 2, 1914, Wilson Papers. See also Wilson to Wallace M. Scudder (*Newark Evening News*), January 5, 1914; Wilson to Solomon B. Griffin (*Springfield* [Massachusetts] *Republican*), January 5, 1914; Wilson to William Allen White (*Emporia* [Kansas] *Gazette*), May 15, 1914; Wilson to E. S. Wilson (Columbus *Ohio State Journal*), May 22, 1914; Wilson to Oswald G. Villard (New York *Evening Post*), August 24, 1914; and Wilson to Frank I. Cobb (New York *World*), March 4, 1915, all in *ibid.,* for other examples.

[64] S. G. Blythe, "Our New President," *Saturday Evening Post,* CLXXXV (March 1, 1913), 49.

[65] S. G. Blythe, "A Talk with the President," *ibid.,* CLXXXVII (January 9, 1915), 3, 37.

[66] Baker, "Wilson," p. 5. I have transposed these sentences.

Miss Tarbell described the "gentleman, who having invited you to his table, treats you as a fellow human being." "The sight of him moving so quietly yet energetically through his exacting daily program," she continued, "treating the grave matters which so dominate him gravely, yet able to turn gayly and with full sense of human values to the lighter matters which are equally a part of his business, humanizes and endears him."[67]

Blythe, Baker, and Miss Tarbell made the best case possible, but they did not convince the reporters who knew the other Wilson. Nor did they convince the American people. To them the President remained a leader they might trust and admire, but they rarely loved him.

[67] Tarbell, *op. cit.*, p. 5.

CHAPTER TWO

Personal Recollections of Woodrow Wilson*

By
Raymond B. Fosdick

The topic which has been assigned me involves the necessity of a some-what autobiographical approach. If I am to discuss my subject, the personal pronoun seems inevitable. I regret this emphasis and I trust that my readers will bear with me and will realize that the framework of my theme makes any other method of discussion almost impossible.

I would also like to say by way of preface that I do not claim to have been an intimate friend of Woodrow Wilson. Very few people ever succeeded in establishing that kind of relationship with him. I was a student of his at Princeton and therefore our paths crossed in a variety of more or less tangential ways. But I cannot say that at any one time my relations with him resembled intimacy or companionship. Certainly there was nothing that bordered on familiarity. He called me by my last name, without the "Mr.," but that was as far as he ever went. On my side, from the day I first met him until he died, he had my whole-hearted admiration and respect.

I first met him, of course, when I was a student at Princeton. I had taken my Freshman and Sophomore years at Colgate University, and I entered Princeton in the fall of 1903 as a member of the Junior class. Three days after I had registered I met Wilson. It was entirely by accident. I saw him approaching on the walk across the front campus, and I recognized him from his pictures. At Colgate it was an ironclad custom for undergraduates to take their hats off to the president, and I assumed, erroneously, that the same tradition held at Princeton. I therefore doffed my hat to him. He smiled and took off his hat to me. Then he stopped and said:

"You're new here, aren't you?"

* Lecture delivered at the University of Chicago, January 30, 1956.

"Yes, sir," I replied.

"And I see you are not a Freshman," he continued, because I was not wearing the prescribed Freshman cap.

I told him I was entering as a Junior, and I answered two or three of his questions about Colgate. He chatted in a friendly manner for a minute or two, and then, as we parted, he said: "I wish you would drop in to see me."

This was my introduction to Princeton, and I am sure that no welcome was ever so stimulating to a lonely and somewhat bewildered student coming to an institution in which he did not know a soul. I assumed that Mr. Wilson meant what he said, and a week or two later I called on him at his house, just as we were accustomed to do at Colgate. It was the beginning of a long and occasionally close association which lasted until his death over twenty years later.

Wilson on first appearance was not what would be called a handsome man. Indeed he was curiously homely. He had what he himself described as a "horse face"—a long, thin, and generally unsmiling visage with strong jaws. He had also an extraordinarily keen gaze, which could sometimes be disconcerting. But his eyes were nevertheless his best feature; they could light up with humor and kindliness, and his whole face would soften as it reflected his thoughts. His figure was tall and lithe, and he held himself erect and walked with a brisk pace. When I first met him he was forty-seven years old, and the mark of leadership was on his face and in his whole bearing.

What I remember initially about him at Princeton was the way he conducted chapel. Attendance at college chapel in my time was compulsory—five days a week and once on Sunday—and the whole business, rooted in Calvinistic traditions, was heartily disliked by the students. Once when a group of undergraduates approached Wilson on the question of making chapel attendance optional, he replied with mock gravity: "Why, gentlemen, it *is* optional. If you wish to go to chapel you may." But when Wilson himself conducted the chapel exercises, as he did once or twice a week, he brought an atmosphere of reverence and sincerity which subdued even the students of Nassau Hall of my boisterous generation. He had a magnificent, resonant voice, and I can still recall his incomparable reading of the Scriptures—his favorite Nineteenth Psalm, for example: "The heavens declare the glory of God; and the firmament showeth his handiwork"; or the thirteenth chapter of I Corinthians: "And now abideth faith, hope, charity, these three."

When these old words came ringing through the chapel, carried by the magnetism of Wilson's voice, I do not say that the students were spellbound, but they were significantly silent.

His prayers were even more compelling, uttered with deep and almost passionate earnestness. They generally had to do with the hope that we young men might be worthy and effective tools in the hands of an omnipotent will. They were always extemporaneous, but, no matter what the occasion, he invariably concluded them with the section from the Episcopal prayer book which begins: "Almighty and most merciful Father, we have erred and strayed from thy ways like lost sheep," and which ends with the sentence: "And grant O most merciful Father, that we may hereafter live a godly, righteous and sober life, to the glory of thy holy Name."

In trying to understand the personality of Woodrow Wilson we have to remember that first and foremost he was a deeply religious man. With the exception of Gladstone, probably no other man in supreme power in the life of any nation was so profoundly imbued by the Christian faith. He came from a Calvinistic background, and he was sturdily and mystically Christian. He believed that God was working out His purposes in this world, and once he made up his mind that a particular course of action represented the will of God, nothing could shake him loose from it. "God save us from compromise," he used to say; or again: "Let's stop being merely practical and find out what's right." I remember when I last saw him, in his house on S Street in Washington, a few weeks before he died, we discussed the recent progress that the League of Nations had been making. With tears rolling down his face, he said: "You can't fight God!" To him the underlying principle of the League of Nations represented the fulfilment of a preordained purpose, and if he took any pride in the situation at all, it was that he had been an instrument—however faulty—in carrying out the will of God.

That this aspect of his character frequently made him appear unyielding and stubborn cannot be denied. That it was one of the great sources of his strength is equally true. He was a man to whom the realities of the life of the spirit were very real, and those of us who heard his occasional lay sermons before the Philadelphian Society in Princeton will never forget the subdued but intense tones of his voice in those evening hours, as with quiet eloquence he upheld the priority of spiritual values in the lives of men.

Personal Recollections of Woodrow Wilson

Of course he was one of the great public speakers of his generation. I would be inclined to say that he was the greatest orator I have ever heard, although the word orator in our day has taken on a somewhat invidious meaning—sound and fury, signifying nothing. But there was no trace of the rotund or of bombast in Wilson's method of speaking, no forensic attitudes, no histrionic gestures. Indeed he employed very few gestures, the only one that I recall being the use of the forefinger of his right hand pointed at his audience. His power lay in the precision of his mind, in the matchless lucidity of his argument, and in his passionate sincerity. His influence on his listeners was almost hypnotic, and he could fairly bring them to their feet with a stirring phrase. I remember one night after his election to the White House, but before he had taken office, he spoke at a dinner in New York City. I do not recall what the occasion was, but in referring to some evil influences or threatening figures in public life he electrified his audience by the grim comment in measured accents: "We'll hang them on a gibbet higher than Haman's."

His addresses were almost invariably extemporaneous, although he prepared his outlines with care. Once when he was asked by some undergraduates to make a speech, he inquired how long it should be. "It doesn't matter," he was told. "It matters to me," he replied. "If you want me to talk for ten minutes, I need two weeks to prepare. If you want me to speak for half an hour I need a day. If you have no time limit I am ready right now." And yet he never memorized an address, and he seldom used notes. The words seemed to flow naturally and logically with uninterrupted cadence.

I heard Lloyd George at the top of his form in the budget debates in the House of Commons in 1909. I heard Asquith and Lord Balfour on several occasions, and William J. Bryan, as well, particularly in his later days. I heard Senator Beveridge and other great speakers of their time. In sheer ability and power it seems to me that Wilson towered above them all. He was a scholar in action, a prophet touched by fire, with unmatched strength to persuade and move the hearts of his listeners.

This ability to express himself in cogent, vivid phrase was one of the reasons, I suspect, why he was so outstanding as a teacher. I have never seen his equal in a classroom, whether the room was a lecture hall, crowded with four or five hundred students, or a curtained-off cubicle for a hastily improvised seminar, or, best of all, his study in Prospect, the president's home at Princeton, with three or four of us asking him

31

questions. More than any other man I have ever met he seemed to personify the dignity and power of ideas. He made the life of the intellect attractive. It was through him that we became aware of our inheritance of the rational tradition that was born in ancient Greece—a tradition of candid and fearless thinking about the great questions of liberty and government, of freedom and control.

Wilson's regular courses were in jurisprudence and in constitutional government, given on the top floor of old Dickinson Hall to a class of perhaps five hundred students. He always started his lectures with the salutation: "Good morning, gentlemen." He generally had a page of notes on the lectern in front of him—notes written in shorthand, for he was a master of shorthand—but he seldom appeared to refer to them. Occasionally he would interrupt his lecture with the remark: "Now gentlemen, I suggest you take this down," and he would dictate slowly and succinctly some idea he had been developing. I still have my old notebooks which I kept in his classes, and I find they contain such sentences as these:

The associated life out of which law springs produces many things: natural ties, ties of habit or affection, ties of interest, a developed set of rules of social morality. Law takes up whatever is in this way completed—whatever has been made ready and reduced to a uniform rule of conduct—and provides it with a compulsive sanction.

Is it any wonder that a man who taught this kind of doctrine should, sixteen years later, describe the proposed prohibition law as unworkable and send it back to the Congress with a stern veto?

Or take this from my notebook, obviously the outline of an idea far more extensively treated:

Morality is a great deal bigger than law. The individual morality is the sense of right or wrong of one man. The social morality must strike an average. This is where reformers make their tragic mistake. There can be no compromise in individual morality; but there *has* to be a compromise, an average, in social morality. There is indeed an element of morality in the very fact of compromise on *social* undertakings.

Here Wilson was posing a difficult question: how to draw a rational line between the individual conscience and social action. The question has plagued the minds of thoughtful men from the days of Plato; and with Wilson's own passionate convictions and fighting spirit, it proved to be the major problem which he had to face again and again.

I can still see his strong, long-jawed, animated face and hear the cadences of his amazing extempory eloquence. No matter how he began them, his sentences always came out in perfect form. Occasionally when he plunged headlong into an involved sentence structure, I would think to myself: "There's a sentence he can't extricate himself from"; but I was always wrong. Not only were his sentences works of art, but his argument was presented with a convincing skill and an intellectual brilliance which held his students spellbound, so that frequently they broke into applause and stamped their feet at the end of his lectures—an almost unheard-of occurrence in the conservative traditions of Princeton.

It was not in his regular lectures, however, but in his informal and sometimes casual contacts with the students that he made his deepest impressions—his occasional talks at Whig Hall, one of the two debating societies on the campus; the more or less informal seminars at which his attendance, because of his administrative duties, was necessarily irregular; and particularly the occasional meetings with small groups in his own home. I remember one evening with particular vividness. He lay on the floor on a rug in front of the fire while his brother-in-law, Stockton Axson, read Wordsworth to us. Wilson was very fond of poetry and read it himself with great effect. I recall on another occasion—just what it was I don't remember—the dramatic earnestness with which he described the Covenanter movement in Scotland in 1638—the forbidding Sunday morning in Greyfriars churchyard, under the shadow of Edinburgh Castle, when the grim and determined citizens signed their names to the Covenant on a flat tombstone just outside the door. Years later, because I had never forgotten his description of it, I went to the churchyard to see for myself the setting and background of the incident. To Wilson it was one of the outstanding events in the long struggle for liberty. It was here that freedom of conscience took root; this was a steppingstone by which the past made its way into a future of wider justice. We who had the privilege of listening to him when he was in this kind of mood always came away feeling that we had been in the presence of someone upon whom had fallen the mantle of the old prophets of liberty.

In Wilson's system of social philosophy, Locke and Bagehot seemed to be the high priests, and in his lectures he quoted them constantly. To some he may have given the impression that he was interested in theory to the exclusion of everything else. But he had a way of illustrating his theory by graphic references to the present; and by indirection he introduced us to a new world of reality in which ideas were put to practical ends. It was through him that many of us received our first impressions of the color and significance of contemporary events. Our academic work largely centered on Latin, Greek, and mathematics. It was the wisdom of the past that preoccupied us. We now entered a realm in which the current Russian-Japanese war was a matter of deep concern, and the question of efficient government on both the local and national level was of intriguing interest.

Of course Wilson had a lighter and gayer side which we students seldom saw, and it was not until later, when I got to know him better, that I realized how real and significant a part of his personality it was. He was a superb raconteur, with an amazing fund of anecdotes and stories. Indeed his dialect stories, told in Scotch, Irish, or Negro accents, were often side-splitting, and a few of them I still recall even after all these decades. Any kind of foolish verse or limerick had a strong appeal to him, and he could recite scores of them. He had, too, a quick and lively wit, and some of his retorts are cherished in the memory of his friends today. For example, the mother of one of his students urged him to make Princeton a coeducational institution.

"Why?" he asked.

"To remove the false glamor with which the two sexes see each other," she replied.

"My dear madam," Wilson shot back, "that is the very thing we want to preserve at all costs!"

In his later years, certainly, he did not hesitate, on informal occasions, to employ a picturesque kind of slang if it suited his purpose; and he could come out with a good healthy "damn" if the occasion required it. But I never heard him go beyond this in the way of expletives, and I doubt if he did. Always he was restrained by a natural fastidiousness, an innate temperance of taste.

I have frequently been asked whether during my student days Wilson was a liberal in his political and social thinking. The word "liberal," of course, is capable of wide definition, but certainly I cannot say that at that time he was in any sense a militant progressive. He seemed to be more of a Federalist than a Democrat, more of a Hamiltonian than a Jeffersonian, and I suspect that at this point in his career he had a kind of intellectual impatience with the practical processes of democracy. For example, he was opposed at that time, and even later, to woman suffrage. "I do not believe in it," he used to say, "but I never argue against it, for there *are* no logical arguments against it." Wilson's awakening to a new social and political awareness came, I am sure, after I graduated. But to the students of my time the words "liberal" or "conservative" had no particular meaning or significance. It was enough for us that Wilson challenged our ability to think and led us to some appreciation of the place and power of ideas in the life of men.

I speak only as a single student at Princeton of over fifty years ago. For me Wilson lit a lamp which has never been put out. All my life I have remembered him as the inspiring teacher who introduced us to the kingdom of the mind and held up before our eyes what Whitehead later called "an habitual vision of greatness."

When I graduated from Princeton in 1905, I went back for a year of postgraduate work. I had the feeling that another year of association with Wilson—even indirect and perhaps remote—would not represent wasted time. I saw him only occasionally. Once our contact had to do with the subject of debating, in which he was very much interested. I had had some experience during my undergraduate years in debating on the intercollegiate level, and one day he sent for me during this postgraduate term and asked me if I would lead the team against Yale. I was reluctant to do it because I had other interests that seemed more important, but he was a very persuasive man, and I yielded to his request. I must tell the whole truth: the Princeton team was beaten, but I had the satisfaction of seeing him jump off his bicycle the next morning on Nassau Street, stride over to the curb where I was standing, and tell me that in his considered opinion the verdict of the judges was unjust. To my lacerated feelings his words were a long-remembered solace and consolation.

At the end of my postgraduate year, I decided to study law. Wilson was not too pleased with my decision, and when I reminded him that this was precisely what *he* had done, he remarked: "It was one of the less happy periods of my career." Thereafter for six years I saw him two or three times only—at his house in Princeton, as I remember, for he continued to live in Princeton even when he was governor of New Jersey.

In 1912 when he had been nominated for the Presidency he wrote me a letter asking me if I would serve as secretary and auditor of the finance committee of the National Democratic Committee. "I should myself feel greatly honored," he added in a warm and gracious sentence, "that a former pupil of mine, who has so distinguished himself in a position of trust, should turn to me at this time." What he was referring to was the fact that I had been serving as Commissioner of Accounts in a rather dramatic reform administration in New York City. Indeed it was to discuss some of my problems in this office that I had visited him at Princeton while he was governor of New Jersey.

Needless to say, I dropped everything to comply with his request, and for two or three months I had offices in the old Fifth Avenue Hotel in New York, the headquarters of the National Democratic Committee. At Wilson's direction we introduced a strict budget system, with lines of accountability definitely established, and with periodic audits. I am quite sure that our methods came as a shock to the old guard of the Democratic party. They were not used to that sort of thing and they doubtless put it down as one of the inexplicable peccadilloes of the man whom in more disparaging moments they referred to as "that Princeton professor."

But it was an interesting lot of people stationed at the headquarters. William G. McAdoo was there, later Secretary of the Treasury, and Josephus Daniels, afterward Secretary of the Navy. Billy McCombs was also there—the tragic figure whose promising career was brought to a swift end by ill health and an ill-adjusted temperament. And then there was a tall, slender, handsome young fellow of great charm—a year older than I was—a man of whom we were all deeply fond. We called him Frank or Franklin. Exactly twenty-one years later we called him Mr. President. Wilson himself occasionally dropped in at the headquarters, and some of us went down to Princeton to get his advice. It was a time of intense excitement. The night before election Wilson spoke before a madly cheering audience at Madison Square Garden. He was hoarse and tired, and the meeting was not the kind of occasion for which he was adapted or which he particularly enjoyed. But he acquitted himself magnificently and sent the crowd away with the feeling that a new kind of intelligence had been recruited to serve the public interest.

A year after he was inaugurated, Wilson asked me to take the position of Commissioner of Immigration at the Port of New York, with headquarters at Ellis Island. (Again I apologize for introducing these personal details, and I emphasize once more that it is only through these details that I can deal with my assigned topic.) I had been in public office in New York City for nearly six years, and it held no illusions for me. Moreover, I was just finishing a book based on a long study I had made of European police systems. I did not want to be Commissioner of Immigration, and I declined the offer. Whereupon the President wrote me urging me to reconsider the matter. "I should not deem myself faithful to my public responsibilities," he said, "if I did not make a very earnest effort to open your mind again on the subject, and to turn it toward acceptance, so strongly do I feel that you are the very man we need for just that place." He asked me to come to Washington to see him if I had further doubts.

With a heavy heart I went to the White House. I knew from long experience how irresistibly persuasive he could be. And it was as I expected. He reverted to his favorite theme of "Princeton in the Nation's service." He drew a vivid picture of what Ellis Island could be made to be. Here hundreds of thousands of immigrants every year got their first impression of America. It must be a good impression—an impression of America at her best. The tawdry surroundings of Ellis Island could be transformed into a kind of laboratory of human relations. We could make these future citizens feel that they were indeed coming to a new home—a home that was glad and proud to welcome them and that would do everything within its power to unite them with the family of democracy. The job required high imagination and patience. It was a challenge—a worthy challenge for a Princeton man.

I do not know how I escaped his spell. I am sure I was not very articulate. He was courteous as always, but I could sense his displeasure, and I left the White House feeling that I had sinned against the light. Even today, more than forty years later, my conscience occasionally troubles me when I recall my stubborn refusal.

Two years later Wilson offered me a post in the Far East, but this time I could decline with a clear conscience, for it was obvious that America would soon be drawn into the European war, and I was deeply involved in a series of studies for the War Department. At the request of the Secretary of War, Newton D. Baker, I had spent the summer of 1916 on the Mexican border, where the National Guard of all the states was mobilized. The question posed was this: What opportunities do men of the armed forces have to make satisfactory and profitable use of their leisure time? Later I made similar studies in Canada. When the United States entered the war in April, 1917, Secretary Baker created a Commission on Training Camp Activities as a branch of the War Department, and I served as chairman. At the suggestion of President Wilson, Secretary Daniels created a similar commission for the Navy, of which I was also chairman. Starting in a small office in the old State, War, and Navy Building, with my secretary and myself as its only occupants, we had five thousand people on the staff before the war was over. We carried on a host of non-military functions which in World War II were taken over by the Special Services Division of the Army and the corresponding branch of the Navy, as well as by the USO. We built scores of theaters in military camps and ran a regular theatrical booking service; we had song coaches and athletic coaches; we had responsibility for the enforcement of Sections 12 and 13 of the Military Draft Act, relating to prostitution and the sale of liquor in the neighborhood of military camps; we co-ordinated the services of a dozen private organizations that were working with the troops; and we carried on a constant warfare with congressional appropriation committees over funds for athletic supplies and all the paraphernalia of normal living for the armed forces. Wilson expressed our function in better words than I can. "The Federal Government," he wrote, referring to our commission, "has pledged its word that as far as care and vigilance can accomplish the result, the men committed to its charge will be returned to the homes and communities which so generously gave them with no scars except those won in honorable warfare."

From the start the President was deeply and personally interested in our work, and I was probably closer to him during this period than at any other time. He wrote me letters about our activities and I frequently conferred with him at the White House. Although I was responsible directly to the Secretary of War and the Secretary of the Navy, in this one respect at least, the President never bothered about official channels. He would ask me to come to see him or he would write me personally with suggestions or complaints that had been brought to his attention. Often these letters he typed on his own typewriter at night. He was concerned, for example, about the problem of race discrimination in the armed forces at Newport News. At another time he thought that we were not giving sufficient attention to the new possibilities of moving pictures. One of his letters I recall had to do with an actress whom he had seen at Keith's theater the night before. The light touch of vaudeville always relaxed him, and he was a frequent attendant at Keith's. His suggestion was that this particular actress might be a successful addition to our theater program in the camps. I am sorry I cannot recall her name, and his letter to me has disappeared. We booked her, of course, and as I remember it she proved to be in great demand, although her artistic temperament involved us in endless difficulties. Perhaps I should add that her name was *not* Elsie Janis, who later, in France, endeared herself to the entire American Army.

As our troops began to embark for Europe, the emphasis of the work of our commission shifted overseas, and I spent some months in 1918 in France and England. After the Armistice, Secretary Baker thought that my permanent headquarters should be with General Pershing, and by rare good fortune I was assigned to the SS "George Washington," which was carrying President Wilson and his associates to the Peace Conference in Paris. That trip, for me so completely accidental, was one of the memorable experiences of my life. I kept a diary of the dramatic events of the voyage, and even today I read it with a feeling of excitement. History was in the process of being made. The curtain was rising on a new era in the human story. Wilson, accompanied by his attractive and charming wife, was thoroughly tired out when he came aboard, but the long, deliberate trip—we went by way of the Azores—seemed to rest him. I had a number of talks with him, and as usual he spoke with the utmost frankness. He was deeply concerned about the spread of Bolshevism—"a poison," he called it. Its absolutism repelled him, and he quoted Jefferson's pledge of "eternal hostility against any form of tyranny over the mind of man." Wilson called himself a liberal, but liberalism must be more liberal than ever before, if civilization is to survive, he said. Conservatism he defined as the policy of "make no change and consult your grandmother when in doubt." "Those who argue for the *status quo ante bellum*," he added, "or for any other *status quo*, are like so many vain kings sitting by the sea and commanding the tide not to rise." In my diary I said, following one of these talks, "I think his mental processes function more easily and logically than in any other man I ever met, and the compelling power of his personality is tremendous."

Wilson's welcome in Paris was accompanied by the most remarkable demonstration of enthusiasm and affection on the part of the Parisians than I have ever heard of, let alone seen. His train from Brest was purposely delayed and arrived at ten o'clock in the morning. The rest of us came through on a fast train that got in at six in the morning. The parade over a four-mile drive consisted merely of eight horse-drawn carriages, preceded by a handful of hussars of the guard. Wilson and Poincaré rode in the first carriage. Troops, cavalry and infantry, lined the entire route, and tens of thousands of persons fought for a glimpse of their hero. The streets were decorated with flags and bunting, and huge banners bearing the words "Welcome to Wilson" or "Honor to Wilson the Just" stretched across the roadways from house to house.

I was in a window in a building on the corner of Rue Royale and the Place de la Concorde. The carriages approached at a trot. We could hear the cheers across the Seine. Wilson was smiling and waving his hat. The noise was deafening. It was all over in a minute and we heard the cheers rolling up the Rue Royale to the Madeleine. The troops started to march, but the crowds broke through, and for an hour the Place de la Concorde was a riot of color and enthusiasm.

My diary ends on a somber note. "Tonight," I wrote, "the boulevards of Paris are still celebrating. An American can have anything he wants today; he owns the city. The girls even try to kiss him on the streets. I wonder—and the thought keeps coming back to me—what will be the greeting of the French when the Peace is finished and Wilson comes to go home. I wish it could be guaranteed that their affection for America and the Americans would be as real and as enthusiastic as it is today. Poor Wilson! A man with his responsibilities is to be pitied. The French think that with almost a magic touch he will bring about the day of political and industrial justice. Will he? Can he?"

During his days in Paris I saw little of the President, although because of the friendships formed on the "George Washington," I took my meals at the Hotel Crillon, the headquarters of the American Peace Delegation. There I was in rather intimate contact with the hectic and frequently stirring events that preceded the Treaty of Versailles. Once, I remember, I went to see Wilson at his house on an errand relating to the Army. It turned out to be rather embarrassing. General Pershing wanted the President to give a silver cup to the final winner of some interdivisional series of athletic sport—whether it was football or boxing I do not recall. To express it more accurately, Pershing wanted Wilson to give his consent to have the cup, for which funds were available, called the "President's cup." When I explained the matter to Wilson, he said: "I should be delighted to do it, but I would want to pay for the cup myself."

"But Mr. President," I expostulated. He cut me off abruptly.

"My dear fellow," he said. "If I give a cup for the Army or for any other object, I am going to pay for it myself. It would look rather shabby if the so-called President's cup was financed from other sources." And that was that; and when I reported it to General Pershing the General growled at me for nearly fifteen minutes.

I returned to the United States the latter part of May, 1919. Hardly had I landed in New York when the State Department called me to say that the President, who was still in Paris, wanted me to accept the position of Undersecretary-General in the new League of Nations. The Covenant of the League provided that the Secretary-General should be Sir Eric Drummond, of the British Foreign Office, and the idea at that time was that there should be an American and a French Undersecretary-General. Jean Monnet, who since then has had a distinguished career in France, was chosen to represent that nation.

To say that I was staggered by the offer is to express my reaction in mild words. Up to that time I had not even heard of the position, and I felt very keenly my own inadequacy. Newton Baker, the Secretary of War, who had become a close friend of mine, urged me to accept, and I did, although with some hesitation—not from any lack of desire to serve, but from a feeling that I was ill-prepared by previous experience for this unique undertaking. I remember Newton Baker's comment on my reservation: "Where in the world would anyone find experience in running a League of Nations?"

On the last day of June, therefore, I left for London, the League's temporary headquarters, exchanging greetings with the President by wireless in mid-ocean, he having sailed from Brest the same day I sailed from New York. Thereafter, during the summer months and into the fall, Drummond, Monnet, and I, with a white sheet of paper in front of us, drew up the tentative organization of the secretariat of the League of Nations. We were indeed pioneers on a far frontier.

In October Drummond asked me to represent the secretariat at the first meeting, scheduled for Washington, of the International Labor Office, which had been set up by a special section of the Treaty of Versailles. I arrived in Washington about the middle of the month. By that time Wilson had made his great fight for the League of Nations and like a soldier in battle had fallen in the field in Pueblo, Colorado—had fallen with a cry that echoed down the years that followed: "My clients are the children; my clients are the next generation!"

Two letters which I wrote my family at the time illustrate the situation as I saw it. "Over everything in Washington," I said in the first letter, "hangs the shadow of the President's illness. The lines of Walt

Whitman's poem keep running through my head: 'Where on the deck my captain lies.' And truly the ship is without a captain, and its precious cargo of hopes for a saner world is in dreadful jeopardy."

In the second letter I made this comment: "After nearly a year's absence the atmosphere in Washington seems strangely different. Of course it was obvious in 1917 and 1918 that the Republicans didn't like Wilson, and I shall always remember how T. R. [it was at a private dinner in New York] referred to the President as 'the gray skunk'; but T. R. was never given to understatement about his political opponents. Anyway, the Republican dislike of Wilson here in Washington has changed to open hatred. In spite of the fact that he is a desperately sick man they still hate him, and the comments you hear at the capitol or in hotel lobbies are almost unbelievable. To hear people talk you would think that Wilson was the chief enemy of his country. It is dreadful to come back from Europe where his name is revered and find this vitriolic feeling at home."

This is not the occasion to discuss the failures of the ruinous months that followed. We were shadowed by a double tragedy: first, the attitude of Senator Lodge and his bloc, who saw the League of Nations only as a God-given opportunity to crush the President; and second, the crippling illness of Wilson which shut him off from outside contacts and deprived us of leadership at a time when we needed it most. We might have survived one or the other tragedy. We could not survive both.

I did not see the President during this period; practically nobody did. And early in the following year I resigned my post as Undersecretary-General when the Senate's position became determinative. Writing to my wife from London, where I had gone to finish up my work with the League, I said: "Before I left America, people kept saying 'What a tragedy for Wilson!' But nobody need be concerned about Wilson. History will vindicate him and will place him among its prophets and heroes. He dared and apparently failed, but that has been the fate of many men whose memories the world reveres. Most generations stone their prophets. This is not Wilson's tragedy. It is America's tragedy. It is the tragedy of the next generation."

I did not see Wilson again until he was living on S Street in Washington after his retirement from the White House, although once or twice I was in contact with him through his secretary. Following my withdrawal from the League, we established here in the United States the League of Nations News Bureau and later the League of Nations Non-Partisan Association, and I undertook to keep Mr. Wilson in touch with the developments at Geneva. One letter from him, received during this period, I particularly cherish. It was couched in warm and affectionate words and was more personal than was his general wont—at least with me. "The League has indeed become," he said, "a vital and commanding force and will more and more dominate international relationships. I am thankful that I had something to do with its institution and I am also thankful, my dear fellow, that it has drawn to its service men like yourself in whose ideals and purposes I have perfect confidence."

Shortly before he died he wrote me asking if I would come in to see him at his house on S Street. "I want to discuss with you," he said, "not a matter concerning the League of Nations, but an educational matter." I immediately went to Washington, and found him in a reminiscent mood about his days as president of Princeton. "It was the best period of my life," he said, "and I begin to realize that my contribution to my generation, if I have made any, was in connection not so much with my political work as with my activities as a teacher and college administrator." I remember he told me a story about the master of Balliol who was asked whether it was not a dreary business to spend twenty years doing the sort of work that the head of any college has to do; to which the master of Balliol replied: "Is it dreary business to run the British Empire?"

Wilson at this moment was dreaming of the possibility of another chance in educational work, another opportunity, as he expressed it, to help American universities to attain the high standards of scholarship which had been reached by Oxford and Cambridge.

It was, of course, the nostalgic dream of an old and crippled warrior as he thinks over the battles of his younger days—a knight with his armor laid aside, sitting by the fire in the late autumn of his life and remembering the blows he had struck for causes that had inspired his youth. Wilson's desire to talk with me about it was due to the fact that at that time I was connected with the General Education Board and had some knowledge of the developments in American colleges. Wilson told me of the philosophy behind the preceptorial system which he had initiated at Princeton and the projected division of the university into small units or colleges—ideas which he said were capable of wide elaboration and application. His body was crippled but his mind flashed with the old fire. In high spirits he reviewed the events of the old days, and his characterizations of some of his contemporaries—particularly those of whom he was not very fond—were couched in vivid and unforgettable words.

I went down to Washington to see him once again, ostensibly on this same errand. It was less than a month before he died, and it was very obvious that his strength was failing, although his mind was keen and alert. When I said to him: "How are you, Mr. President," he quoted a remark by John Quincy Adams in answer to a similar query: "John Quincy Adams is all right, but the house he lives in is dilapidated, and it looks as if he would soon have to move out." On this occasion Wilson talked very little about education. His whole thought centered on the League of Nations, and I had never heard him speak with deeper or more moving earnestness. In his weakness the tears came easily to his eyes and sometimes rolled down his cheek, but he brushed them impatiently away. I think he had a premonition that his days were numbered—"The sands are running fast," he told me—and perhaps he wanted to make his last testament clear and unmistakable. The League of Nations was a promise for a better future, he said, as well as an escape from an evil past. Constantly his mind ran back to 1914. The utter unintelligence of it all, the sheer waste of war as a method of settling anything, seemed to oppress him. "It never must happen again," he said. "There is a way out if only men will use it." His voice rose as he recalled the charge of idealism so often used against the League. "The world is *run* by its ideals," he exclaimed. "Only the fool thinks otherwise." The League was the answer. It was the next logical step in man's widening conception of order and law. The machinery might be changed by experience, but the core of the idea was essential. It was in line with human evolution. It was the will of God.

That was my last glimpse of him. With his gray, lined face, his white hair, his grim, determined jaw, he seemed like the reincarnation of one of the prophets—an Isaiah, perhaps—crying to his country in the words which Wilson had so often read to us in the chapel at Princeton years before: "Awake, awake, put on thy strength, O Zion; put on thy beautiful garments, O Jerusalem!"

Many harsh allegations were made against Woodrow Wilson by his enemies, and some of these allegations still survive in the folklore of today. It was said, for example, that he wanted only flattery from his associates and that he did not take kindly to frankness or dissent. It was said that he was a cold, distant, and arrogant man who reached his decisions not by rational processes but by intuition and who formed his conclusions in isolation.

To me these allegations seem completely preposterous. They do not fit in with any experience I ever had with him, although admittedly my contacts were limited. That he was a man of steely determination who allowed no compromise on what he regarded as a matter of principle is transparently true. No one could meet him without sensing the driving power of his mind and the flame of his spirit. Equally true is the fact that he had too little appreciation of what Ray Stannard Baker called "human lubricants": the need of explanation, conference, and team play, the ability to keep differences of opinion on an impersonal level. He did not suffer fools gladly—neither fools nor people with untidy minds. There was an element of intellectual impatience in his makeup, and more than a dash of volatile temper. It was not easy for him to forget or forgive. In other words, he was a human being, and like all of us he had his temperamental and physical limitations.

But in the end, what difference does it make? All the world's heroes and prophets have had their limitations, too. The great leaders and idealists who in strange bursts of power have lifted the spirits of men from age to age have been made of human stuff. In retrospect we do not focus on their inadequacies. History has its own methods of achieving perspective, of sifting the gold from the dross. The last word does not belong to the cynics or the scoffers.

So with Wilson. From his grave his ideals have ruled the future. The hope of the world today, tenuous as it may seem, is a hope which more than any other man he helped to shape. And *we* are the future over which he brooded. We are his clients—the children of the next generation. It is *our* world that he sought to serve and tried to save. We have lived in the presence of greatness, and in this year of remembrance we rekindle our personal recollections of the kind of man he was and cherish, as the future will cherish them, the tenacity of his faith and the constancy of his courage.

CHAPTER THREE

The Development of Woodrow Wilson's Theory of the Presidency: Continuity and Change*

By
A. J. Wann

In his autobiography, Dr. Stephen S. Wise relates that he once asked Woodrow Wilson, "When did you first think or dream of the Presidency?" The answer was "startlingly simple," according to Dr. Wise, for Wilson replied that there was never a time after his departure from Davidson College in 1874 "when I did not expect and did not prepare myself to become President."[1]

Those who expect the normal preparation for the Presidency to consist of a rather lengthy apprenticeship in other national or state government positions may find it difficult to understand the "preparation" to which Wilson referred in this statement. He had never held any political office, elective or appointive, nor had he presented himself before an electorate as a candidate until he ran for governor of New Jersey in 1910, only two years before his election as President.[2] Although he had been vitally interested in political affairs from youth onward, he had remained almost completely aloof from participation in practical politics prior to his successful gubernatorial campaign. Before 1910, his writings and speeches and his controversial conduct as president of Princeton had achieved a national reputation for Wilson rather than any overt political activity on his part. It was mainly be-

* Paper delivered at the Annual Meeting of the American Political Science Association, Washington, D.C., September, 1956.

1 Stephen Samuel Wise, *Challenging Years* (New York: G. P. Putnam's Sons, 1949), p. 161.

2 Wilson was appointed in 1906 as a member of the New Jersey Commission on Uniform State Laws. This was his first public office, but it was in no way a political one. See Arthur S. Link, *Wilson: The Road to the White House* (Princeton: Princeton University Press, 1947), p. 103.

cause of this growing national reputation[3] that the Democratic leaders of New Jersey selected Wilson as their candidate for governor, thus starting him on an active political career at the advanced age of fifty-four.

It is in what Wilson wrote before his belated entry into politics that evidence is found of the "preparation" for the Presidency which he probably had in mind in his reply to Dr. Wise. That he had been preoccupied for many years with analyzing the nature and problems of the Presidency can be seen in many of his works, from an early article, "Cabinet Government in the United States,"[4] published in 1879 while Wilson was in his senior year at Princeton, down to his book, *Constitutional Government in the United States*,[5] written in 1907. No other President prior to his election has set forth such a comprehensive theory regarding the role of the President in the American governmental system as did Wilson.

In studying the development of Wilson's theory through the years, one finds a considerable degree of continuity in his consistent reiteration of certain fundamental concepts. Regarding several aspects of the Presidency, however, Wilson's writings reveal that his views underwent a very substantial amount of change.

Wilson began his article, "Cabinet Government in the United States," by discussing the anxiety prevalent at the time about the future of American institutions. "A marked and alarming decline in statesmanship, a rule of levity and folly instead of wisdom and sober forethought in legislation, threaten to shake our trust not only in the men by whom our national policy is controlled, but also in the very principles upon which our government rests. Both state and national legislatures are looked upon with nervous suspicion, and we hail an adjournment of Congress as a temporary immunity from danger."[6] After denying that the principal cause was to be found in universal

[3] Wilson had already been the subject of considerable discussion as a potential presidential candidate as early as 1906 when George B. M. Harvey, editor of *Harper's Weekly* and an influential Democrat, first proposed him as an excellent Democratic nominee for the 1908 election. See Ray Stannard Baker, *Woodrow Wilson: Life and Letters* (New York: Charles Scribner's Sons, 1946), II, 196–200.

[4] *International Review,* VI (August, 1879), 146–63. Also found in R. S. Baker and W. E. Dodd (eds.), *The Public Papers of Woodrow Wilson* (New York: Harper & Bros., 1925–27), I, 19–42 (hereinafter cited as *Public Papers*).

[5] New York: Columbia University Press, 1908.

[6] *Public Papers,* I, 19.

manhood suffrage, as was being charged by many, Wilson stated that the real cause was "to be found in the absorption of all power by a legislature which is practically irresponsible for its acts."[7]

It was Wilson's belief that representative government, when properly constituted, is the best form to enable free people to govern themselves. He maintained, however, that under the representative system of the United States, government had actually come to be carried on by irresponsible and secret congressional committees.

Because of this system of "Committee Government," the President and his cabinet could not provide the effective and responsible leadership which Wilson believed necessary. "The President can seldom make himself recognized as a leader; he is merely the executor of the sovereign legislative will; his Cabinet officers are little more than chief clerks, or superintendents, in the Executive departments. . . ."[8] Instead, almost absolute power over the government had fallen into the hands of men—the Speaker of the House of Representatives and the chairmen of the congressional committees—who did not "speak for the nation" and whose conduct was not subject to suitable control by the people of the country.

The underlying reason for this situation, in Wilson's view, was that the doctrine of separation of powers had been applied too rigorously by the writers of the Constitution. According to Wilson, the separation is "so complete as to amount to isolation."[9] As a remedy, Wilson proposed that a system of responsible cabinet government should be adopted in the United States whereby the heads of the executive departments should hold seats in Congress and should have the privilege of initiating legislation. This could best be done, Wilson believed, by requiring the President to select his cabinet from members of the House of Representatives or the Senate.

Under a responsible cabinet system, the President and his cabinet would determine the national policies of the party they represent; it would be the function of Congress to debate, then reject or accept the proposals which cabinet members would introduce. Such a system would provide a badly needed link between the executive and legislative departments. For the proper functioning of the government, Wilson believed this to be absolutely necessary. "The Executive is in constant need of legislative cooperation; the legislative must be aided by an Executive who is in a position intelligently and vigorously to

[7] *Ibid.,* p. 20.   [8] *Ibid.,* p. 36.   [9] *Ibid.,* p. 25.

execute its acts."[10] This change would make the President and his cabinet the responsible leaders of the government, and the President "would then be in fact, and not merely in name, the head of the government."[11] Thus, cabinet government would insure responsible presidential leadership. In these early statements setting forth the necessity of such leadership, Wilson first expressed a view which was to continue to be fundamental to all his later thinking about the Presidency.

Wilson's second article on American government was written about four years after the first, following his attendance at the School of Law of the University of Virginia, his unhappy and unsuccessful year in the practice of law at Atlanta, Georgia, and his return to academic life at the Johns Hopkins University. Soon after he became a Johns Hopkins graduate student in 1883, Wilson wrote "Committee or Cabinet Government?"[12] which was, for the most part, only an expanded version of the views expressed in its predecessor. Wilson again urged that responsible leadership should be provided in the government by replacing the dominant power of the congressional committees with a system of cabinet government. He stated:

Let ... the leaders of parties be made responsible. ... This can be done by making the leaders of the dominant party in Congress the executive officers of the legislative will; by making them also members of the President's Cabinet, and thus at once the executive chiefs of the departments of State and the leaders of their party on the floor of Congress; in a word, by having done with the standing committees, and constituting the Cabinet advisers both of the President and of Congress.[13]

The first of Wilson's books, *Congressional Government*,[14] was written at Johns Hopkins during 1883 and 1884 and published in 1885. Wilson submitted this work in 1886 as his dissertation in fulfilling the requirements for the Ph.D. degree at Johns Hopkins, but that had not

---

[10] *Ibid.*, p. 41. [11] *Ibid.*, p. 38.

[12] *Overland Monthly*, III (January, 1884), 17–33. Also found in *Public Papers*, I, 95–129.

[13] *Ibid.*, p. 112. Wilson also outlined in this article a simple constitutional amendment which would remove the only legal obstacle to cabinet government. He proposed the addition of merely four words to the second clause of section 6 of Article I of the Constitution, so that instead of reading, "no person holding any office under the United States shall be a member of either House during his continuance in office," the amended article would read, "and no person holding any *other than a Cabinet* office under the United States shall be a member of either House during his continuance in office." According to Wilson, this would be the only change needed for the introduction of his cabinet system. *Ibid.*, p. 113.

[14] Boston: Houghton Mifflin Co.

been his original motivation for writing it. After the favorable way in which the article "Committee or Cabinet Government?" was received, particularly among his professors and fellow graduate students at Johns Hopkins,[15] Wilson decided to proceed with a project which he had seemingly been turning over in his mind for several years: to write a full treatment of the American national government, centered upon the same theme as that of his two articles—the need for effective and responsible leadership. His analysis of the weaknesses then existing in the government remained essentially the same as in the articles. In *Congressional Government*, however, Wilson presented a much more comprehensive treatment of the Presidency than he had done previously.

Wilson introduced his discussion of the role of the President by restating his belief that the Congress was virtually supreme in the American government and operated practically without restraint upon its actions. The men who wrote the Constitution had expected the President to be an effective restraint upon the power of Congress, for the President, Wilson wrote,

. . . was constituted one of the three great coordinate branches of the government; his functions were made of the highest dignity; his privileges many and substantial . . . and there can be little doubt that, had the presidential chair always been filled by men of commanding character, of acknowledged ability, and of thorough political training, it would have continued to be a seat of the highest authority and consideration, the true centre of the federal structure, the real throne of administration, and the frequent source of policies.[16]

In the early days of the government's operation, the President *was* of primary importance. "Washington and his cabinet commanded the ear of Congress, and gave shape to its deliberations; Adams, though often crossed and thwarted, gave character to the government; and Jefferson, as President . . . was the real leader of his party. But the prestige of the presidential office has declined with the character of the Presidents."[17] In Wilson's opinion, however, this decline in the character of the presidents was not the cause, but "only the accompanying manifestation, of the declining prestige of the presidential office."[18]

Undoubtedly one of the main reasons for the loss of presidential

[15] See Baker, *Woodrow Wilson*, I, 212–13.

[16] *Congressional Government*, p. 41.

[17] *Ibid.*, pp. 41–42.   [18] *Ibid.*, p. 43.

power and prestige had been that Congress increasingly realized how extensive its powers could be. In organizing to exert these powers, Congress had divided itself into standing committees which exercised almost complete control over legislative initiative and action. Not content with this, Congress had also attempted through these committees to administer the government. As time went on, Congress had entered more and more into all aspects of administration, until it had "virtually taken into its own hands all the substantial powers of government."[19] Thus, the prevailing situation in the American government had usually been one in which the "executive was losing and Congress gaining weight."[20]

According to Wilson, another major factor in the decline of presidential power and prestige had been the change from the congressional party caucus method of nominating presidential candidates to the national convention method. After political parties became firmly established in the United States by 1800, presidential nominations were made by congressional caucus until the breakdown of the method in the controversial election of 1824 led to its abandonment. In Wilson's view, "nominating the chief magistrate by Congressional caucus . . . was a very logical mode of party government," which failed only because "it was not an open enough way."[21] Wilson believed that nomination by congressional caucus was preferable to nomination by the national convention method; however, he stated emphatically that the caucus never should have made its selections by secret, hidden methods behind closed doors, as had been the custom. Instead, each party should have decided upon its presidential candidate openly by selecting a man who had won high place in the party through past services and accomplishments.

Wilson regarded it as inevitable that the character and leadership of the presidents should have declined after presidential candidates came to be selected by party nominating conventions. Under the operation of the convention system it was

absolutely necessary in the eyes of politicians, and more and more necessary as time went on, to make expediency and availability the only rules of selection . . . when the presidential candidate came to be chosen, it was recognized as imperatively necessary that he should have as short a political record as possible, and that he should wear a clean and irreproachable insignificance. "Gentlemen," said a distinguished American public man, "I would make an excellent President, but a very poor candidate." A decisive career which gives

[19] *Ibid.*, p. 45.　　　[20] *Ibid.*, pp. 46–47.　　　[21] *Ibid.*, pp. 247–48.

a man a well-understood place in public estimation constitutes a positive disability for the presidency; because candidacy must precede election, and the shoals of candidacy can be passed only by a light boat which carries little freight and can be turned readily about to suit the intricacies of the passage.[22]

Another serious weakness of the convention method noted by Wilson was the complete inability of the convention which selected a presidential candidate to do anything to control his course of action after he became President. A convention performs its function of nominating a man for the Presidency and then goes out of existence. Wilson contrasted this with the continued responsibility found in the English cabinet system whereby the House of Commons not only puts prime ministers into office but deposes them as well. In the United States, however, ". . . nothing short of a well-nigh impossible impeachment can unmake a President, except four successions of the seasons. As has been very happily said by a shrewd critic, our system is essentially astronomical. A President's usefulness is measured, not by efficiency, but by calendar months. It is reckoned that if he be good at all he will be good for four years. A Prime Minister must keep himself in favor with the majority, a President need only keep alive."[23]

In Wilson's estimation, there was no suitable training ground for presidents in the American government. In a cabinet system, a man gets to be prime minister because of the eminence he attains in his party through devoted service in the legislature and in subordinate positions in the cabinet. By contrast, "A nominating convention does not look over the rolls of Congress to pick a man to suit its purpose; and if it did it could not find him, because Congress is not a school for the preparation of administrators. . . ."[24] Unfortunately, Wilson continued, "it required diligent inquiry to find out what many of our Presidents had been before they became candidates; and eminence in legislative service has always been at best but an uncertain road to official preferment."[25]

Since its was not desirable, in Wilson's opinion, that men should go to the Presidency from congressional service, he hailed it as a "rational tendency" that presidents should be drawn increasingly from among the governors of the states. "This is the only avenue of subordinate place through which the highest place can be naturally reached," for "the Presidency is very much like a big governorship. Training in the duties of the one fits for the duties of the other."[26]

22 *Ibid.*, p. 43. 24 *Ibid.*, p. 251. 26 *Ibid.*, p. 253.
23 *Ibid.*, p. 249. 25 *Ibid.*, p. 252.

Woodrow Wilson's Theory of the Presidency

Wilson preferred the "still more natural line of promotion . . . under the cabinet governments abroad,"[27] but, in the absence of that method, he regarded experience in state administration as the best preparation for service in the Presidency. This was particularly true, Wilson said, because most of the business of the President is

> *mere* administration, mere obedience of directions from the makers of policy, the Standing Committees. Except in so far as his power of veto constitutes him a part of the legislature, the President might, not inconveniently, be a permanent officer; the first official of a carefully-graded and impartially regulated civil service system, through whose sure series of merit promotions the youngest clerk might rise even to the chief magistracy. He is part of the official rather than of the political machinery of the government and his duties call rather for training than for constructive genius.[28]

As most of the work of the President was "mere administration," Wilson believed that the importance of administrative ability and training was seriously underestimated in the selection of presidential candidates. People were far too prone to think

> the work of administration easy enough to be done readily, with or without preparation, by any man of discretion and character. No one imagines the dry-goods or the hardware trade, or even the cobbler's craft, can be successfully conducted except by those who have worked through a laborious and unremunerative apprenticeship, and who have devoted their lives to perfecting themselves as tradesmen or as menders of shoes. But . . . administration is regarded as something which an old soldier, an ex-diplomatist, or a popular politician may be trusted to take to by instinct. No man of tolerable talents need despair of having been born a Presidential candidate.[29]

A proper regard for the administrative duties of the position would indicate that "even Americans are not Presidents in their cradles," and that "one cannot have too much preparatory training and experience who is to fill so high a magistracy."[30]

In discussing the lack of influence of the President and his cabinet, Wilson observed:

> In so far as the President is an executive officer he is the servant of Congress; and the members of the Cabinet, being confined to executive functions, are altogether the servants of Congress. The President, however, besides being titular head of the executive service, is to the extent of his veto a third branch of the legislature. . . . The President is no greater than his prerogative of veto makes him.[31]

---

[27] *Ibid.*

[28] *Ibid.*, p. 254.

[29] *Ibid.*, p. 256.

[30] *Ibid.*, p. 255.

[31] *Ibid.*, pp. 260, 266.

In the early days of the government, presidents and their cabinet members were able to exercise considerable guidance and leadership in the formulation of policies by Congress. As the standing committees gained power, however, the influence of the presidents waned. The relationship between the executive and Congress had deteriorated to such an extent that Congress had come to look "upon advice offered to it by anybody but its own members as gratuitous impertinence."[32]

Wilson concluded his discussion of the Presidency in *Congressional Government* by stating his conviction that ". . . if there be one principle clearer than another, it is this: . . . *somebody must be trusted,* in order that when things go wrong it may be quite plain who should be punished," as "*power and strict accountability for its use* are the essential constituents of good government."[33] It was a serious defect of the American governmental system that power was so divided and accountability so confused. Consequently, it was essential, in Wilson's eyes, that power and accountability should be brought together by making the President and his cabinet the responsible leaders of the Congress.[34]

Wilson's second book in the field of political science was published in 1889. This was *The State*,[35] one of the first comparative government textbooks written in the United States. This "dull fact book," as Wilson called it,[36] contained only one paragraph of significance in tracing the development of his theory of the Presidency. In discussing Article II, section 3, of the United States Constitution, which provides that the President "shall, from time to time, give to the congress information of the state of the union, and recommend to their consideration such measures as he shall judge necessary and expedient," Wilson wrote:

[32] *Ibid.,* p. 270. [33] *Ibid.,* pp. 283–84.

[34] In 1887, while teaching at Bryn Mawr, Wilson wrote his pioneering article on administration: "The Study of Administration," *Political Science Quarterly,* II (June, 1887), 197–222; reprinted in *Political Science Quarterly,* LVI (December, 1941), 481–506; also found in *Public Papers,* I, 130–58. This article, a discussion of administration in general and theoretical terms, did not deal specifically with the Presidency. However, Wilson did amplify further the views expressed in *Congressional Government* regarding the interrelationship of power and responsibility: "And let me say that large powers and unhampered discretion seem to me the indispensable conditions of responsibility. . . . There is no danger in power, if only it be not irresponsible. If it be divided, dealt out in shares to many, it is obscured; and if it be obscured, it is made irresponsible. But if it be centered . . . it is easily watched and brought to book." *Public Papers,* I, 148–49.

[35] Boston: D. C. Heath & Co. [36] Baker, *Woodrow Wilson,* I, 102.

Washington and John Adams interpreted this clause to mean that they might address Congress in person . . . and their annual communications to Congress were spoken addresses. But Jefferson . . . being an ineffective speaker, this habit was discontinued and the fashion of written messages was inaugurated and firmly established. Possibly had the President not so closed the matter against new adjustments, this clause of the Constitution might legitimately have been made the foundation for a much more habitual and informal, and yet at the same time much more public and responsible, interchange of opinion between the Executive and Congress. Having been interpreted, however, to exclude the President from any but the most formal and ineffectual utterance of perfunctory advice, our federal executive and legislature have been shut off from cooperation and mutual confidence to an extent to which no other modern system furnishes a parallel.[37]

This clearly foreshadows the action which Wilson was to take years later when he shattered the long-established custom by appearing before the Congress in person to deliver his presidential messages.

Eighteen years elapsed after publication of *The State* before Wilson wrote his next political science book, *Constitutional Government in the United States*. During this period a number of journal articles and speeches constitute the main sources of information concerning his views on the Presidency.

Grover Cleveland, whose conduct as President made a strong impression upon Wilson, was the subject of two of these articles. The first, "Mr. Cleveland's Cabinet,"[38] was published in 1893 shortly after Cleveland began his second term. Although commending Cleveland highly as "an altogether exceptional man, a real leader . . . ,"[39] Wilson felt compelled to offer some "friendly criticisms" of Cleveland's cabinet appointments. He thought it regrettable that Cleveland had placed only one well-known Democratic party leader in the cabinet. Though he did not feel much trepidation over this situation under Cleveland, because he believed Cleveland would dominate his cabinet as other strong presidential leaders such as Jackson and Lincoln had dominated theirs, Wilson feared that Cleveland's example might provide a dangerous "precedent to his successors, who may not have like ability and discretion."[40] Thus the country might find itself with a cabinet composed exclusively of non-party leaders serving under a weak President who had been chosen in haste through the compromises or sudden

---

[37] *The State,* pp. 565–66.

[38] *Review of Reviews* (American Edition), VII (April, 1893), 286–97. Also found in *Public Papers,* I, 198–222.

[39] *Public Papers,* I, 217.   [40] *Ibid.,* p. 215.

impulses of a nominating convention. The only way to eliminate this possibility, Wilson concluded, was for the parties to make certain that they "choose the men who really lead them for Presidents, and Presidents . . . must give us responsible party government by surrounding themselves with a cabinet . . . made up from among party men whom the people have known and have shown themselves disposed to trust."[41]

The second article, "Mr. Cleveland as President," was written in March, 1897, as Cleveland was leaving the Presidency.[42] Wilson began with effusive praise:

Mr. Cleveland has been President in ordinary times, but after an extraordinary fashion; not because he wished to form or revolutionize or save the government, but because he came fresh to his tasks without the common party training, a direct, fearless, somewhat unsophisticated man of action. In him we got a President, as it were, by immediate choice from out the body of the people, . . . and he has refreshed our notion of an American chief magistrate.[43]

Nevertheless, he went on to acknowledge that Cleveland had not been the type of strong party leader Wilson had always advocated for the Presidency. "The Democrats, in fact, did not recognize him as their leader, but only as their candidate for the office of President . . . he had been chosen as a man, not as a partisan—taken up by his own party as a likely winner rather than as an acceptable master."[44]

In addition, Cleveland had not at the outset regarded the Presidency as a place for strong political leadership in determining matters of policy. Cleveland at first believed his proper function was to be essentially administrative, except for approving or vetoing bills passed by Congress. Outgrowing these earlier predilections, however, he became a leader of policy after all, "as if in spite of himself. . . . He could not keep to his role of simple executive."[45] Particularly during his second term, Cleveland had come to exemplify much of what Wilson thought a President should be:

The habit of independent initiative in respect of questions of legislative policy was growing upon him. . . . It was singular how politics began at once to centre in the President, waiting for his initiative. . . . Power had somehow gone the length of the avenue, and seemed lodged in one man . . . the Democrats in the House were made conscious that the eye of the country had been

41 *Ibid.*, p. 221.

42 *Atlantic Monthly,* LXXIX (March, 1897), 289–300. Also found in *Public Papers,* I, 286–310.

43 *Public Papers,* I, 287. 44 *Ibid.*, p. 292. 45 *Ibid.*, p. 296.

withdrawn from them in matters of policy, and Washington seemed full of Mr. Cleveland, his Secretary of the Treasury and his Secretary of State.[46]

Thus, Grover Cleveland had revealed to Wilson that a man of strong intellect and strong character could still exercise strong presidential leadership.

Although deeply impressed by Cleveland's performance, Wilson regarded it as a notable exception to the generally prevailing rule of presidential mediocrity. That Wilson still retained a considerable degree of pessimism about the operation of the American system can be seen clearly from two other works written in 1897. The first of these was an article, "The Making of the Nation,"[47] which appeared in the *Atlantic Monthly*. The second, titled "Leaderless Government,"[48] was an address which Wilson delivered before the Virginia State Bar Association.

Toward the end of "The Making of the Nation," Wilson returned to his old theme of responsible government and again expressed concern about why, after a century under the Constitution, the country still did not possess adequate means of formulating national policy. He said:

> . . . we have made no provision for authoritative national leadership in matters of policy. The President does not always speak with authority, because he is not always a man picked out and tested by any processes in which the people have been participants, and has often nothing but his office to render him influential. Even when the country does know and trust him, he can carry his views no further than to recommend them to the attention of Congress in a written message which the Houses would deem themselves subservient to give too much heed to.[49]

The leaderless structure of American government had been concealed for a time, according to Wilson, by the practical political habits and the sagacity of the American people. In the early days of the country's history it was virtually taken for granted that the outstanding leaders of the nation would find their way into the Presidency because nominations of presidential candidates were worked out in congressional caucus by the men in whose hands rested both the conduct of the government and the determination of party policy. Although he stated that it was probably inevitable that this system of

[46] *Ibid.*, pp. 298–300.

[47] *Atlantic Monthly*, LXXX (July, 1897), 1–14. Also found in *Public Papers*, I, 310–36.

[48] *Public Papers*, I, 336–60.   [49] *Ibid.*, p. 329.

congressional nomination should have come to an end, Wilson reiterated his belief that "rejecting that system to pass to the use of nominating conventions . . . rendered it . . . in the highest degree unlikely—that our Presidents should ever be leaders again."[50]

To Wilson's way of thinking, the nominating convention had been instrumental in separating Congress and the President even more than the makers of the Constitution intended and had eliminated the earlier traditions of party leadership. Wilson concluded his criticisms thus:

> If you would have the present error of our system in a word, it is this, that Congress is the motive power in the government and yet has in it nowhere any representative of the nation as a whole. Our Executive, on the other hand, is national: at any rate may be made so, and yet has no longer any place of guidance in our system. It represents no constituency, but the whole people; and yet, though it alone is national, it has no originative voice in domestic national policy.[51]

It is significant, however, that Wilson for some time had not advocated the adoption of cabinet government as the way to remedy this situation. Instead, he urged the parties to nominate only tried and tested party leaders of national reputation for the Presidency. This would enable the President, as the unquestioned leader of his party, to exercise an authoritative initiative in proposing national policies to the Congress.

It was in 1900 that Wilson wrote a brief statement which showed most clearly that significant changes were taking place in his views concerning the Presidency. This was the Preface which he prepared for the fifteenth edition of *Congressional Government*.[52] A careful rereading of the book, Wilson indicated, had convinced him that it should not go through another printing without the addition of a few words "with regard to the changes which our singular system of Congressional government has undergone."[53] He asked those who might read the book in the future to remember that it was written in the years 1883 and 1884, and that the description which it gave of the government of the United States "is not as accurate now as I believe it to have been at the time I wrote it."[54]

Discussing the developments which had taken place, Wilson stated: "Much the most important change to be noticed is the result of the

[50] *Ibid.*, p. 344.

[51] *Ibid.*, p. 357.

[52] Boston: Houghton Mifflin Co., 1900.

[53] *Ibid.*, p. v.

[54] *Ibid.*

war with Spain upon the lodgment and exercise of power within our federal system: the greatly increased power and opportunity for constructive statesmanship given the President . . . which has been that war's most striking and momentous consequence."[55]

According to Wilson, this had been an almost inevitable change. "When Foreign affairs play a prominent part in the politics and policy of a nation, its Executive must of necessity be its guide: must utter every initial judgment, take every first step of action, supply the information upon which it is to act, suggest and in large measure control its conduct."[56] As a consequence of the war, the relative importance of the President in the government had grown profoundly, and Wilson had high hopes for what this change might portend:

> The President of the United States is now, as of course, at the front of affairs, as no president, except Lincoln, has been since the first quarter of the nineteenth century. . . . Interesting things may come out of the singular change. . . . It may be . . . that the new leadership of the Executive, inasmuch as it is likely to last, will have a very far-reaching effect upon our whole method of government. It may give the heads of the executive departments a new influence upon the action of Congress. It may bring about, as a consequence, an integration which will substitute statesmanship for government by mass meeting. It may put this whole volume hopelessly out of date.[57]

Although Wilson wrote nothing pertaining directly to the Presidency between 1900 and 1907, these years were most important ones in the development of his ideas. The views expressed in 1907 in *Constitutional Government in the United States*[58] show that his thinking about the Presidency had been extensive during this time. As might have been anticipated from the 1900 Preface to *Congressional Government*, Wilson continued to subject many of his earlier opinions to careful re-examination and some of them underwent radical transformation.

Wilson initiated his discussion of the Presidency in *Constitutional Government in the United States* by saying that "it has been one thing at one time, another at another, varying with the man who occupied the office and with the circumstances that surrounded him."[59] The makers of the Constitution provided that the President should serve

---

[55] *Ibid.*, p. xi.   [56] *Ibid.*, pp. xi–xii.   [57] *Ibid.*, pp. xii–xiii.

[58] Wilson originally prepared the materials in this book for a series of lectures which he gave at Columbia University in 1907.

[59] *Constitutional Government*, p. 57.

mainly as the government's chief executive officer whose primary responsibility would be the faithful execution of the laws enacted by Congress. His only "check" on Congress was his veto over legislation; this gave him an effective power to prevent bad laws, but he was not given adequate authority to introduce good ones. Nevertheless, because of the strong leadership of some of the presidents and changing historical circumstances, the Presidency had become considerably more than the Constitution originally provided. "Greatly as the practice and influence of Presidents has varied, there can be no mistaking the fact that we have grown more and more inclined from generation to generation to look to the President as the unifying force in our complex system, the leader both of his party and of the nation."[60] To Wilson, this development was both necessary and desirable because governments must "work out the close synthesis of active parts which can exist only when leadership is lodged in some one man or group of men."[61]

Wilson advanced several views in this book which were quite different from some he had expressed earlier. For one thing, he had come to believe that a President becomes automatically the leader of his party through his selection by a nominating convention. Although Wilson granted that the procedure of a convention in choosing a candidate appeared to be "somewhat haphazard," which was certainly a mild charge compared to some of the earlier strictures he had leveled at the nominating conventions, in actuality, "there is much more method, much more definite purpose, much more deliberate choice in the extraordinary process than there seems to be."[62]

Along with this reformation in his attitude toward the nominating convention, Wilson expressed another idea which was sharply at variance with his previous views. He said:

It must be remembered also that our political system is not so coordinated as to supply a training for presidential aspirants or even to make it absolutely necessary that they should have had extended experience in public affairs. . . . If the matter be looked at a little more closely, it will be seen that the office of President, as we have used and developed it, really does not demand actual experience in affairs so much as particular qualities of mind and character which we are at least as likely to find outside the ranks of our public men as within them.[63]

[60] *Ibid.,* p. 60.
[61] *Ibid.,* pp. 60–61.

[62] *Ibid.,* p. 63.
[63] *Ibid.,* p. 65.

In selecting a presidential candidate, therefore, a nominating convention need not choose a successful party leader of long experience, as Wilson had previously advocated, but a "man who will be and who will seem to the country in some sort an embodiment of the character and purpose it wishes its government to have—a man who understands his own day and the needs of the country, and who has the personality and the initiative to enforce his views both upon the people and upon Congress."[64] Once a nominee is selected, he will stand before the country as the symbol of the party. It is inevitable that the party must be led by its presidential candidate during the campaign, because "Sometimes the country believes in a party, but more often it believes in a man."[65] Thus, the role of party leader is literally thrust upon a presidential nominee when he is nominated.

Once a President is elected, "he cannot escape being the leader of his party except by incapacity and lack of personal force, because he is at once the choice of the party and of the nation. He is . . . the only party nominee for whom the whole nation votes."[66] This should also make the President the leader of the nation, or at least he

. . . has it in his choice to be. . . . His is the only national voice in affairs. Let him once win the admiration and confidence of the country, and no other single force can withstand him, no combination of forces will easily overpower him. . . . If he rightly interpret the national thought and boldly insist upon it, he is irresistible; and the country never feels the zest of action so much as when its President is of such insight and calibre. Its instinct is for unified action, and it craves a single leader. . . . A President whom it trusts can not only lead it, but form it to his own views. . . . If he lead the nation, his party can hardly resist him. His office is anything he has the sagacity and force to make it.[67]

The President's leadership of Congress must be exercised through persuasion and through appeals to public opinion, according to Wilson, for the President has no proper means of compelling Congress to do anything. Wilson had little regard for those presidents who had failed to use the full power of persuasion which they might legitimately have used in dealing with Congress. Some of the presidents "have acted as if they thought that Pennsylvania Avenue should have been even longer than it is; that there should be no intimate communication of any kind between the Capitol and the White House."[68] Such a view had no place

---

[64] *Ibid.*

[65] *Ibid.*, p. 66.

[66] *Ibid.*, p. 67.

[67] *Ibid.*, pp. 67–69.

[68] *Ibid.*, p. 70.

in Wilson's thinking, for to him "The President is at liberty, both in law and conscience, to be as big a man as he can. His capacity will set the limit; and if Congress be overborne by him, it will be no fault of the makers of the Constitution . . . but only because the President has the nation behind him, and Congress has not."[69] The messages and policy recommendations which the Constitution authorizes the President to present to Congress should never be transmitted in a perfunctory manner. Instead, the President should back them up with all the personal force and influence he may possess.

Changes which had taken place in the relationship of presidents to their cabinets provided an excellent illustration, in Wilson's view, of the fact that the President was not only the legal and executive head of the government but had also become the political leader of the nation. In the early days of the government, it was customary for a President to fill his cabinet with the outstanding leaders of his party— a practice which Wilson strongly commended in his earlier writings. Later years had brought a decided change in this custom. Some of the more recent presidents, notably Cleveland and Theodore Roosevelt, had not regarded the cabinet as primarily a council of party advisers. Instead, they looked upon it as essentially an administrative rather than a political body; they appointed to cabinet positions not those whom party affairs had brought into prominence but men who had given proof of their executive abilities in private rather than in public life. Wilson expressed approval of this practice, contrary to his earlier views, because he believed the President no longer had time to be the actual executive himself. Consequently, a President should appoint men with outstanding legal and business abilities to act in his place and depend upon them to administer the government. The President would then be free to devote the major part of his energies to the political leadership of his party, the Congress, and the nation.

Wilson reaffirmed in this book the opinion he had expressed earlier that the President's power over foreign relations provides one of his most important avenues for exercising leadership. "The initiative in foreign affairs, which the President possesses without any restriction whatever, is virtually the power to control them absolutely."[70] While it is true that the President cannot conclude a treaty without senatorial approval, he may yet direct every step of diplomatic negotiations in such a way that the government and the Senate are virtually com-

[69] *Ibid.*   [70] *Ibid.*, p. 77.

mitted, according to Wilson. (Of course, he was to learn eleven years later from bitter experience that a President's diplomatic negotiations do not *always* commit the Senate.)

In concluding his discussion of the Presidency, Wilson expressed concern about the continued expansion of presidential functions which had made the President the most heavily burdened officer in the world. He wrote, "Men of ordinary physique and discretion cannot be Presidents and live, if the strain be not somehow relieved. We shall be obliged always to be picking our chief magistrates from among wise and prudent athletes—a small class."[71] Wilson was of the opinion, however, that presidents themselves could secure substantial relief from severe strains of the office by proper delegation of their administrative duties to subordinates. Such delegation would become increasingly necessary, in Wilson's estimation, because "We can safely predict that as the multitude of the President's duties increases, as it must with the growth and widening activities of the nation itself, the incumbents of the great office will more and more come to feel that they are administering it in its truest purpose and with greatest effect by regarding themselves as less and less executive officers and more and more directors of affairs and leaders of the nation."[72]

In his earlier discussions of the Presidency, Wilson feared that three historical factors had so divided and hidden power and responsibility in the American government that only a major change could provide the kind of presidential leadership which he deemed necessary. These factors were: (1) an overzealous application of the doctrine of the separation of powers by the framers of the Constitution; (2) the rise of powerful and irresponsible standing committees in Congress; and (3) the innovation of the party nominating convention as the method of selecting presidential candidates. Wilson's early writings were filled with criticisms of congressional domination of the governmental process and the inability of the President to lead in the formulation of national policies. He earnestly advocated a change to a modified form of cabinet government patterned after the English model, which he admired greatly. If recognized leaders of the President's party in Congress served at the same time as the President's cabinet, Wilson believed responsible party government under presidential leadership would be assured.

[71] *Ibid.*, p. 80.   [72] *Ibid.*, p. 81.

Many of Wilson's early views gradually underwent significant revision with the passage of time. Although he was still criticizing the "leaderless government" of the United States until nearly 1900, he no longer proposed the adoption of cabinet government as a necessary step. Instead, he stressed the need of bringing the President and the Congress closer together in their work. According to Wilson, this could be achieved primarily through an increased recognition of party leadership in the selection of presidential candidates and cabinet members. He urged nominating conventions to choose only established party leaders as presidential nominees, and presidents to select cabinet members exclusively from those with long records of devoted party service. Because of the increased sense of party responsibility and discipline which would result, the President and his cabinet would be the acknowledged leaders of their party and of Congress. This would insure that Congress would accord the President's policy recommendations the respect to which they should be entitled.

By the time he wrote *Constitutional Government in the United States,* Wilson no longer maintained that the existing governmental system made it extremely difficult, if not impossible for a President to exercise proper leadership. In contrast to his earlier opinions, he had eventually come to the conclusion that a President could lead his party, the Congress, and the entire nation if he was a man of ability and force who would use all the means at his disposal wisely and well.

The changes in Wilson's views probably resulted to considerable extent from his always alert attention to what was taking place on the national political scene. Four influences may be singled out as particularly determinative: (1) Grover Cleveland's conduct in the presidential office, especially during his second administration; (2) the increased importance of the President's role during and after the Spanish-American War; (3) the dynamic initiative brought to the Presidency by Theodore Roosevelt; and (4) the beginning of some discussion in political circles of Woodrow Wilson as a presidential possibility.

The first two of these factors stand out from Wilson's writings as obvious influences in shaping his later attitudes. The last two are not so apparent, but it is reasonable to infer that they were undoubtedly of importance.

Wilson wrote very little about Theodore Roosevelt, and he held a rather low opinion of Roosevelt's conduct, thinking of it as often undignified.[73] In spite of this, he must have been impressed by Roosevelt's vigorous performance as President. To at least some degree, Wilson's growing assurance that strong presidential leadership was not only possible but that it would be favorably received by the country was doubtless based upon his observation of Roosevelt's success in the White House.

As previously mentioned,[74] Wilson first received serious attention as a presidential possibility early in 1906. Although he outwardly disclaimed any interest in presidential politics at that time, Wilson's long-diverted political ambitions were stimulated by this discussion of himself as a possible candidate.[75] Consequently, there may well have been a tendency for him to think in 1907 not merely as a political scientist but as a man who was being talked about as a potential President of the United States. It seems likely that this may have prompted Wilson to write of the Presidency as he would try to conduct it if the efforts started in his behalf should eventually develop into a winning presidential campaign.

Certainly many of Wilson's views had changed profoundly. From his indictment of the nominating convention as a disastrous device for selecting presidential candidates, he had turned to its defense.[76] From a demand that presidents should always be chosen from among established party leaders with long records of public and party service, he had come to hold that presidential candidates need not be prominent party men at all; instead, men who have earned the respect of the country in private as well as public life should be selected if their qualities make them excellent representatives of the nation. From the view that the President had no effective power over Congress except his limited right to veto legislation, he had changed to the belief that the President could be the true leader of legislative policy through forceful messages to Congress backed up by persuasive appeals to public opinion. From

[73] For some of Wilson's views on Roosevelt, see Link, *op. cit.,* pp. 107, 112, 468–69, 475–76. Also, James Kerney, *The Political Education of Woodrow Wilson* (New York: The Century Co., 1926), pp. 63, 125, 145.

[74] See note 3.

[75] See Link, *op. cit.,* pp. 99–103; also, Baker, *Woodrow Wilson,* II, 197–99.

[76] Later, as President, Wilson was to urge that the nomination of presidential candidates should be made directly by the voters of the parties in primary elections. He wanted the national party conventions to be retained, but only for the formulation of party platforms. See "First Annual Address to Congress," delivered December 2, 1913, *Public Papers,* III, 76; and "A Second Term for Presidents," letter to A. Mitchell Palmer, February 5, 1913, *ibid.,* p. 23.

his conception of the President's duties as essentially "mere administration," he had changed to the opinion that the President was less an administrative figure and more the national guide and spokesman in the determination of all important courses of action. From his criticism of the parties for often naming presidential candidates who were in no way recognized as party leaders, he had changed to the view that the selection of a presidential nominee automatically makes him the undisputed leader of the party. From a view of the Presidency as the weakest, most ineffectual branch of the government, completely under the domination of Congress, he had changed to a belief that the President had sufficient means at his command to be the powerful leader of the Congress, of the national administration, of his party, and of the nation.

Beneath the many changes, however, Wilson's fundamental concept—that strong, responsible leadership is essential for good government—remained the same. Although his views varied greatly through the years regarding the details of how best to guarantee that presidents would function as effective leaders, he emphasized continuously that such presidential leadership was absolutely necessary if the government was to operate properly. By paraphrasing an old French proverb, one may conclude that the more Wilson's theory of the Presidency seemed to change, the more it continued to be the same.

CHAPTER FOUR

Woodrow Wilson and the Presidency*

By
Richard P. Longaker

Woodrow Wilson wrapped his Presidency tightly in his own contradictions—not the least were the contradictions of his theory of the Presidency. The purpose of this paper is to try to avoid stressing the contradictions in favor of the main emphases in theory and action which were, in the end, his gift to later presidents. The present analysis is not a detailed description of Wilson in the presidential office, nor is it concerned with his agonizing journey from confidence to disillusion. It is an attempt to discuss briefly Wilson's theory of the Presidency and to speculate about the major elements of Wilsonian theory and experience which were passed on to his successors. Harding, Coolidge, and Hoover drew little from the experience of their Democratic predecessor, for neither the times nor their impulses demanded positive leadership. F. D. R., Harry Truman, and to some extent Eisenhower, however, have absorbed many of the lessons of Wilson's incumbency. There is much evidence of conscious adoption in which Wilson's name and actions are mentioned. Of greater importance, however, is the twentieth-century image of the Presidency which Wilson created and which his strong successors have consciously—and frequently unconsciously—adopted.

Wilson's theory of the Presidency was never hidden under a bushel. His knowledge of executive power was based on years of scholarly preparation, a period as president of Princeton, and a term as governor of New Jersey—events too well known to require retelling here.[1] There was abundant raw material for the construction of a sound the-

---

* Paper delivered at the Annual Meeting of the American Political Science Association, Washington, D.C., September, 1956.

[1] See Arthur S. Link, *Wilson: The Road to the White House* (Princeton: Princeton University Press, 1947).

ory of presidential power. As a historian Wilson was well aware of the most significant contributions of the strong Presidents of the past, and from them he drew much of his theory:[2] from Washington, the President as a symbol of national unity and as chief of state; from Jefferson, the President as party leader; from Jackson, the President as tribune; from Lincoln, the Presidency as a place of moral leadership; from Cleveland, presidential jealousy of the separation of powers; and from his rambunctious predecessor, a refined version of the stewardship theory. Walter Bagehot, as Wilson was the first to recognize,[3] had a profound influence on Wilson in his younger days, and his method, as Wilson described it, of finding "the living reality" of a constitutional system rather than the "paper description" pervades Wilson's two greatest scholarly contributions, *Congressional Government* and *Constitutional Government in the United States*.[4] Nor did he soon forget Bagehot's declaration that "The efficient secret of the English Constitution may be described as the close union, the nearly complete fusion, of the executive and legislative powers."[5] Nevertheless, Bagehot has been given a more impressive position than he deserves in influencing Wilson's view of presidential power. More credit should be given to Henry Jones Ford, whose *Rise and Growth of American Politics* Wilson called "lucid and convincing,"[6] to T. R., who aroused Wilson's competitive sense,[7] and to Wilson's knowledge of American history.

[2] Louis Brownlow, *The President and the Presidency* (Chicago: Public Administration Service, 1949), p. 10. See Wilson's essay, "A Calendar of Great Americans," in *Mere Literature and Other Essays* (Boston and New York: Houghton Mifflin Co., 1896); his essays on Washington, Lincoln, Jefferson, and Cleveland in R. S. Baker and W. E. Dodd (eds.), *The Public Papers of Woodrow Wilson* (New York: Harper & Bros., 1925–27), Vols. I and II (hereinafter cited as *Public Papers*); and Walter Lippmann's Introduction to *Congressional Government* (New York: Meridian Books, 1956), pp. 13–14.

[3] Charles Seymour (ed.), *The Intimate Papers of Colonel House* (Boston: Houghton Mifflin Co., 1926–28), I, 121.

[4] Ray Stannard Baker, *Woodrow Wilson: Life and Letters* (Garden City: Doubleday, 1927–39), I, 214.

[5] Walter Bagehot, *The English Constitution* (New York, 1908), p. 78.

[6] "Hide and Seek Politics," *Public Papers*, II, 212.

[7] Roosevelt's strong leadership appealed to Wilson. According to David Lawrence, Wilson commented on Roosevelt in class at Princeton as follows: "Whatever else we may think or say of Theodore Roosevelt, we must admit that he is an aggressive leader. He led Congress—he was not driven by Congress. We may not approve of his methods but we must concede that he made Congress follow him." Lawrence, *The True Story of Woodrow Wilson* (New York, 1924), p. 39.

All helped him to adjust scholarly assumptions to the realities of the American political system.

In turn, too much has been made of the influence of *particular* British practices on Wilson. His threats to resign and talk of votes of confidence were minor anachronistic by-products of his earlier days. If, during his Presidency, he believed the transformation could be made to an indigenous cabinet system, he realized it would take place only in the distant future.[8] He did succeed, however, in making much of what Bagehot called "the simple essence" of the British system—executive responsibility, co-ordination between the executive and the legislature, and party leadership—more familiar and acceptable to Congress and the American public. Regardless of the extent of influence of each, Bagehot, Ford, and Roosevelt provided a heady mixture for a man about to become President.

Wilson believed, with Bagehot, Ford, and Roosevelt, that the executive should be "the vital place of action"[9] in a modern constitutional system. His basic insight was that the American political system could not operate effectually without vigorous presidential leadership. Leadership, Wilson contended, was based on public opinion, and the President was the only true representative of the nation's sentiment. "Opinion," he wrote, "is the great, indeed the only coordinating force in our system," and the President draws his power and his duty from "his close and special relation to opinion the nation over."[10] His duty is to represent, lead, and interpret public opinion which is represented only imperfectly in Congress. The people are generally wise, Wilson assumed, but particularly wise in centering their attention and expectations on the chief magistrate, for, by so doing, they promote clear responsibility and efficiency in government. When the power of initiative and direction of public policy lies in a single person leading a disciplined party, the people can rest assured that the power will be used responsibly. He believed that the unity of power and responsibility would bring an end to the irresponsible "hide and seek" government which had reigned in the era of legislative supremacy.[11]

Since opinion was the co-ordinating force in government and a dis-

[8] Wilson to A. Mitchell Palmer, February 5, 1913, *Public Papers,* III, 24.

[9] *Constitutional Government in the United States* (New York: Columbia University Press, 1908), p. 73.

[10] *Ibid.,* pp. 171–72.

[11] "Hide and Seek Politics," *Public Papers,* II, 204–24.

ciplined party the vehicle of presidential articulation of this force, the role of the legislature was to criticize, to represent localism and group interest, and—in the face of overwhelming public sentiment—to stand back. Wilson did not believe that the delaying function of an independent legislative force had value in itself. More than once he suggested that the Constitution was a Newtonian invention wallowing in a Darwinian age.[12] He wanted to substitute, and he believed events would demand the substitution of, a "Darwinian" fluidity and co-ordination for the mechanical and rigid Newtonian system of mutual restraint. As Wilson declared, "synthesis, not antagonism, is the whole art of government, the whole art of power."[13] The President, of course, as leader of the party and leader of the nation, was to be the synthesizer.

Certainly Wilson did not contend that the Presidency would rise inevitably to this new role, although he realized America's new international position tipped the balance to the executive.[14] But the decisive factor was still the personality in the office. Given public following and a party majority in Congress the office required a complex co-ordination of technique—the adroit use of the weapons of leadership—and will. Typically, Wilson emphasized will over technique. As he noted in an address to the Economic Club of New York in 1912, "The place where the strongest will is present will be the seat of sovereignty. If the strongest will is present in Congress, then Congress will dominate the government; if the strongest guiding will is in the Presidency, the President will dominate the government . . ."[15] or, to cite his famous not-so-truism, "The President is at liberty, both in law and conscience, to be as big a man as he can."[16] It was this expansive interpretation and oversimplification of presidential power which caused him difficulty in the last years of his Presidency.

No President before or since Wilson has had his incumbency sliced in such rich portions of failure and success, victory and defeat. Partly because his success was so brilliant and his failure so tragic, Wilson left

[12] Address at the Annual Banquet of the Economic Club, New York, *ibid.*, p. 434; *Constitutional Government*, p. 56.

[13] *Ibid.*, p. 106.

[14] *Ibid.*, p. 79; Preface to the fifteenth edition of *Congressional Government* (Boston: Houghton Mifflin Co., 1900), pp. xxii–xxiii.

[15] *Public Papers*, II, 434–35.

[16] *Constitutional Government*, p. 70.

a deep impression on the office. At the risk of oversimplification it may
be said that Wilson's positive contributions correspond roughly with
his activities as a war President and reform President while his negative contributions fall largely in the period of 1918–19. In some respects
this severe division is deceptive, for Wilson was following the same
theory of presidential power throughout; also more than one negative
contribution appears during his period as President.[17] But, for present
purposes, the important factor is that his strong successors saw two
Wilsons and learned lessons from each. The Wilson of 1919 taught
them caution, the Wilson of 1913 the fruitful consequences of adroit
leadership and presidential initiative.

With the possible exceptions of 1932 and 1936, the political conditions in 1913 were as ideal as they have ever been for the application of
a Wilsonian theory of executive leadership. Even though Wilson was a
minority President, the Democrats had a majority of seventy-three in
the House and seven in the Senate and the apparent backing of popular
sentiment for reform stirred up in the three-way presidential contest in
1912. There were, as well, undernourished Democrats eager to be fed
patronage held in store since 1896. With popular and party sympathy
behind the President, the party in Congress was only too willing to appear co-operative. Wilson was blessed as well by the reduction of the
power of the Speaker of the House, which followed the revolt against
Cannon in 1910 and the corresponding rise to power of a co-operative
majority leader, Oscar Underwood, who, as chairman of the Committee on Ways and Means, appointed other committees and dominated
the party caucus.[18] Also, for the brief period 1913–17 strong party cau-
causes in the Senate and House were able to maintain in an unparalleled number of cases almost perfect party unity.[19] Party obedience
fitted perfectly with Wilson's view of unity of action under presidential guidance. As he wrote to one recalcitrant senator in 1913:

I feel there are times, after every argument has been given full consideration and men of public conscience have conferred together, when those who

[17] For example, one negative contribution apparently influenced F. D. R.; that is
Wilson's reluctance to prepare for war. See Frank Freidel, *Franklin D. Roosevelt:
The Apprenticeship* (Boston: Little, Brown & Co., 1952), pp. 287–89, and John
Gunther, *Roosevelt to Retrospect* (New York: Harper & Bros., 1950), p. 13. For
Wilson's reluctance see Seymour, *op. cit.,* I, 298.

[18] George B. Galloway, "The Majority Leader of the House of Representatives,"
Congressional Record, 84th Cong., 2d sess., p. A2490.

[19] George B. Galloway, *The Legislative Process in Congress* (New York: Thomas
Y. Crowell Co., 1953), p. 330.

are overruled in caucus should accept the principle of party government . . . and act with the colleagues through whom they expect to see the country best and most permanently well served.[20]

A disciplined party in Congress, an abundance of patronage, and favorable public opinion account for the success of Wilson's early attempt at legislative-executive "synthesis." It was the President, however, not the party organization, who gave the machinery direction and provided the fuel. Wilson denied that he "drove" members of Congress; he only "led and stimulated them to what all the country knows to be their duty."[21] Their duty, of course, was to vote with the President and for his program.

Wilson was aware that the country was ripe for leadership in 1913 and realized the situation would never again be so favorable. The first year, he confided, was the year of his "greatest efficiency and it was now or never."[22] His conviction that the vital opportunity might be lost accounts for Wilson's ambitious legislative program in 1913 and the urgency of the special session of Congress called in April, 1913, to pass the Underwood tariff; it explains as well Wilson's driving leadership in the next year, which produced the Federal Reserve Act, the Clayton Act, the Fair Trade Act, and—perhaps his most impressive victory—the repeal of the Panama tolls.[23] All the elements of strong legislative leadership so familiar today were used with unequaled force and finesse: direct and constant contact with members of Congress,[24] personal appearances on Capitol Hill—both formal and informal—imaginative use of patronage, executive formulation of bills, and direct appeals to the public against special interests and legislative localism.

The President combined leadership in Congress with leadership of public opinion when he re-established personal appearances before

[20] Wilson to Senator John R. Thornton, July 15, 1913, Baker, *Woodrow Wilson,* IV, 125.

[21] Wilson to Mrs. Hulbert, September 21, 1913, *ibid.,* p. 182. His tone was different in conversation with one of his House leaders during the fight over the shipping bill: "I am tired of this obstruction. We need the ships. It is time for Congress to get behind the matter. I want the House, for the moral effect of it, to pass that shipping bill and send it to the Senate, and I want you to see that it is put through." *Ibid.,* V, 132.

[22] *Ibid.,* p. 137.

[23] See Arthur M. Link, *Woodrow Wilson and the Progressive Era, 1910–1917* (New York: Harper & Bros., 1954), pp. 90–93. Both Speaker Clark and Wilson's majority leader, Oscar W. Underwood, were opposed to the President on this issue.

[24] In 1913 Wilson apparently installed a special telephone to facilitate contact with members of Congress. Baker, *Woodrow Wilson,* IV, 123.

Congress, a weapon of leadership which had rusted since John Adams' second annual message. It was after his personal appearance in Congress that Wilson, aware of his "red corpuscled" competitor, told his wife, "Yes, I think I put one over on Teddy."[25] Wilson used this technique not so frequently as to ruin its effect but only for issues of pressing national importance. Speaking to his "colleagues" he focused national attention on Congress, the issue, and himself. They were not portmanteau messages of the Theodore Roosevelt variety but were brief and contained a single, well-prepared request.

The proposals were kept alive by subsequent presidential pressure; for Wilson did not set Congress adrift after his speech from the throne. One need only recall his appearance on Capitol Hill to consult with the Senate Finance Committee the day following his special message to Congress on the tariff.[26] He followed floor strategy, actively opposed unfavorable amendments, cajoled, and—when necessary—compromised. Although at first he was opposed, Wilson realized, after a long talk with Postmaster Burleson, that patronage would have to be used to generate enthusiasm for his program. Burleson, House, and Joseph Tumulty with his "Black Book," were the principal presidential agents in such matters.[27] The President distributed the loaves and fishes reluctantly but not without effect. As he himself declared, the presidential office is "not a rosewater affair. This is an office in which a man must put on his war paint. . . ."[28]

The legislative struggle, Wilson realized, was not limited to the halls of Congress. The President's leadership had to be double edged, alerting public opinion and soliciting public enthusiasm as a foundation for legislative maneuver. The President's grass-roots appeal through the press against the first major grass-roots lobby during the tariff fight is a case in point;[29] others are the belated and only partially successful

[25] *Ibid.*, p. 109. David Lawrence maintains that a newspaper reporter, Oliver P. Newman, suggested the idea of a personal appearance to the President-elect (*op. cit.*, pp. 81–83). Whatever the origin of the idea, it was in harmony with Wilson's theory of leadership.

[26] Baker, *Woodrow Wilson,* IV, 109, 111.

[27] See John M. Blum, *Joe Tumulty and the Wilson Era* (Boston: Houghton Mifflin Co., 1951), pp. 73–74; Seymour, *op. cit.,* I, 84. Burleson convinced the President that patronage was the price he had to pay for leadership in Congress. Baker, *Woodrow Wilson,* IV, 44–49.

[28] *Ibid.*, III, 430.

[29] In this message the President virtually identified himself as the people's lobbyist. See *Public Papers,* III, 36.

preparedness tour in 1916 and the tragic League tour in 1919. The same intense purposiveness existed in all cases: to appeal to the people against the shortsightedness of Congress. In a letter written during the fight for the Federal Reserve Act, bemoaning the fact that he would have no vacation, Wilson epitomized the burden of the active Presidency: "Not an hour can I let it out of my mind. Everybody must be seen: every right means used to direct the thought and purpose of those who are to deal with it and those who, outside of Washington, are to criticize it and form public opinion about it."[30]

It is interesting that Wilson, in the process of legislative leadership, adjusted his technique to the unpleasant reality he had condemned in *Congressional Government* many years before. He did not try to by-pass those islands of power, congressional committees, but worked through them and collaborated with the chairmen—as he did with Carter Glass and Senator Robert L. Owen during the congressional battle over the Federal Reserve Bill. In the heyday of his leadership Wilson effected an interesting compromise between the ideas of his *Congressional Government* and *Constitutional Government*. Neither the President nor the congressional committees could stand alone. Working through the party they were, in Wilson's words, co-operative colleagues.

This was the pattern of Wilson's legislative leadership, soundly based on theory, adroitly applied in practice. His leadership in the first eighteen months of his first administration is a textbook example of unalloyed presidential success which was repeated with less frequency in the years that followed—the Adamson Act, the shipping bill, and the Lever and Overman acts are testimony to his later success. Nonetheless, the "Eighteen months" stands with the Hundred Days as an impressive example of executive vigor and especially of what has been described above as harmony of presidential will and technique. Wilson provided a brilliant model for those of his successors who felt the same impulse toward leadership.

Wilson's three other major contributions to the twentieth-century Presidency provided the motive power behind his legislative leadership. All are familiar today: the President as moral leader, the President as trustee of national prosperity, and the President as war leader. It is not the purpose of this paper to discuss what Wilson meant by "moral leadership" or "prosperity." It need only be said that Wilson

[30] Wilson to Mrs. Hulbert, June 22, 1913, Baker, *Woodrow Wilson,* IV, 170.

judged political actions in the light of their moral effect. He believed that the dominant pattern of self-interest in international and domestic politics could be replaced, with the proper leadership and institutional change, by a new moral order. As for prosperity, Wilson did not restrict his definition to mere economic health but extended it to include evenly distributed social "justice."[31] Neither view of presidential obligation, the moral or the social, was new—as Lincoln, Jackson, and Roosevelt attest—but, once again, Wilson theorized, publicized, and ingrained in the national consciousness these presidential responsibilities.

Behind all Wilson's executive actions lay an intense feeling of moral purpose, and it is not surprising that his leadership was invariably expressed in moral terms whether in international politics or domestic. Of the sincerity of Wilson's belief that politics should be directed toward great moral ends, there can be no question. But as an astute politician, and perhaps quite unconsciously, Wilson doubtless sensed that the legislative mill rolls more easily when greased with moralism. Moralism led to near tragedy in Mexico and to confusion in World War I when the President threw a sentimental curtain around the reality of America's position. Although his morality in these instances was self-righteous, oversimplified, and contradictory, in others it was used effectively as a technique and basis for leadership. The President believed that he should represent and interpret national morality, that he should draw raw sentiment from the nation and, as national preacher, articulate the nation's moral sense. As he told a Methodist audience, "If I can speak for you and represent you and in some sense hand on the moral forces that you represent, then I am indeed powerful."[32] Later Presidents absorbed this function; one need only recall F. D. R.'s declaration that the Presidency is "preeminently a place of moral leadership," or the Great Crusade. Sometimes the morality has been genuine, sometimes shoddy, sometimes cloying, as it frequently was with Wilson; but it has been generally effective, particularly if the President has been able to pluck the string of majority sentiment.

Of considerable influence, too, was Wilson's sense of responsibility for the economy. "I am," he said in 1913, "the trustee of national prosperity in council."[33] His leadership in the legislative quest for the New

[31] Address to the Senate, January 22, 1917, *Public Papers,* IV, 407–14; "Benevolence or Justice," in *The New Freedom* (Garden City: Doubleday, 1913), pp. 215–22.

[32] Address before the Annual Conference of the Methodist Protestant Church, April 18, 1915, *Public Papers,* III, 298.

[33] Baker, *Woodrow Wilson,* III, 432.

Freedom was based on his conviction that he should intervene actively to promote the interests of national economic health. In the campaign of 1912 he declared, ". . . the trouble with our present political condition is that we need some man who has not been associated with the governing classes and the governing influences of this country to stand up and speak for us; we need to hear a voice from the outside calling upon the American people to assert again their rights and prerogatives in the possession of their own government."[34] This statement has the same ring as Harry Truman's declaration that he alone could represent the interests of the consumer above the demands of special interests; for Wilson, presumably, the President was the "voice from the outside."

During the war, the President requested and received legislation involving him deeply in the economy, and, although the legislation was largely for war ends, the lesson was not lost for future crises whether of an economic or a military nature.[35] Wilson's economic power during the war, however, should not obscure his prewar and postwar sense of responsibility for economic and social welfare. In addition to preparing a legislative program, he acted—not with great success—to co-ordinate government efforts toward economic readjustment after Sarajevo and intervened in industrial disputes. In a telegram to striking anthracite miners, Wilson gave reassurance that he was "personally and officially interested in promoting the welfare of every man who has to work for a living."[36] Aided by Roosevelt's precedents Wilson took a large step toward capturing for the Presidency the exclusive title of Protector of the National Welfare.

Finally, Wilson's war Presidency was in itself a major positive contribution to the modern Presidency. Lincoln had established the war power of the President, but Wilson determined its twentieth-century character: legislative delegation of responsibility to the President during emergencies. As war President, Wilson acted unilaterally and without legislative sanction to establish war agencies (the WIB, WLB, and Committee of Public Information), seized private property (the Smith and Wesson Co.), and armed American merchantmen. These precedents were useful for later Presidents. Undoubtedly the most marked

[34] "Freedmen Need No Guardians," in *The New Freedom,* pp. 67–68.

[35] See Franklin D. Roosevelt's first inaugural address for the merging of war powers with the President's obligation as trustee of the economy. Samuel I. Rosenman (ed.), *The Public Papers and Addresses of Franklin D. Roosevelt* (New York: Random House, 1938), II, 11–16.

[36] *Public Papers,* VI, 501.

change was in congressional delegation of power. The Lever Act and the Overman Act are only two of the statutes passed during Wilson's war Presidency which delegated unparalleled legislative powers to the President.[37]

It is of more than passing interest that the Congress which surrendered power was sharply rebuffed by the President when it attempted to establish a committee on the conduct of the war, the President declaring that this project would be "fatal to the unity of the executive."[38] He fought successfully to defeat those who, in his words, were "doing their best to get their hands on the steering apparatus of the government."[39] Wilson, right or wrong, was unwilling to permit the creation of an extraordinary committee to oversee the administration of extraordinary legislation. His views on the appropriateness of untrammeled presidential discretion in modern emergencies appeared in his speech to Congress in 1916 requesting congressional approval for the arming of merchantmen and the use of other "instrumentalities and methods" necessary to protect United States vessels and citizens on the high seas. "I believe," Wilson stated, "that the people will be willing to trust me to act with restraint and prudence."[40] The modern tone of this statement is unmistakable. The war experience was a dress rehearsal with the atmosphere dominated by the expansion of discretion and a reliance on self-restraint.

One might assemble a long list of lesser contributions during Wilson's Presidency. Some found their way into the briefs of Attorneys-General, for example, the landing of troops at Veracruz (anachronistically cited in the Great Debate in 1951). Wilson's fight for Brandeis' appointment to the Supreme Court was an incitement to presidential courage in later appointment contests; and, if little else had happened in Wilson's Presidency, he would deserve the gratitude of later chief executives for support given to the Budget and Accounting Act. Also, by opposing vigorously the Gore and McLemore resolutions he protected executive supremacy in foreign affairs.

In the stream of presidential history, Wilson's most enduring contributions are found in his legislative leadership, the aspects of the war

[37] See Edward S. Corwin and Louis W. Koenig, *The Presidency Today* (New York: New York University Press, 1956), p. 33, and Clinton Rossiter, *Constitutional Dictatorship* (Princeton: Princeton University Press, 1948), pp. 243–45.

[38] Wilson to John Sharp Williams, September 1, 1917, Baker, *Woodrow Wilson*, VII, 252.

[39] Wilson to John J. Fitzgerald, September 4, 1917, *ibid.*, p. 258.

[40] Address to Congress, February 26, 1917, *Public Papers*, IV, 431.

Presidency discussed above, and his efforts to fulfil his obligations as moral leader and guardian of the economy. The other Wilson, the Wilson of tragedy, shortcoming, and defeat, was not lost upon later Presidents. The element of tragedy, in fact, makes Wilson's legacy of failure more penetrating. The lesser mistakes were mistakes of judgment with the exception of Wilson's illness, where little presidential judgment was involved. The regency of Mrs. Wilson and Dr. Grayson was doubtless a dramatic lesson for the Eisenhower regents in 1955. It is impossible to say conclusively at this time whether Sherman Adams, James C. Hagerty, and Richard Nixon were influenced by the short-sighted handling of Wilson's case,[41] but the silence during Wilson's illness can be compared unfavorably to the sometimes excessive out-pouring of information on President Eisenhower's indisposition. The later regency certainly satisfied Wilson's often repeated test of "pitiless publicity."

It is more certain that Wilson's shortcomings in the protection of civil liberties were influential in determining a more careful pattern of operations during World War II. The invasions of personal liberty by both Postmaster Burleson and Attorney-General Palmer were not the occasion of spirited presidential protest during and after World War I. With the not inconsiderable exception of the treatment of Japanese-Americans, the Roosevelt administration quite consciously attempted to avoid the excesses of its Democratic predecessor.[42]

Ultimately, however, the greatest failure, and the most significant negative contribution, was based on Wilson's theory of the Presidency, not on a question of judgment. There is no need here to review the familiar story of Wilson's efforts to force Senate acceptance of the Versailles Treaty and United States membership in the League of Nations. The President's greatest personal defeat can be attributed to many things: bad timing, the personal enmity between Wilson and Lodge, the President's overdependence on public opinion and yet his failure to inform and organize the public. Even though the people seemed hostile or indifferent, Wilson prepared sentiment in Congress

[41] In a letter to the author, dated August 14, 1956, Mr. Hagerty said: "I did not have a study made, nor did I seek information concerning President Wilson's illness in 1919. That was not necessary. I had been aware for some time of the situation that existed during the illness of President Wilson. As a matter of fact, my father, who was then a political reporter for The New York Times, covered the President during a portion of his illness, and in talking together as fathers and sons do, I had received a fairly complete fill-in many years ago."

[42] Robert E. Cushman, "American Government in War-Time: Civil Liberties," *American Political Science Review*, XXXVII (February, 1943), 49.

and the country haphazardly; his appeal to the country in the grinding tour of 1919 was not the culmination of a carefully worked out strategy of consultation and maneuver but a desperate eleventh-hour attempt to overcome past neglect of technique. We shall never know if the President's illness contributed decisively to the debacle, although general bad health certainly weakened his judgment and shortened his temper.[43] But beneath all was a controlling weakness of theory.

First of all, Wilson's strong theoretical attachment to party government and his undoubted success as a party leader contributed to three of his basic errors in the last years of his Presidency: the appeal for a Democratic party victory in 1918; the refusal to give strong Republican representation in the American peace commission; and his tacit approval of the slogan, "He kept us out of War," used in the campaign of 1916. In all cases Wilson failed to make the crucial distinction between the President as party leader and the President as chief of state. His belief that the chief executive required a unified party majority led him to appeal, in the name of national necessity, for a Democratic Congress in 1918; party demands in an election year permitted him to tolerate the deception of "He kept us out of war"; and a deeply ingrained partisan spirit led to his conviction that Republicans could not be trusted on the peace commission. The President could not or would not see that a constitutionally governed country cannot afford to make the vital issues of foreign policy a party matter. In fairness to Wilson it must be said that during the war and the League fight he stated that issues of war and peace should not be partisan. He acted, however, as if they were. No better example of party excess can be cited than Wilson's statement of Shadow Lawn during the campaign of 1916 praising the Democrats as the party of peace and warning that "the certain prospect of the success of the Republican Party is that we shall be drawn in one form or another into the embroilments of the European war."[44] Partisanship was forgotten once the election had been won and the war came, but once again in the last two years of his Presidency

[43] Blum, *Joe Tumulty and the Wilson Era,* pp. 208, 213–16.

[44] *New York Times,* October 1, 1916. At one point Wilson apparently was more direct: "If you elect my opponent you elect a war." See Edward S. Corwin, review of Merlo J. Pusey's *Charles Evans Hughes* in *American Political Science Review,* XLVI (December, 1952), 1169. In the heat of the campaign of 1940 Roosevelt forgot at least one of Wilson's errors of judgment in his Boston speech on October 30: "I have said this before, but I shall try it again and again: Your boys are not going to be sent into any foreign wars." In neither case, 1916 or 1940, was the statement justified except, no doubt, politically. See Samuel I. Rosenman, *Working with Roosevelt* (New York: Harper & Bros., 1952), pp. 242–43, for a weak defense of Roosevelt's statement.

the roles of chief of state and party leader became hopelessly entangled with the result that the government and the party suffered equal frustration.

Second, Wilson's expansive view of the Presidency led him in the end to underestimate the power of Congress. He foreshadowed 1919 in 1907 when he wrote of the "very absolute" power of the President in foreign affairs. "He need disclose no step of negotiation until it is complete. And when in any critical matter it is completed the government is virtually committed. Whatever its disinclination, the Senate may feel itself committed also."[45] This assertion anticipates Wilson's statement at Madison Square Garden, on his return home from Paris in 1919, implying that the League Covenant was so closely tied to the treaty of peace that it could not be rejected. The President believed, as he had in the past, that his will could overcome the will of Congress. The basic miscalculation that led to all the others was his conviction that "the President is at liberty both in law and conscience to be as big a man as he can."

The statement, as Winston Churchill once said, referring to the words of another President, is true but not exhaustive. Its spirit is generous to the President and forgetful of Congress; it exaggerates the factor of will and underestimates technique. It assumes that opinion is easy to determine and, although it correctly appreciates "the coordinating force" of opinion once determined, it ignores the fact that Congress, too, engineers and directs sentiment. The effect of Wilson's error on later Presidents is obvious. Franklin D. Roosevelt, in Sherwood's words, was "haunted by the ghost of Woodrow Wilson," and both Truman and Eisenhower have expressed an awareness of the same ghost.[46] Even Harding, nothing if not a party man, was careful to appoint a bipartisan senatorial delegation to the Washington Arms Conference in 1921. It is ironical that Wilson, the apologist for the dominant Presidency, clarified, if he did not establish, the crucial role of the legislature in foreign affairs. In his day of relatively small appropriations that role lay with the Senate, in our own it is with the entire Congress. To use

[45] *Constitutional Government,* pp. 77–78. His advice in the same volume (p. 44), a volume touched by other contradictions, was for Presidents to keep "in confidential communication with the leaders of the Senate," to avoid a "final challenge and contest."

[46] Robert E. Sherwood, *Roosevelt and Hopkins* (New York: Harper & Bros., 1948), pp. 360, 227, 697; Harry S. Truman, *Memoirs by Harry S. Truman* (Garden City: Doubleday, 1955–56), I, 323, and, with allowance for historical inaccuracy, 272; II, 243; Robert J. Donovan, *Eisenhower: The Inside Story* (New York: Harper & Bros., 1956), p. 313.

Wilson's own figure, in his Darwinian quest he forgot the Newtonian nature of our constitutional scheme.

Wilson's historical position, at the watershed of the Presidency, accounts in part for his errors in judgment and theory as well as for the depth of his influence. With an awareness of the traditions of the office, he consciously applied his own positive theory of executive power to twentieth-century conditions of reform and war. The result was a new image of the Presidency. As legislative leader, trustee of the national welfare, as moral leader, and as war President, Wilson produced heightened expectations in the public mind and many lessons for his successors. In the short run his overly rich leadership was partly responsible for the executive doldrums of the 1920's. In the long run the same leadership set a pattern for later Presidents who were able and inclined to lead and, equally, enhanced the role of Congress. Success and failure have helped to remind later Presidents of the necessity for a balance of technique and will. Wilson's positive contribution, in sum, was to entrench in popular and executive consciousness a concept of the Presidency as "the vital place of action" in our governmental system; his negative contribution still stands as a tragic reminder of the caution Presidents must exercise.

If, by and large, Presidents have profited by Wilson's experience, they are nevertheless struggling with some of the same riddles. Partial answers have ben found for a few problems. The fine line between the President's role as chief of state and party leader is not so elusive as it was in Wilson's day. Also, the use of concurrent resolutions by Congress has modified, if only slightly, presidential autonomy in the use of delegated legislative power. The riddle of presidential disability, of course, has not been solved. But of deeper significance are two other interrelated questions which Wilson struggled with and passed on to his successors unanswered. When in quest of public support, to what extent should a President use the pleasant moral argument at the cost of obscuring less palatable justifications for public policy? And, what degree of deference should a President show to public opinion? when be its follower, when be its guide? Reference to Wilson's own thinking shows that he was confused on this matter.[47] Once again, by his excesses, Wilson doubtless tempered the working solutions of later Presidents; but, quite understandably, like Wilson, none has found conclusive answers.

[47] See Baker, *Woodrow Wilson*, VI, 457, 503; VII, 447–48; Seymour, *op. cit.*, II, 49, 50, 60–61, 376–77.

PART TWO

WILSON

AND THE NEW FREEDOM

CHAPTER FIVE

Wilson in the Campaign of 1912*

By
John Wells Davidson

It has been standard practice for most people writing American political history covering the second decade of the twentieth century to pay tribute to the eloquence with which Woodrow Wilson presented his case to the electorate in the presidential campaign of 1912. It is also standard practice for the historian if he wishes to garnish his text with a few samples of Wilson's campaign utterances to quote from *The New Freedom*,[1] that little book compiled by William Rayard Hale and first published in 1913. Nor have Wilson's 1912 campaign speeches failed to draw praise from the political scientists. One paper read at the 1956 meeting of the American Political Science Association in Washington even went so far as to say, "Along with the Lincoln-Douglas debates, Woodrow Wilson's campaign speeches of 1912 are the only election documents which will have a lasting place in the history of American political thought."[2] However, the scholar who made this statement based much of his paper on Hale's compilation, perhaps oblivious of the fact that this volume contained less than 25 per cent of the 1912 campaign speeches. Richard Hofstadter in writing his brilliant *Age of Reform*,[3] a Pulitzer Prize winner, depended mostly on Hale's compilation for material on which to base his analysis of Wilson's program and ideology as set forth in the campaign of 1912.

It is not the purpose of this paper to chastise American historians for passing judgment on Wilson time and again since 1912 without

---

* A paper read at the Twenty-second Annual Meeting of the Southern Historical Association, Durham, N.C., November 15, 1956. A portion of the paper appeared in the *Saturday Review,* December 22, 1956.

[1] Woodrow Wilson, *The New Freedom* (Garden City: Doubleday, 1913).

[2] Andrew Hacker, "Is the 'New Freedom' Obsolete?" p. 1.

[3] *The Age of Reform: From Bryan to F.D.R.* (New York: Alfred A. Knopf, 1955), pp. 223–47, *passim.*

seeking a more thorough knowledge of what he said in that memorable campaign. But I cannot refrain from wondering why they did not heed more carefully the caveat in the Preface to Hale's book itself, to wit, Wilson's own warning that *The New Freedom* "is not a book of campaign speeches." Wilson only offered the volume to the public under his imprimatur as a book containing "in their right sequences the more suggestive portions of my campaign speeches," without any guaranty that all of it came from his 1912 campaign speeches. In fact, close examination reveals that, in addition to extracts from the presidential campaign, it also contains selections from Wilson's 1910 gubernatorial and 1912 preconvention campaigns.

A few historians, it is true, have not been content with Hale's compilation. Arthur S. Link in writing his *Wilson: The Road to the White House* made extensive, though by no means exhaustive, use of newspaper texts of Wilson's 1912 campaign utterances.[4] But press coverage was far from complete, for Wilson delivered his speeches extemporaneously—all except his Speech of Acceptance—thus rendering it difficult for the newsmen to make their deadlines. The newspaper reports of Wilson's utterances were often scanty or inaccurate.

Fortunately Wilson had with him as his shorthand reporter during the 1912 campaign a young man named Charles L. Swem. Although Swem was then only nineteen years old, his speed and efficiency in shorthand had already attracted national attention and eventually would win him two world's championships. Most of the typewritten transcripts he made of Wilson's 1912 campaign speeches have been lost, but his stenographic notes themselves have been preserved. Some of these, covering sixty-odd long and short speeches, Ray Stannard Baker secured from Swem and had transcribed by Mrs. Inez C. Fuller. He made limited use of these in his *Woodrow Wilson: Life and Letters*[5] but did not have access to Swem's notes of forty-odd other speeches delivered by Wilson during the 1912 campaign. These, in some way mislaid for a time, Swem eventually donated to the Princeton University Library, along with his notebooks covering Wilson's presidential years.

My efforts during the last three years have in a large measure been directed toward assembling and preparing for publication accurate

---

[4] (Princeton: Princeton University Press, 1947), pp. 467–528, *passim.*

[5] Ray Stannard Baker, *Woodrow Wilson: Life and Letters* (8 vols.; Garden City: Doubleday, 1927–39), III, 364–412.

texts of Wilson's 1912 campaign speeches.[6] This entailed enlisting the aid of shorthand experts for the work of transcribing materials in the Swem notebooks at Princeton and revising Mrs. Fuller's transcripts in the Ray Stannard Baker Papers at the Library of Congress, as well as gathering numerous newspaper texts of Wilson's speeches to facilitate the deciphering of the stenographic notes. Mr. Swem himself, official shorthand reporter for the Supreme Court of New York, very generously helped in the transcribing of the most difficult passages in his shorthand notes.

My purpose in this paper is not to give a complete history of Wilson's role in the campaign of 1912 but to show how a reading of his speeches, many of which have not been easily accessible to scholars, will help to clear up some of the misunderstandings regarding his New Freedom program of 1912 and even his personality itself.

The first point I would like to examine here is how Wilson stood on the question of extending the powers of the federal government in the interest of the people of the United States. Some scholars describe the Wilson of 1912 as an ardent progressive ready to use the powers of government to promote the welfare of the people. On the other hand, even such a sound scholar as George E. Mowry portrays the Wilson of 1912 as a kind of narrow Jeffersonian wedded to the idea that the best government is that which governs least.[7] Professor Link takes a position between these two extremes, picturing Wilson as a progressive leaning toward conservatism in 1912 but for political reasons becoming an "advanced progressive" in 1916.

The second point that I have endeavored to explore is how Wilson stood on the question of social justice in 1912. Professor Link has described the New Freedom of 1912 as virtually devoid of social aims. In his *Woodrow Wilson and the Progressive Era* he makes this statement: "The divergence in Wilson's and Roosevelt's views on the role government should play in human affairs was more vividly revealed, however, by Wilson's savage attacks on Roosevelt's proposals for social welfare legislation."[8] Those who would have challenged Link on this point have been handicapped by the fact that Hale's compilation for the most

[6] See John Wells Davidson (ed.), *A Crossroads of Freedom: The 1912 Campaign Speeches of Woodrow Wilson* (New Haven: Yale University Press, 1956).

[7] *Theodore Roosevelt and the Progressive Movement* (Madison: University of Wisconsin Press, 1947), p. 277.

[8] Arthur S. Link, *Woodrow Wilson and the Progressive Era, 1910–1917* (New York: Harper & Bros., 1954), p. 21.

part underscores Wilson's advocacy of economic and political rather than social reforms. Nevertheless, there have been challengers. One is Richard L. Watson, who in an article in the *South Atlantic Quarterly* points out, among other things, that Wilson in his first inaugural address advocated government intervention "in safeguarding the health of the nation, the health of its men and its women and its children."[9]

The third point I hope to make is that Wilson's 1912 speeches are a valuable source for those seeking to understand his personality, the more so because all except one of the speeches were extemporaneous—that is, they were not read from prepared texts. Allowance has to be made for the fact that these are campaign orations, but anyone who reads the words Wilson actually uttered on the stump in 1912 must unavoidably gain striking insights into the kind of man he was.

In discussing how Wilson stood on the question of the use of governmental powers, it is interesting to see how one of his sentences has been taken out of context and used to buttress the interpretation that he was advocating a narrow Jeffersonianism. This was a remark Wilson made at the New York Press Club, September 9, 1912: "The history of liberty is a history of the limitation of governmental power, not the increase of it." Professor Mowry quotes this sentence in his *Theodore Roosevelt and the Progressive Movement* to indicate that Wilson was a narrow Jeffersonian, and it appears again to support the same kind of interpretation in the 1956 American history textbook of Hicks and Mowry.[10] Mowry does not cite a text of Wilson's speech at the New York Press Club. He contents himself with referring to the *New York Times* of September 16, 1912, which carries the sentence in question in an editorial.

What needs to be examined in this case, therefore, is the history behind Wilson's "history of liberty" remark. Wilson had issued an advance text (actually a lightly edited version of an address delivered at Buffalo a few days previously), but the speech he made extemporaneously at the New York Press Club was an entirely different one.[11]

The paper that carried more of the text of the extemporaneous speech than any other that I have searched was the *New York Trib-*

[9] Richard L. Watson, Jr., *South Atlantic Quarterly*, LIV (January, 1955), 111–12.

[10] Mowry, *op. cit.*, p. 277; John D. Hicks and George E. Mowry, *A Short History of American Democracy* (Boston: Houghton Mifflin Co., 1956), p. 620.

[11] For a copy of the advance text of Wilson's New York Press Club speech, see *Philadelphia Record*, September 10, 1912.

une, a copy of which came into Theodore Roosevelt's hand when he stopped in Ogden, Utah, on a tour of the West.[12] Soon thereafter, on September 14, at San Francisco the Bull Moose leader used the "history of liberty" statement as the text of a major speech picturing Wilson as an advocate of outmoded political and economic ideas.

After mentioning that he had read the stenographic report of the New York Press Club address in the *Tribune,* Roosevelt charged that the "history of liberty" statement was "the key to Mr. Wilson's position," calling it "laissez-faire doctrine of the English political economists three-quarters of a century ago," capable of being applied with profit "only in a primitive community under primitive conditions." To apply it to the United States at the beginning of the twentieth century, he contended, "means literally and absolutely to refuse to make a single effort to better any one of our social or industrial conditions."

Then he went on to contrast his own plan to Wilson's:

Our proposal is to increase the power of the people themselves and make the people in reality the governing class. Therefore Mr. Wilson's proposal is really to limit the power of the people and thereby to leave unchecked the colossal, embodied privileges of the present day. Now, friends, you can adopt one philosophy or the other. You can adopt the philosophy of laissez-faire, of the limitation of governmental power and turn the industrial life of this country into a chaotic scramble of selfish interests, each bent on plundering the others and all bent on oppressing the wageworker.

This is precisely and exactly what Mr. Wilson's proposal means; and it can mean nothing else. Under such limitation of governmental power as he praises every railroad must be left unchecked, every great industrial concern can do as it chooses with its employees and with the general public; women must be permitted to work as many hours a day as their taskmasters bid them; great corporations must be left unshackled to put down wages to a starvation limit and to raise the price of their products as high as monopolistic control will permit. The reverse policy means an extension, instead of a limitation, of governmental power; and for that extension we Progressives stand.[13]

Now, the significant thing is that the text of Wilson's New York Press Club speech as Theodore Roosevelt read it in the *Tribune* entirely omitted a long and highly important passage immediately preceding the "history of liberty" statement. An examination of a transcript of Swem's shorthand notes, in the Princeton University Library, reveals that in this part of his address Wilson was denouncing the close alliance

[12] See *New York Tribune,* September 10, 1912, for partial text of Wilson's New York Press Club speech. For news story telling of Roosevelt's obtaining the *Tribune*'s text of Wilson's speech, see *ibid.,* September 15, 1912.

[13] Quoted from text of Roosevelt's speech in *San Francisco Examiner,* September 15, 1912.

between the federal government and big business, a relation which he predicted would be perpetuated if Roosevelt should be elected and if his plan to regulate monopoly were put into effect. "Who will guarantee to us," the Democratic candidate asked,

that this machine will be just and pitiful? Do we conceive social betterment to lie in the pitiful use of irresistible power? Or do we conceive it to arise out of the irresistible might of a body of free men? Has justice ever grown in the soil of absolute power? Has not justice always come from the press of the heart and spirit of men who resist power?

Liberty has never come from the government. Liberty has always come from the subjects of the government. The history of liberty is a history of resistance. The history of liberty is a history of the limitation of governmental power, not the increase of it. Do these gentlemen dream that in the year 1912 we have discovered a unique exception to the movement of human history? Do they dream that the whole character of those who exercise power has changed, that it is no longer a temptation? Above all things else do they dream that men are bred great enough now to be a Providence to the people over whom they preside?[14]

It is quite evident that in effect Roosevelt quoted the "history of liberty" statement out of context. Also it is interesting to note that both of these candidates were emphasizing the people as the source of governmental power in a democratic society. And it is perhaps significant that Roosevelt failed to call Wilson's political philosophy Jeffersonian in that such a label would have resulted in his identifying his opponent with a noted advocate of the people.

To get a fuller understanding of Wilson's attitude toward the extension of governmental power, we have to read some of the addresses he made later in the 1912 campaign when his ideas were more fully developed and organized. We should keep in mind that the campaign was part of Wilson's political education. Roosevelt's sharp attack in his San Francisco address apparently did Wilson a service. It made him realize the necessity of stating his position more carefully and of answering his opponent.

Two weeks after his New York Press Club appearance Wilson, at Scranton, Pennsylvania, answered the charge of Roosevelt and other Progressive Republicans that he opposed an extension of the federal powers in the interest of the people. After saying he was against "the mere presentation to audiences of the abstract conceptions of government," he put himself on record as hostile to a narrow Jeffersonianism.

[14] Davidson, *op. cit.*, pp. 129–30.

Of course, this was intended to be a government of free citizens and of equal opportunity, but how are we going to make it such? That is the question. Because I realize that while we are followers of Jefferson, there is one principle of Jefferson's which no longer can obtain in the practical politics of America. You know that it was Jefferson who said that the best government is that which does as little governing as possible, which exercises its power as little as possible. That was said in a day when the opportunities of America were so obvious to every man, when every individual was so free to use his powers without let or hindrance, that all that was necessary was that the government should withhold its hand and see to it that every man got an opportunity to act if he would. But that time is past. America is not now, and cannot in the future be, a place for unrestricted individual enterprise. It is true that we have come upon an age of great cooperative industry. It is true that we must act absolutely upon that principle.[15]

Wilson then went on to point out that conditions of the twentieth century were so different from those of Jefferson's time that problems relating to labor and property could no longer be dealt with by the old standards. He argued that the laws had to be broadened to safeguard the interests of human beings, citing as an example that the city of Glasgow in order to protect the interests of its citizens had decided to treat the entries and hallways of the great tenements as public streets. Then he summed up his answer to Roosevelt and the others who had distorted the meaning of his "history of liberty" statement:

What I am illustrating for you is this: it is something that our Republican opponents don't seem to credit us with intelligence enough to comprehend. Because we won't take the dictum of a leader who thinks he knows exactly what should be done for everybody, we are accused of wishing to minimize the powers of the government of the United States. I am not afraid of the utmost exercise of the powers of the government of Pennsylvania, or of the Union, provided they are exercised with patriotism and intelligence and really in the interest of the people who are living under them. But when it is proposed to set up guardians over these people to take care of them by a process of tutelage and supervision in which they play no active part, I utter my absolute objection. Because the proposal of the third party, for example, is not to take you out of the hands of the men who have corrupted the government of the United States but to see to it that you remain in their hands and that government guarantees to you that it will be humane to you.[16]

Wilson, however, repeatedly contended that Roosevelt's plan for regulation of monopoly called for the delegation of too much power to the proposed trade commission and would result in a government of men. The very vigor with which Roosevelt championed the regulation

---

[15] *Ibid.*, p. 234.   [16] *Ibid.*, p. 237.

of corporations and the fact that he did advocate the delegation of considerable power to the regulatory commission made him vulnerable to Wilson's attack. In fact, Wilson's hammering on this point appears to have made such an impression on Roosevelt that during the latter part of the campaign he sought to clarify his position. Even while he lay in a Chicago hospital recovering from the wound he had received in Milwaukee, Roosevelt issued a statement, through Francis Heney, declaring that he favored an amendment to the Sherman Antitrust Act that would define specifically what practices should be regarded as illegal. "If, for instance," so reads this statement, "a corporation should be found crushing out competition by refusing to sell when the patron bought of competitors, or by underselling in districts, or in the dozen of other ways that Congress should learn were being practised and should say were illegal, I would have the statute say point blank, with no loophole for escape, that the corporation was guilty."[17] By this statement Roosevelt put himself very close to the position that Wilson had taken in his New Haven address. At this stage, the main difference between the two candidates on the trust question was that Roosevelt was more specific and emphatic in his declaration of intention to have the proposed trade commission given the necessary powers to enforce the new law. Noteworthy is the fact that Roosevelt at this point in the campaign ruled out the delegation of discretionary powers to a commission for the purpose of determining which trade practices would be outlawed.

Another thing that has undoubtedly contributed to the notion of Wilson as an enemy of strong federal government is his well-known distrust of commissions and experts. Although it seems clear from his 1912 speeches that he was not an advocate of narrow Jeffersonianism, we should at the same time recognize that he tended to be more cautious than Roosevelt regarding the extension of the powers of the federal government. He went into the campaign with a distinct distrust for governmental commissions. Before very long (probably owing to Brandeis' influence) he admitted the advisability of establishing a commission to regulate competition, being careful, however, to specify that the powers of the commission should be defined precisely by law. Perhaps the best statement of his position on this question is to be found in the following paragraphs from his New Haven address:

[17] For text of Roosevelt's statement see *New York Tribune,* October 20, 1912.

The Democratic party does not stand for the limitation of powers of government, either in the field of the state or in the field of the federal government. There is not a Democrat that I know who is afraid to have the powers of the government exercised to the utmost. But there are a great many of us who are afraid to see them exercised at the discretion of individuals. There are a great many of us who still adhere to that ancient principle that we prefer to be governed by the power of laws, and not by the power of men.

Therefore, we favor as much power as you choose, but power guided by knowledge, power extended in detail, not power given out in the lump to a commission set up as is proposed by the third party and unencumbered by the restrictions of law, to set up a "constructive regulation," as their platform calls it, of the trusts and monopoly. But we wish a law which takes its searchlight and casts its illuminating rays down the secret corridors of all the processes by which monopoly has been established and polices those corridors so that highway robbery is no longer committed on them, so that men are no longer waylaid upon them, so that the liberty of individuals to compete is no longer checked by the power of combinations stronger than any possible individual can be. We want to see the law administered. We are not afraid of commissions.[18]

Pursuing this point further, Wilson acknowledged that under existing conditions an individual had to have courage to go to the courts and challenge the power of those in control of industries. Hence he readily admitted that there might be a need for "special tribunals" and "special processes," but he was "absolutely opposed to leaving it to the choice of those tribunals what the processes of law shall be and the means of remedy."[19]

Related to Wilson's original skepticism about governmental commissions were his doubts about the role of experts in government. Taken out of context, some of the jibes he directed toward "experts" during the 1912 campaign might even be used as evidence of a kind of anti-intellectualism. Careful examination of his speeches, however, shows that he was objecting to the determination of governmental policy by experts isolated from public opinion, or to the uncritical acceptance of the advice of experts without regard to the totality of a given problem. That he was not opposed to experts per se is evidenced by the fact that he favored a governmental program that would provide the farmers with scientific information for the improvement of their agricultural methods.[20]

In his Labor Day speech at Buffalo he denounced as undemocratic

[18] Davidson, *op. cit.*, pp. 264–65.

[19] *Ibid.*, p. 265.   [20] *Ibid.*, pp. 46–47.

the idea of a small number of experts taking care of the people of the United States. "What I fear, therefore," he declared, "is a government of experts. God forbid that in a democratic country we should resign the task and give the government over to experts. What are we for if we are to be scientifically taken care of by a small number of gentlemen who are the only men who understand the job? Because if we don't understand the job, then we are not a free people."[21]

At Sioux City, Iowa, two weeks later, Wilson criticized Roosevelt for relying too much on the advice of the Remsen Board in the handling of the pure food problem. A narrow approach to this question, he contended, had resulted in the continued use of benzoate of soda to conceal putrefaction of food. It is in this connection that Wilson again expressed his distaste for government by experts:

> I want to warn the people of this country to beware of commissions of experts. I have lived with experts all my life, and I know that experts don't see anything except what is under their microscope under their eye. They don't even perceive what is under their nose. An expert feels in honor bound to confine himself to the particular question which you have asked him.[22]

This belief of Wilson's that each important problem facing the nation should be considered in its totality rather than in dissevered parts was a long-standing one with him. As president of Princeton he had insisted that technical training alone could not prepare a man to cope with the problems of the world. "The managing minds of the world, even the efficient working minds of the world," he asserted in his inaugural address as president of Princeton, "must be equipped for a mastery whose chief characteristic is adaptability, play, and initiative which transcends the bounds of mere technical training." He believed that the "truly educated man" must always be mindful of the "subtle and yet universal connections of things."[23]

But there was more than this behind Wilson's objections to government by experts. He saw in it a threat to what he called "government by discussion," a phrase probably derived from Walter Bagehot's *Physics and Politics*.[24] In an address at Pittsburgh on October 19, 1912, he drew a contrast between "government by discussion" and "government by control":

[21] *Ibid.*, p. 83.   [22] *Ibid.*, pp. 160–61.

[23] R. S. Baker and W. E. Dodd (eds.), *The Public Papers of Woodrow Wilson* (6 vols.; New York: Harper & Bros., 1925–27), I, 445, 457.

[24] (Boston: Beacon Press, 1956), pp. 114–48.

Wilson in the Campaign of 1912

I have been trying all day to find some phrase in which to tell you my own impression of what it is that the United States, particularly the most thoughtful people in the United States, desire to see done. The nearest I have come to it is this: that they desire to see discussion supersede control. We have had a government not by public opinion, not by diffused and general public opinion, but by private concert of action. We have had government by control instead of government by discussion, and government by control must always sooner or later fall under just suspicion; whereas government by discussion must always be blown through with a pure air of outdoors and the influences that come from the great bodies of the people itself. Not all of this control has been sinister in intention. I like to believe that very little of it has been sinister in intention.[25]

Now, what about Wilson and social justice in 1912? The claim has been put forward that he did not espouse social justice as such until 1916. Wilson's speeches show clearly that though he did give priority to *economic* reform he also undoubtedly advocated the principles of social justice in 1912 as part of his campaign. "The interest of this country," he declared in his speech at the Yorkville Casino in New York City, September 4, 1912, "is founded, in the last analysis, upon its material prosperity and its social justice." He placed material prosperity first, he said, because, "you can't attend to your spiritual interests unless you are at least physically sustained."[26]

Far from savagely attacking Roosevelt's proposals for social justice legislation, Wilson had words of praise for this part of his opponent's program. Believing that a minimum-wage law would result in a lowering of wages, he did object to Roosevelt's proposal to establish a minimum wage for women;[27] but he did not combat social justice itself. What he did oppose most forcefully, time and again during the campaign, was having the Progressive Republican party, which he charged with being an ally of big business, in control of a social reform program. This, he said, would not result in the establishment of social justice, which would come only from below, but in paternalism, in justice dispensed from above and willed by the great corporations.

At the Parade Grounds in Minneapolis, September 18, 1912, he discussed at some length the need to conserve the human resources of America and advocated improvement of working conditions in the factories. He warned that this would only come after a change in the

[25] Davidson, *op. cit.*, p. 454.

[26] *Ibid.*, p. 107.   [27] *Ibid.*, pp. 76–77.

point of view of government. While denying that the Progressive Republicans should be trusted to carry out a program of social reform, he indorsed most of their aims in these words:

I want to say here, as I have said on so many other occasions, that there is a great deal in the program of the new third party which attracts all public-spirited and hopeful men, that there is a great program of human uplift included in the platform of that party. A man would be niggardly and untrue to himself who would not say that. But when I ask myself who is going to carry out this program, then the thing wears another aspect.[28]

At New Haven Wilson discussed some of the things that needed to be done to conserve the nation's human resources:

Then there is the matter of the regulation of hours of labor, of the conditions of labor, of the sanitation of factories, of the limitation of the hours of work for women and children, of the limitation of hours for men, questions which are in part state questions but also in part federal questions. All of these matters have to be treated by knowledge and pursued by a constancy of purpose which no special interests should be allowed to stand in the way of. And the government of the United States under the Democratic party will attempt to put all through this nation the structural steel of law, so that no man can doubt what his rights are, or doubt the stability of the thing that he is walking on.[29]

Near the end of the campaign in a speech at Newark, New Jersey, October 29, 1912, Wilson admitted that "one branch of the Republican party" had "some very persuasive arguments in favor of social justice." In this connection he made the following comments:

Now, I hope I do not have to say to you that I am in favor of social justice, but I want to know who is going to get it for you and when. Does anybody suppose that either branch of the Republican party can possibly control the next House of Representatives, plus the next Senate, plus the next Presidency? Doesn't everybody know that the only possible way of uniting those three forces in a common enterprise is to vote the Democratic ticket? If you want social justice, when do you want it? Now, two years from now, four years from now? I tell you solemnly, ladies and gentlemen, we cannot postpone justice any longer in the United States.[30]

In the face of the evidence presented above, it seems that any interpretation of Wilson in 1912 suggesting that he was indifferent to social justice needs to be modified. Wilson was then actively talking and thinking in terms of social justice. It should be remembered that Wilson, instead of being hostile to Roosevelt's social justice program, was in favor of it. He was, it is true, undecided about just how much should

---

[28] *Ibid.*, p. 192.   [29] *Ibid.*, p. 266.   [30] *Ibid.*, pp. 500–501.

be done by the federal government and how much by the states. He deferred his decision on that point to a later date.

Last of all, let us now consider Wilson's 1912 speeches as a source of clues to his personality. For this purpose these extemporaneous utterances are very rewarding. They show that he was no doctrinaire, in this respect being very much like Jefferson. Although he had certain guiding principles in 1912, he kept his New Freedom program elastic rather than rigid. And his speeches reveal that he was fully aware that his political views had changed considerably within the space of a few years. When Roosevelt and other Republican Progressives quoted some of his 1907 utterances to prove that his conversion to progressivism was recent,[31] he made the following reply in his Cleveland speech:

These gentlemen [the Republican Progressives] say that if the Democratic party gets into power it will follow the old Jeffersonian idea of taking its hands off, that what we need is more power, not less power. Why, Mr. Roosevelt has had a great deal of amusement expounding what he believes to be my political philosophy. He is going a long journey, and I bid him welcome to that jungle. I am not interested in my political philosophy; I am interested in what he is going to do and in what he is thinking about, and . . . I would invite him to be interested in what I am thinking about and am going to do.[32]

The profound elasticity of Wilson's mind, exemplified by the way in which the New Freedom grew and took shape during the campaign of 1912 and still later during his first administration, is too often ignored. To many people he still looms up as the stern Scottish Covenanter, the stubborn man in the White House who, impervious to reason, was unwilling to compromise even while he lay on his sick bed. Mr. Charles Seymour has done history a service by demonstrating in his recent article in the *Virginia Quarterly Review* that even at the Paris Peace Conference Wilson was willing to learn and compromise, *and did*. Mr. Seymour says that Wilson was "educable"; that he was proud of his ability to yield to reason. It is my belief that Wilson was also "educable" in 1912 and that a reading of his major campaign speeches of that year will confirm this.[33]

Again, inconsistent with the picture of Wilson as the stern, mono-

[31] See Roosevelt's remarks at Houghton, Michigan, as quoted in *Chicago Daily Tribune,* October 10, 1912.

[32] Davidson, *op. cit.,* pp. 423–24.

[33] "The Paris Education of Woodrow Wilson," *Virginia Quarterly Review,* XXXII (Autumn, 1956), 578–93, *passim.*

lithic personality is the extemporaneous humor which crops out again and again in his 1912 campaign speeches. At Union City, Indiana, for instance, he was pressed into making a rear-platform speech. Although this kind of campaigning was not to his taste, he delighted his small audience in the following manner.

I am very much obliged to you for this greeting which I did not expect. I have a rather strong objection to talking from the back platform of a train. I believe that the back platform just now belongs to the Republicans and not to the Democrats. We belong on the front platform. Not only that, but this is the kind of platform that I don't like to stand on. It changes too often. It moves around and shifts its ground too often. I like a platform that stays put.[34]

Also the introductory passages of these speeches often contain passages of rippling humor. At New Haven, after Governor Baldwin of Connecticut had introduced him to an audience in especially glowing terms, Wilson responded in the following manner:

The introduction reminds me by contrast with the remark made to me by a gentleman a good many months ago after I had appeared before a good many audiences. He said that he ventured to say that if I had an opportunity to add a petition to the litany it would be: "From all introducers and traducers, Good Lord, deliver us." But I would own, for I had had other experiences like this evening, that I counted myself peculiarly happy in my introducers and that I could not have more prudently chosen my traducers if I had chosen them myself.[35]

And of course there are other examples of Wilson's wit in these speeches.

There are also numerous superb passages which typify Wilson's lofty idealism. One of these, his peroration at Scranton, describes the mission of America:

The vision of America will never change. America once, when she was a little people, sat upon a hill of privilege and had a vision of the future. She saw men happy because they were free. She saw them free because they were equal. She saw them banded together because they had the spirit of brothers. She saw them safe because they did not wish to impose upon one another. And the vision is not changed. The multitude has grown, that welcome multitude that comes from all parts of the world to seek a safe place of life and of hope in America. And so America will move forward, if she moves forward at all, only with her face to that same sun of promise. Just so soon as she forgets the sun in the heavens, just so soon as she looks so intently upon the road before her and around her that he does not know where it leads, then will she forget what America was created for; her light will go out; the nations will grope

---

[34] Davidson, *op. cit.,* p. 154.   [35] *Ibid.,* p. 259.

again in darkness and they will say: "Where are those who prophesied a day of freedom for us? Where are the lights that we followed? Where is the torch that the runners bore? Where are those who bade us hope? Where came in these whispers of dull despair? Has America turned back? Has America forgotten her mission? Has America forgotten that her politics are part of her life, and that only as the red blood of her people flows in the veins of her polity shall she occupy that point of vantage which has made her the beacon and the leader of mankind?"[36]

Last of all, I wish particularly to quote a passage illustrating Wilson's essential humility, his realization of himself as a fallible human being, subject to the judgment of posterity. These were the words in which he told his audience at Detroit on September 19, 1912, how it felt for the historian to play a role in important historical events:

I pity the man who in the year 1912 promises the people of the United States anything that he cannot give them. I used to say sometimes when I was attempting to write history that I could sit on the side lines and look on with a certain degree of complacency upon the men who were performing in the arena of politics; because, I said, after the game is over, some quiet fellow like myself will sit down in a remote room somewhere and tell the next generation what to think of you fellows, and they will think what he tells them to think. He assesses; he sums up. You may talk yourselves tired, and your own estimate of yourselves will be discounted.

And now that I am myself exposed, I think of that quiet jury sitting in those rooms surrounded by nothing but shelves and books and documents. I think of the anticipated verdict of another generation, and I know that the only measure and standard by which a man can rise or fall is the standard of absolute integrity; that he can deceive nobody but himself and his own generation for a little space.[37]

So it was that Wilson, like Winston Churchill, realized that history alone held the final answer.

[36] *Ibid.*, p. 242.   [37] *Ibid.*, p. 212.

CHAPTER SIX

Woodrow Wilson: Political Leader and Administrator*

By
Arthur W. Macmahon

Durably impressive in themselves, Woodrow Wilson's achievements as a political leader and practical administrator may also be used as a measure of the development of Wilson's own thought and of the possibilities and progress in the institutions upon which he left his imprint.

While he was governor of New Jersey and already a possible presidential candidate, Wilson remarked in an address before the Commercial Club of Portland, Oregon:

> The whole country, since it cannot decipher the methods of its legislation, is clamoring for leadership; and a new role, which to many persons seems a little less than unconstitutional, is thrust upon our executives. The people are impatient of a President or a governor who will not formulate a policy and insist upon its adoption. They are impatient of a governor who will not exercise energetic leadership, who will not make his appeals directly to public opinion and insist that the dictates of public opinion be carried out in definite legal reforms of his own suggeston.

It was indeed a prospectus typical of the times; Charles Evans Hughes in New York was talking and acting in these terms. Wilson's own state leadership helped to make it typical.

On the eve of entering the White House, Wilson dealt with the Presidency in a public letter to A. Mitchell Palmer.[1] The purpose was to sidetrack a proposed amendment for a single, six-year presidential term. This proposal had been indorsed by the Democratic platform,

---

* Paper, slightly abridged, prepared for seminar on "Wilson, the Administrator and Politician," led by Arthur W. Macmahon, University of Chicago, February 1, 1956.

[1] The text appeared in the daily press of February 6, 1913. It is given in R. S. Baker and W. E. Dodd (eds.), *The Public Papers of Woodrow Wilson* (New York: Harper & Bros., 1925–27), III, 21–25 (hereinafter cited as *"Public Papers"*).

and a resolution of amendment had already passed the Senate and had been reported favorably in the House. In opposing it, Wilson pointed to what he believed was the transitional condition and the still uncertain destination of the Presidency. Such uncertainty, he argued, made any early constitutional amendment undesirable. "I must speak with absolute freedom and candor in this matter, or not speak at all," Wilson wrote, "and it seems to me that the present position of the Presidency in our actual system, as we use it, is quite abnormal and must lead eventually to something very different." Why should the President, who is expected to be the leader of the party and spokesman of policy, be responsible to no one for four years, let alone six? "Sooner or later, it would seem, he must be made answerable to opinion in a somewhat more informal and intimate position—answerable, it may be, to the Houses whom he seeks to lead, either personally or through a Cabinet, as well as to the people for whom they speak." He added: "But this is a matter to be worked out—as inevitably it will be—in some natural American way which we cannot yet even predict."

To speak in these vague terms in February, 1913, was probably both tactical and honest. It bulwarked the argument that the Presidency was in unresolved transition while equally unresolved for him, and it retained elements of Wilson's earlier preoccupation. It left Wilson free to emphasize what was immediate and practical: that the President "is expected by the Nation to be the leader of his party as well as the Chief Executive Officer of the Government, and the country will take no excuses from him." This assumption was the basis for the crucial point in the argument. "The present fact," Wilson wrote, "is that the President is held responsible for what happens in Washington in every large matter, and so long as he is commanded to lead he is surely entitled to a certain amount of power—all the power he can get from the support and convictions and opinions of his fellow countrymen; and he ought to be suffered to use that power against his opponents until his work is done." Limiting the President to a single, six-year term, he argued, would seriously embarrass the fighting power of a President who is a true spokesman for the people.

In such passages we are given a working plan on the eve of its stupendous application. Thereafter we can glean only the barest hints of Wilson's later thinking about constitutional change. There is little to offset the verdict that, as man of action, he helped history to pronounce: namely, that the practice of real presidential leadership reduced the possibility of evoking legislatively responsible cabinets.

As for clues to Wilson's later thinking about responsibility, it is true that on November 5, 1916, he wrote to Secretary Lansing that, if Hughes was elected, he proposed to appoint him Secretary of State and then to resign along with the Vice-President so that Hughes could become President without delay. "All my life long," Wilson wrote to Lansing,

I have advocated some such responsible government for the United States as other constitutional systems afford as of course, and as such action on my part would inaugurate, at least by example. Responsible government means government by those whom the people trust, and trust at the time of decision and action. The whole country has long perceived, without knowing how to remedy, the extreme disadvantage of having to live for four months after an election under a party whose guidance has been rejected at the polls.[2]

But President Wilson was speaking here of a special aspect of the problem of responsibility. The Twentieth Amendment has eased this angle of the problem by cutting the length of the interregnum in half.

On the question of President Wilson's ultimate views about political responsibility through a cabinet, David F. Houston reported that "after he went to Washington, I never heard him refer to the proposal."[3] Houston added his guess that "Wilson had never really thought through this problem which interested him for so many years." Houston did not believe that Woodrow Wilson quite realized how far his own successful practice of his immediate working code had helped to remove the dilemma by closing the doors on any other course for the Presidency.

Against this glancing evidence must be put the equally slight clue given by Colonel House's dictated diary note about a dinner conversation with the President on April 29, 1917. "The President," House recorded,

declared his intention of writing some things which were on his mind, after he retired from office. . . . He said he had no notion of writing about his administration, but expressed a desire to write one book which he had long had in mind and which he thought might have some influence for good. . . . He talked of the proposed book and its contents. I thought that if he would bring out clearly the necessity for a more responsible form of government, and the necessity for having Cabinet members sit in the House of Representatives, it

[2] Ray Stannard Baker, *Woodrow Wilson: Life and Letters* (Garden City: Doubleday, 1927–39), VI, 292–93. Baker remarks: "There is no doubt that he would have carried on his purpose in resigning in case Hughes had been elected" (p. 293).

[3] David F. Houston, *Eight Years with Wilson's Cabinet* (Garden City: Doubleday, 1926), II, 198.

would be worth while. He agreed that if the Cabinet officers sat in the House, the outcome would be that the President would have to take his material for the Cabinet from Congress. This, in the end, would give the Cabinet more power, and would have the further effect of bringing into Congress the best talent in the country. It would eventuate in something like the British system.[4]

But what we have quoted is Colonel House, self-consciously leading; it is not Woodrow Wilson speaking directly. Moreover, so far as the report goes and is accurate, it merely says that the President "agreed" about the consequences likely to follow the imagined first step. It does not necessarily commit the President to belief in these ultimate consequences.

A more practical issue was the way Wilson as President conceived and dealt with the interfused, double representative roles of the office. Undoubtedly his inaugural address stated the core of his thought about the instrumental relation of majority processes and party rule to the changing national consensus. "The success of a party," he said on March 4, 1913, "means little except when the Nation is using the party for a large and definite program. No one can mistake the purpose for which the Nation now seeks to use the Democratic Party. It seeks to use it to interpret a change in its own plans and point of view."[5] The same conception was reflected in an article—an interview, it should perhaps be called—that appeared in a magazine on March 8. "I am bidden," he said, "to interpret as well as I can the purposes of the people of the United States, and to act, in so far as my purpose determines the action, through the instrumentality of persons who likewise represent that choice." He drew the conclusion: ". . . I shall not be acting in a partisan spirit when I nominate progressives—and only progressives. I shall be acting as a representative of the people of this great country."[6]

We shall have occasion in examining Wilson's legislative methods to note the importance of his decision to work with the regular leaders and officers of the Democratic party in Congress. This crucial choice of tactics was qualified but not renounced in such statements as his remark in a Jackson Day talk in January, 1915, "that politics in this country does not depend any longer upon the regular members of either party."[7] He contended that the Democratic party was two-thirds

---

[4] Charles Seymour (ed.), *The Intimate Papers of Colonel House* (Boston: Houghton Mifflin Co., 1926–28), III, 47.

[5] The text of the address is given in *Public Papers,* III, 1–6.

[6] *Collier's Weekly,* L (March 8, 1913), 8; *Public Papers,* III, 27–30.

[7] *Ibid.,* p. 238.

"progressive," the Republican party one-third "progressive." In the spring of 1916 he said at a Jefferson Day banquet: "Party politics, my friends, sometimes plays too large a part in the United States. . . . the country demands service which is essentially and fundamentally non-partisan." He added that he was referring as much to domestic as to foreign affairs "for in saying 'non-partisan' I do not mean merely as between parties and political organizations, but also and more fundamentally as between classes and interests."[8]

Later, in the congressional campaign of 1918, the President's appeal for the return of a Democratic majority seemed to project something basic to his thinking about the role of party in responsibility. The recollections of his cabinet associates indicate that they understood his appeal would be couched in terms of support for his policies.[9] Colonel House, however, noted in his diary on September 24: "The President spoke of politics in general and expressed an earnest desire that a Democratic Congress should be elected. He said that he intended making a speech or writing a letter about two weeks before the elections, asking the people to return a Democratic House."[10] Colonel House added: "I did not express any opinion as to the wisdom of this." On October 25, when the President's statement was issued and before the election, Colonel House did confide to his diary that he was "greatly disturbed by the President's appeal" and that "I am sorry now I did not discuss it with him to a finish." It is true that the President's statement on October 25 sought to avoid the charge that he was complaining of lack of support of the war.[11] "I have no thought," he said, "of suggesting that any political party is paramount in matters of patriotism." But his appeal was frankly in terms of party. He went on to say that "the leaders of the minority in the present Congress have unquestionably been pro-war, but they have been anti-administration." He charged that they had been constantly seeking "to take the conduct of the war out of my hands and put it under the control of instrumentalities of their own choosing." Pleading that "this is no time for divided counsel or for divided leadership," the President said to the voters: "If you have approved of my leadership and wish me to continue to be your unembarrassed spokesman in affairs at home and abroad, I earnestly beg that

[8] *Public Papers,* IV, 144.

[11] The text is given in *Public Papers,* IV, 286–87.

[10] Seymour, *op. cit.,* IV, 68.

[9] Baker, *Woodrow Wilson,* VIII, 513–14.

you will express yourselves unmistakably to that effect by returning a Democratic majority to both the Senate and the House of Representatives." It should be noted that the President based this appeal largely on the importance of being unembarrassed by divided counsel and controls. There was no commitment to stop striving when he added: "I am your servant and will accept your judgment without cavil, but my power to administer the great trust assigned me by the Constitution would be seriously impaired should your judgment be adverse, and I must frankly tell you so because so many critical issues depend upon your verdict."

Writing later in a personal letter, Wilson said of his action: "I have no idea that the President is sacrosanct in any way, and being the leader of the country and under our system necessarily the leader of a party, he certainly ought not to be rendered dumb on a point of taste at a critical moment."[12]

Woodrow Wilson himself recognized the relation of the moving consensus of cumulative thinking and agitation to the legislative dynamic of party action and executive leadership within and through a party. In a letter on April 23, 1911, toward the close of the fruitful New Jersey legislative session of Wilson's first year as governor, he wrote that it was "just a bit of natural history. I came to the office in the fulness of time, when opinion was ripe on all these matters, when both parties were committed to these reforms, and by merely standing fast, by never losing sight of the business for an hour, but keeping up all sorts of (legitimate) pressure *all the time*, kept the mighty forces from being diverted or blocked at any point."[13] Governor Wilson's contemporary view of himself is echoed by Arthur S. Link as historian: "He succeeded because he marshaled into a coherent unit the force of public opinion, because he was a competent party leader, but above all because the necessary fundamental agitation had already been accomplished by other men."[14]

To say that Woodrow Wilson learned his politics in New Jersey (as he said) and revealed there his methods of leadership in their relation to a critical stage in the maturing of agreement does not deny important differences in the depth of controversy on state and national issues. It does not belittle the importance and bitterness of the choices

[12] Baker, *Woodrow Wilson*, VIII, 552.

[13] Wilson to Mrs. Hulbert, Baker, *Woodrow Wilson*, III, 169–71.

[14] *Wilson: The Road to the White House* (Princeton: Princeton University Press, 1947), p. 272.

that remain even when there is general agreement that something must be done about some long-discussed matter—currency, say. Harvesting —even if it were no more than that—is not the least nor the least tricky of the skills of husbandry.

It is timely to pass to a closer examination of the methods of legislative leadership followed by President Wilson and to observe him in a role which, as has been noted, he viewed as distinctively political. Later we shall turn to the administrative views and methods of the man who in 1887 wrote a pioneering essay on the importance of administration and its study in the modern state.

"Woodrow Wilson," Lawrence Chamberlain has remarked, "was the first President to develop systematically the legislative powers of his office. Coming in a period of peace and prosperity, his first administration offered an unusually favorable climate in which to test the theory of presidential synthesis and he was equipped by training, experience, and purpose to develop his concept of the office to its fullest."[15] This statement is doubtless true both in point of Wilson's historic contribution in the development of legislative leadership and also in point of the relative importance of domestic statutory policy in 1913 and 1914.

It does not diminish the importance of the events of the early years to note Ray Stannard Baker's comment (which indeed Wilson whimsically anticipated in an offhand remark before he took the oath of office, after a campaign in which foreign affairs were hardly mentioned): "Such was the irony of fate that from the Cabinet meeting on March 7 . . . until Congress assembled in April—and long afterwards—Wilson's attention was largely absorbed by the clamorous problems of Mexico, China, Japan, Panama, the Philippine Islands, Nicaragua."[16] Along the same line, David Houston, Secretary of Agriculture, in a notation on May 20, 1913, about cabinet meetings, wrote:

Somebody pointed out that all our discussions, or nearly all, had been over foreign matters; that domestic problems of importance such as the tariff and currency were never raised by the President. Lane, in particular, was critical. I pointed out that the President had evidently and of necessity given his thoughts primarily to pressing foreign questions, that he regarded this as his particular field, one in respect to which he had unusual powers and responsibilities, that he was evidently depending upon the heads of departments ini-

[15] L. H. Chamberlain, *The President, Congress, and Legislation* (New York: Columbia University Press, 1946), p. 17.

[16] Baker, *Woodrow Wilson,* IV, 56.

tially to handle domestic economic questions each in his particular field, and that he complimented us by presenting many matters for discussion and advice while some heads of departments did not.[17]

Colonel House, of course, saw it from a different perspective. He dictated a grumbling note for his diary on June 24, 1915: "To my mind, the President has never appreciated the importance of our foreign policy and had laid undue emphasis upon domestic affairs. I thoroughly approved this up to the end of the special session of Congress, when the tariff, banking, and such other measures were involved. . . ."[18]

The methods by which the President advanced the domestic legislative program were of course endlessly varied. Nevertheless it is possible to identify certain main characteristics.

1. President Wilson used his legislative influence selectively. He pushed one measure at a time. But the pressure kept coming. While the special session that met on April 7, 1913, was concentrating on tariff, the House committees generally were not organized. Nevertheless, the Committee on Banking and Currency was chosen so that Carter Glass (busy with a preliminary draft of banking legislation even before the election) could go ahead as duly constituted chairman. The tariff bill was not ready for signature until October, but in late June the President addressed Congress on the need for banking legislation. In the field of antitrust, House hearings began in December, with the ground already laid in conversations with the Democratic leaders.[19] A presidential message in January indicated the five points for legislative action.

Overlapping selective pressure of this sort was an effective though partial answer to Wilson's long-standing complaint. "Legislation is conglomerate," he had written in 1885.[20] "The absence of any concert of action amongst the Committees leaves legislation with scarcely any trace of determinate party courses. No two schemes pull together."

2. The President's legislative approach was studiously collaborative. In addressing Congress personally on April 8, 1913, he opened by saying that the President should not be viewed as "a mere department of the government hailing Congress from some isolated island of jealous power . . . that he is a human being trying to cooperate with other human beings in a common science." The President added that "after

[17] Houston, *op. cit.*, I, 68.   [18] Seymour, *op. cit.*, I, 177.

[19] Chamberlain, *op. cit.*, p. 36.

[20] *Congressional Government* (Boston: Houghton Mifflin Co., 1885), p. 325.

this pleasant experience I shall feel quite normal in all our dealings with one another."

There were hazards in going to the Hill. As President-elect, Wilson asked Josephus Daniels: "Did you ever hear of a President occupying a room in the Capitol called the President's Room? What would be thought of it, if, instead of asking Senators with whom I wished to consult to call at the White House, I should occupy that room for conference?"[21] Daniels did not think the senators would like it, and he recalled later that Senator Simmons exclaimed: "My God . . . tell him not to do it. It would be resented by the Senators." But the favorable reaction to the personal delivery of his tariff message prompted the President to meet next day in the President's Room.

Ray Stannard Baker records illustratively the frequent and varied nature of the President's congressional contacts. "He was constantly receiving delegations of senators at the White House and he often visited the President's Room at the Capitol. We have an account of one instance, June 12th, when he inquired for twenty-one senators, only seven of whom could be found. . . . On June 18th he was again at the Capitol conferring with twenty-three different senators. He asked to have a special telephone put in so that he might, on occasion, reach senators quickly and directly from the White House."[22]

3. The President's legislative approach was frankly through party as the instrument for the reshaped purposes of the nation. In his tariff message he said: "I have called the Congress together in extraordinary session because a duty was laid upon the party now in power at the recent elections which it ought to perform promptly." In his message in June on banking legislation he said: "I have come to you, as the head of the Government and the responsible leader of the party in power, to urge action, now while there is time to serve the country deliberately and as we should, in a clear air of common counsel." Factional rifts reflecting different viewpoints within the party were clearly in sight on all the major, early, and outstanding legislative undertakings—the tariff currency, and antitrust. "Nevertheless"—to quote John M. Blum's summary of a presidential choice that was in fact many-sided—"in keeping with his theories of government, and on the advice of Burleson and Daniels, Wilson decided to work through his party rather than to attempt to construct a progressive coalition. The implementation of

[21] Josephus Daniels, *The Wilson Era* (Chapel Hill: University of North Carolina Press, 1944), I, 100.

[22] Baker, *Woodrow Wilson*, IV, 123.

this decision called for the recognition of each important Democratic function in the assignment of political largess. This worrisome task fell largely to Postmaster General Burleson, Secretaries Bryan and Mc-Adoo, and Tumulty. . . ."[23]

4. In seeking results through party, not coalition, the President chose to work with the regularly constituted party leaders and organs. The crucial demonstration of this tactic and its success was in bowing to seniority and accepting Senator Simmons as chairman of the Senate Finance Committee. Originally, facing protective tendencies in certain southern and western Democrats, the President had thought that an effort should be made to sidetrack Simmons in favor of a more militantly low-tariff chairman. He yielded to the counsel of Daniels and others, however, and gained in Simmons an unusually effective supporter in defending the reductions. Another example came during the war when the President relied on the help of Claude Kitchin, who in 1914 replaced Oscar Underwood as Democratic floor leader in the House. Kitchin had voted against the declaration of war and indeed, as Alex Arnett put it, in the mood of revisionist history-writing in the thirties, had been "able, in fact, to lead a majority of his colleagues *almost* to the point of blocking the President's tragic course."[24] After hostilities began, however, Arnett notes, "Kitchin never questioned his duty to do all in his power, consistent with his principles, to prosecute the war to a successful conclusion."[25] Nothing came of the rumor that the President would throw his influence against Kitchin's re-election as floor leader. He was indeed approved unanimously by the Democratic caucus. On the President's side there was doubtless a favorable carry-over from his earlier attitude as described by Arnett: "Although their personal contacts were infrequent, Wilson was cordial toward Kitchin when they met, respected his judgment, and admired his sincerity."[26]

On the debit side, to be sure, a consequence of working through the regular party machinery was the deepening of southern influence. John Blum reminds us of Tumulty's growing concern about this condition. He concludes that "by 1917 it was too late to overcome the Southern predominance in Congress and in party councils."[27]

[23] John M. Blum, *Joe Tumulty and the Wilson Era* (Boston: Houghton Mifflin Co., 1951), p. 69.

[24] Alex M. Arnett, *Claude Kitchin and the Wilson War Policies* (Boston: Little, Brown & Co., 1937), p. viii.

[25] *Ibid.*, p. 241.   [26] *Ibid.*, p. 41.   [27] Blum, *op. cit.*, p. 159.

5. The use of the caucus was a further feature of the plan of working through party, not through coalition. On the tariff measure, a caucus of House Democrats in April, "after tumultuous debate,"[28] voted to support the bill, and on the following day it was reported by the Ways and Means Committee, passing in the following month with only five Democrats against it. On the Senate side, where the majority in the chamber was a scant seven, the President was at first unsuccessful in his attempt to secure caucus indorsement. Later, however, the first Democratic senatorial caucus or party "conference" in many years, at least, discussed the tariff bill over more than a fortnight and, by declaring it a party measure, substantially defended the integrity of the House bill. The currency bill was debated "behind closed doors"[29] in the House Democratic caucus for two days in September; the measure passed the House later that month by 285 to 85. In this caucus the administration bill had to face the dissident views of so potent a Democrat as the chairman of the Rules Committee. In securing overwhelming caucus support for a middle degree of central guidance in the proposed reserve system, the administration had Bryan's aid, especially after it was agreed that the Federal Reserve Board should be wholly public in membership, not partly banker-chosen.

In view of the President's public statement of his gratification at the action of House committee and the caucus in handling the currency bill, it is a bit puzzling to read Carter Glass's recollections about the use of the caucus in pushing the currency bill in the Senate after a divided committee had reported the measure without recommendation. Glass recalled that Wilson was at first "disposed to assert vigorously his established aversion to 'rule by caucus.'" Glass's account goes on to emphasize the indispensability of caucus action. Had he persisted in his attitude, Glass writes, "there might have been no reform of currency for years. . . . the practical politicians finally convinced the President that there must be a caucus or abandonment of all hope for legislation."[30] So a "conference" was held and the President, Glass adds, "did the cleverest kind of work among the Senators in healing differences and imparting a new and militant spirit to the whole movement." As to the initial reluctance about a Senate caucus thus strangely attributed by Glass to the President, it is true that Wilson had always extolled open debate. In his first book he discussed the caucus as a corrective of legis-

---

[28] Chamberlain, *op. cit.*, p. 115.   [29] *Ibid.*, p. 319.

[30] Carter Glass, *An Adventure in Constructive Finance* (Garden City: Doubleday, 1927), p. 195.

lative incoherence but observed: "The fact that makes this defense of the caucus not altogether conclusive is that it is shielded from all responsibility by its sneaking privacy."[31] However it is doubtful whether these tentative scruples (conceived in his earlier writings against the background of an imagined main alternative) had much weight against the necessities and methods of 1913.

6. Essential in the President's tactics was the well-timed public appeal. When the tariff bill faced a crucial test in the Senate hearings, Wilson, apparently without consulting either Cabinet or congressmen, gave to the press his statement against rampant lobbies that could be offset only by an alert public opinion.

7. The President was willing to fight for legislative proposals. In connection with the movement for merchant fleet development begun in 1915, Secretary of the Treasury McAdoo recalled that "when I saw the President again, he was strongly in favor of the plan that I had submitted. He handed me back the draft of the bill that I had submitted and said with a smile, 'We'll have to fight for it, won't we?' "[32] McAdoo adds that, when he replied, "We certainly shall," the President said, "Well, then, let's fight." The fight lasted eighteen months.

But against this evidence of mood and manner may be put the sort of tone in Wilson's letter to Secretary of War Lindley Garrison on January 17, 1916, before the latter's resignation. The President wrote, "I am not irrevocably or dogmatically committed to any one plan of providing the nation with such a reserve, and am cordially willing to discuss alternative proposals." He added: "Any other position on my part would indicate an attitude toward the Committee on Military Affairs of the House of Representatives which I should in no circumstances feel at liberty to assume. It would never be proper or possible for me to say to any committee of the House of Representatives that, so far as my participation in legislation was concerned, they would have to take my plan or none."[33]

8. President Wilson's intervention in the legislative handling of particular measures was characteristically selective. During the debate on the tariff, John Sharp Williams told the Senate that the President had actively concerned himself with decisions on two items only. One was clearly sugar, where firmness was needed against protective pressures

[31] *Congressional Government,* p. 329.

[32] William Gibbs McAdoo, *Crowded Years: The Reminiscences of William G. McAdoo* (Boston: Houghton Mifflin, 1931), p. 296.

[33] Houston, *op. cit.,* I, 172.

from Louisiana and Colorado. Moreover, on other bills the President allowed leeway for permissive language that seemed unlikely to disturb the substantial policy the administration was advocating. Carter Glass recalled how they agreed to such a provision in the Federal Reserve Act. His account reports the President saying: ". . . if we can hold to the substance of the thing and give the other fellow the shadow, why not do it, if thereby we may save our bill?"[34]

Generally speaking, it may be said that in legislative leadership it was Woodrow Wilson's theory and practice, within a selective strategy in identifying certain policies for active support, to supply not draftsmanship but rather a stream of influence, public and personal, and aid in defense or adjustment at a few crucial points. Illustratively, Henry Parker Willis, in his detailed story of the Federal Reserve Act, remarks in summary: "President Wilson's service to the country, important and absolutely fundamental as it was, had nothing to do with the development of any essential feature of the measures and his most important effect upon its content was seen in the change made for the purpose of satisfying the Bryan element in the administration and in Congress." Willis added: "This statement in no wise underestimates the importance of President Wilson's service in connection with the adoption of the law—indeed it could never have become an act without his steady, persistent, and insistent support of it."[35]

One finds in Wilson's writings little direct generalization about the administrative side of government after he published the prescient essay on "The Study of Administration," in 1887 while he was at his first full-time teaching post.[36] Emblematically, Saul Padover's little anthology of Wilson's sayings, which on most matters draws passages from many stages of Wilson's life, quotes only from the 1887 essay under the heading "administration."[37]

[34] Glass, *op. cit.*, p. 125.

[35] *The Federal Reserve System: Legislation, Organization and Operations* (New York: Ronald Press, 1923), pp. 531–32.

[36] *Political Science Quarterly*, II (June, 1887), 197–222. The text is given in *Public Papers*, I, 130–58. Dwight Waldo has noted: "This essay has received much attention in recent years because so much of it seems so modern it could have been written yesterday. It seems not to have exerted much influence, even attracted much attention, for many years." *The Administrative State* (New York: Ronald Press, 1948), p. 26 n.

[37] Saul K. Padover (ed.), *Wilson's Ideals* (Washington: American Council on Public Affairs, 1942), pp. 30–38.

Wilson: Political Leader and Administrator

Wilson in 1887 identified in executive power what was to be the generally accepted focal point of administrative study, agitation, and progress in the three decades that followed. He deplored the fact that the English race had long and successfully "studied the art of curbing executive power, to the constant neglect of the art of perfecting executive methods." He alluded to the growing complexity of the tasks of government. He declared that "large powers and unhampered discretion seem to me the indispensable conditions of responsibility." He pointed out that "administration in the United States must at all points be sensitive to public opinion," and public opinion must be the "authoritative critic." The methods of control, however, must learn to separate the essentials of liberty from its accidents. "The ideal for us," he wrote, "is a civil service cultured and self-sufficient enough to act with sense and vigor, and yet so intimately connected with the popular thought, by means of elections and constant public counsel, as to find arbitrariness or class spirit quite out of the question." Since in all governments the legitimate ends of administration are the same, we should not be frightened at looking into foreign systems for suggestions.

In these affirmations of 1887, the core idea of executive integration was present but the structural and procedural corollaries were not worked out. The essay was a contribution to perspective, as well as exhortation, in declaring that "the science of administration is the latest fruit of that study of the science of politics which was begun twenty-two hundred years ago." Administration, Wilson wrote, is "the executive, the operative, the most visible side of government, and is of course as old as government itself." But the science of administration "is a birth of our century, almost of our own generation." Such a science, he declared, is needed "to straighten the path of government, to make its business less unbusinesslike; to strengthen and purify its organization, and to crown its duties with dutifulness."

Wilson's preoccupation was always with political leadership. Increasingly he emphasized the role of the elective chief executive in such leadership. This emphasis helps to explain why he did not elaborate the postulates and prescriptions of a science of administration. But his assumptions about political leadership dictated his working theory of executive organization and devolution. It was the simple and cogent theory of reliance upon the heads of departments.

1. Wilson's application of the theory was fairly consistent. It was the more thorough because of the President's absorption in state papers

and foreign policy. In carrying out his theory of devolution Wilson consciously avoided discussing the affairs of other agencies when dealing with a single department head. Early in the first administration Colonel House described and indorsed this restraint. "I told Page," he wrote, "that the President consulted with the individual members of his Cabinet about their departments, but he did not consult with them on matters affecting their colleagues, and I thought he was right." House added: "If he did this, he would soon have every Cabinet officer meddling with the affairs of the others, and there would be general dissatisfaction."[38] Later, reminiscing about the President's wartime practice, Hurley wrote that, although he "found him ready and willing to receive suggestions," the President "was very much opposed to having one member of the Cabinet interfere with the work which came under the head of another; and to receiving suggestions as to how another man's department should be conducted."[39] Hurley, too, thought the President was right, noting also that an interchange was possible in the so-called war cabinet. One sees that the net effect of such scruples in working through the departmentalization helped agency morale. Its incidental effect probably increased the compartmentalization of the system.

Houston, with opportunity to observe from two cabinet posts, commented on the degree to which the President relied upon his subordinates in other fields than foreign affairs. He qualified his praise of Wilson's practice by suggesting that devolution does not mean inattention. Houston in his memoirs phrased his estimate as follows: "It is good administration for a chief to select the right sort of subordinates and then to trust them, but he must and will, if he possesses administrative ability of the highest order, be alert to know their problems; to be aware of the extent to which they handle them properly and to get rid of them if they do not do so. Because of this defect, Mr. Wilson was not an administrator of first rank, but, as an administrator, I should say he was superior to Lincoln."[40]

2. Wilson's emphasis upon the departmental system inclined him against the expansion of presidential staff. This negative attitude can be traced in various directions. For example, the Bureau of Efficiency,

[38] Seymour, *op. cit.*, I, 128.

[39] E. N. Hurley, *The Bridge to France* (Philadelphia: J. B. Lippincott Co., 1927), p. 177.

[40] Houston, *op. cit.*, II, 169.

though created by statute in 1916 as an independent agency separate from the Civil Service Commission, was never fully drawn into the executive orbit; its informal senatorial link was never broken. Another example was the fact, as we shall note in tracing budgetary reform, that the stress was for some time on congressional committee reorganization, not executive staffing.

It is true that in the later stage of the war an outstanding bit of staff work was provided by the Central Bureau of Planning and Statistics. It was organized early in June 1918 in response to the President's request in a letter to Bernard Baruch for the creation of an organization that would provide "a conspectus of all the present war activities and upon that base a periodical checking up of the actual operations and results." This unit operated as an agency directly under the President though reporting through Bernard Baruch, chairman of the War Industries Board. It was headed by Edwin F. Gay, who also headed and co-ordinated the planning and statistical divisions of the War Industries Board, the Shipping Board, and the War Trade Board. It included a central statistical clearinghouse. Altogether, from its apex in the presidency outward, this complex of reporting and control services involved the work of about a thousand employees.[41]

Summarizing on the point of executive staff, we may say that Wilson's avowed wish to proceed through departmental heads, who in their fields would also be the President's chief advisers, showed a sound instinct against short-circuiting at the top. Only in foreign affairs where several special and on the whole regrettable conditions entered did such short-circuiting occur through Colonel House.

In speaking thus we are not pronouncing against the institutional developments that have taken place since Wilson's time. Some needs that were felt then and partly met presaged later forms of clearance under the President. For instance, on the question of haphazard speaking by the heads of departments, Colonel House reported late in 1913: "The President was pleased when I told him I had spoken to a sufficient number of the Cabinet to ensure the adoption of my suggestion that no speeches should be made in the future without his consent, and only when he thought the occasion demanded it."[42]

3. The President's belief in action through a departmental system

[41] The National Archives, *Handbook of Federal World War Agencies and Their Records, 1917–1921* (1942), pp. 64–65.

[42] Seymour, *op. cit.*, I, 138.

did not prevent the increase of permanent, independent commissions. The administrative issue about departures from hierarchy does not seem to have been raised and decided in broad, theoretical terms. Special circumstances were in play in connection with each of the entities created in a period of innovative zest.

In the case of the Federal Reserve Board it should be noted that the final arrangement was integrative in the double sense that the board was to be wholly public and that it was to contain two ex officio members. Furthermore there is evidence that Wilson on at least one occasion was prepared to remove members of the Board if it went ahead with its rumored intention in 1915 to abolish four of the reserve banks. Carter Glass, writing twelve years later, declared: "There can be no possible doubt that the Board would have been summarily reorganized by the President under his power of removal had it taken next day the action which was contemplated." The President, Glass said, looked to the law and "wholly concurred in the view that such action by the Board would constitute an intolerable usurpation of power, without either textual or implied legal sanction."[43] Glass added that he knew of no other time when Wilson approached the point of executive intervention with the affairs of the Federal Reserve Board. On the contrary, members of the Board had complained to him of the President's indifference to the Board. Glass recalled that when he mentioned this complaint to the President, Wilson said that he "wanted the Board to feel perfectly free to pursue its course of action within the law without a particle of constraint or restraint from the Executive."[44] The President added: "The very moment that I should attempt to establish close relations with the Board, that moment I would be accused of trying to bring political pressure to bear."

4. When it came to war organizations, it was deemed impossible to stay within the regular departmental frame. The President's inclina-

[43] Glass, op. cit., p. 271. Robert E. Cushman, in The Independent Regulatory Commissions (New York: Oxford University Press, 1941), p. 681, mentions the instance cited by Glass but does not offer other support for his generalizations: "President Wilson made plain his attitude towards the independent commissions on more than one occasion. . . . There is no doubt that Wilson with his 'prime minister' theory of the nature of the presidential office felt that he was entitled to impress his policies on the independent commissions and to expect their conformity to those policies."

[44] Glass, op. cit., p. 272. Houston in his recollections made the general observation: "He respected the independence of such bodies as the Interstate Commerce Commission, the Civil Service, the Federal Trade, and the Tariff Commission" (op. cit., II, 189).

tions ran toward simplicity: "We are in danger of creating too much machinery,"[45] he wrote in April, 1917. Nevertheless, he was ready to see a positive virtue in separating the temporary controls. In these terms the public statement in May when the food control law was passed extolled the intention "to draw a sharp line of distinction between the normal activities of the Government represented in the Department of Agriculture with reference to food production, conservation, and marketing on the one hand and the emergency activities necessitated by the war in reference to the regulation of food distribution and consumption on the other."[46]

Meanwhile a matrix was at hand in the Council of National Defense and its Advisory Commission. The President himself had helped by a modest request in his message of December, 1915, to give an impetus to the statutory creation of the Council in the following year, when pressure came also from two voluntary movements to mobilize the country's resources. After war was declared Congress placed $100 million at the President's disposal for national security and defense. In 1918, when asking for another flexible emergency fund of half the size, the President told the chairman of the House Appropriations Committee: "I have used considerable sums for the maintenance of the Food Administration, the Fuel Administration, and for the War Trade Board, and for the maintenance of the proper agencies for the allocation of labor."[47] He pointed out that as soon as these agencies had been thoroughly organized," their support had been shifted to regular appropriations.

The final step in the maturing of the war machinery was the consolidation of Bernard Baruch's position as chairman of the reconstituted War Industries Board—a designation which in the face of some opposition on the ground that Baruch was a speculator, not a production expert, showed the President's instinct for chancy action under stress.[48] In a different setting and in another way he had sounded this note in his secret talk to officers of the fleet on August 11, 1917. "Please leave out of your vocabulary altogether the word 'prudent,'" he said, and he pointed out that "nobody ever before conducted a war like this and

[45] Baker, *Woodrow Wilson*, VII, 14.

[46] *Public Papers*, V, 42.   [47] *Ibid.*, p. 213.

[48] Blum, *op. cit.*, p. 142. Carter Field, *Bernard Baruch, Park Bench Statesman* (New York: McGraw-Hill, 1944). See also Bernard M. Baruch, *American Industry in the War: A Report of the War Industries Board* (New York: Prentice-Hall, 1941).

therefore nobody can pretend to be a professional in a war like this. . . ."[49]

5. Wilson fought to keep control of the war organization. The hazards he saw were of two kinds: a congressional committee on the conduct of the war and statutory action to inject a small, plenary war cabinet.

As to the first, his objections were set forth in letters to Senator Owen in August and to Senator Simmons in September, 1917. To the latter he wrote that "an additional authority put alongside of me on this already tremendous task of directing the administrative activities of the government is just the thing which would create confusion and make any task twice as complex as it is."[50] And in May of the following year when it was proposed to authorize the Senate Military Affairs Committee to be in effect a committee on the conduct of the war, the President wrote, "I deem it my duty to say that I would regard the passage of this resolution as a direct vote of want of confidence in the administration."[51] He declared roundly, "Such activities on the part of a particular committee of the Senate . . . would constitute nothing less than an attempt to take over the conduct of the war, or at the least so superintend and direct and participate in the executive conduct of it as to interfere in the most serious way with the action of the constituted executive."

The second attack, led by Senator Chamberlain, chairman of the Military Affairs Committee, took the form of a bill introduced early in 1918 to create a war cabinet of "three distinguished citizens of demonstrated executive ability," to be appointed by the President and Senate and to be supervised only by the President and to be in full control of the conduct of the war.[52] About this time the President wrote to Colonel House: "It is the Junkertum trying to creep in under cover of the patriotic feeling of the moment. They will not get in. They have now no examples of happy or successful coalition to point to. The nominal coalition in England is a Tory Cabinet."[53] And from another angle of objection, the President wrote to the head of the United States Chamber of Commerce, "The faith that some people put in machinery is childlike and touching, but the machinery does

[49] *Public Papers*, V, 82–88.

[50] Baker, *Woodrow Wilson*, VII, 251.   [52] *Ibid.*, VII, 485.

[51] *Ibid.*, VIII, 143.   [53] Daniels, *op. cit.*, II, 285.

not do the task; particularly is it impossible to do it if new and unexpected elements are added."[54]

6. The successful countering of these measures secured the passage in May of the administration-sponsored Overman Act. It authorized the President "to take such redistribution of functions among executive agencies as he may deem necessary, including any functions, duties, and powers hitherto by law conferred upon any executive department, commission, bureau, agency, office, or officer, in such a manner as in his judgment shall seem best fitted to carry out the purposes of this act. . . ." While the bill was awaiting floor consideration after a favorable report, the President wrote to Senator Overman. "Senator after Senator has appealed to me most earnestly to 'cut the red tape.' I am asking for the scissors."[55] The act by its terms was geared to war needs and the war period. The leeway it allowed was used by the President in that spirit. Nevertheless, as a technique the precedent had general bearing.

Apart from this limited emergency approach to executive rearrangement, the Wilson administration did not push for any general administrative reorganization. To be sure, the President in his regular message of 1914 spoke of the piecemeal growth that had been characteristic of the government and said: "I think it is generally agreed that there should be a systematic reorganization and reassembling of its parts." But it was consonant with Wilson's policies that he should add the warning: "The people of the United States do not wish to curtail the activities of this Government; they wish, rather, to enlarge them." Such an appeal, though it might be in terms of truest efficiency, was not likely to seem exigent. Finally, under interregnum conditions of 1920, a measure for a joint congressional body on administrative reorganization went into effect without the President's signature.

7. As for personnel, Wilson took for granted the ideals of career service. He came to the Presidency aware of the burdens of the appointing process. "The mere task of making appointments to office, which the Constitution imposes upon the President," he wrote in 1908, "has come near to breaking some of our Presidents down, because it is a never-ending task in a civil service not yet put upon a professional footing, confused with short terms of office, always forming and dis-

[54] *Ibid.*, p. 503.   [55] Baker, *Woodrow Wilson*, VIII, 41.

solving."[56] He sought at the outset to refuse himself to see applicants; the responsibility must be devolved. But, as Ray Stannard Baker summed it up, "First and last the business of appointments was Wilson's greatest burden. It was often near to overwhelming him."[57]

As a politician he must compromise. Burleson, according to Ray Stannard Baker's account, asked the President to clear certain postmaster appointments. Wilson asked to see the entire list. Burleson sent over the documents relating to two score of pending appointments— letters, recommendations, petitions, protests. Burleson, we are told, contended that the President "would not need to yield his position. . . . all that he needed to do was to adopt a policy of harmony and observe the laws of human nature." The argument went on for two hours. The President kept the papers another week. When the conference was resumed, he said he would not appoint the man recommended by a certain congressman. Burleson explained the facts and, in Baker's words, "all of the complicated elements of politics in a democracy were bound up in this one trivial appointment." The President said, "I will appoint him."[58] This was not the end, but it was a point on the difficult and shadowy border zone where the administrator, in the name of political leadership, became the practical politician.

8. It remains to consider budgetary reform in the Wilson administration. In January, 1913, the President-elect wrote rather loosely to Senator Tillman: "Ever since I was a youngster I have been deeply interested in our methods of financial administration. Ever since then I have insisted upon the absolute necessity of a carefully considered and wisely planned budget, and one of the objects I shall have most in mind when I get to Washington will be conferences with my legislative colleagues with a view to bringing some budget system into existence."[59]

But what kind? The President was seeking to collaborate through the party with a Congress that had disregarded, even rebuffed, President Taft's attempt to submit a budget. Congressional leaders, if they acted at all even under the changed political situation, were likely to stress a strengthened reassemblage of the scattered committee jurisdiction over appropriation bills. In December, 1914, the President's second

[56] *Constitutional Government in the United States* (New York: Columbia University Press, 1908), p. 79.

[57] Baker, *Woodrow Wilson*, IV, 53.

[58] *Ibid.*, p. 47.   [59] *Ibid.*, IV, 212.

annual message indicated that the time was at hand for more attention to administrative reform. "Our program of legislation with regard to the regulation of business is now virtually complete,"[60] he said, and he then mentioned "two topics, much discussed out of doors." One was government expenditures, not so much keeping them down as making sure that the money went for approved objects and was "being applied with good business sense and management." These were "large and general standards," as the President said; they were not a plan.

In 1915 a committee of the Democratic caucus—still concentrating upon control at the legislative end—concluded that action in that Congress would be impracticable. Significantly, the Democratic platform of 1916 confined its plank on economy to the machinery in Congress. It favored "a return by the House of Representatives to its former practice of initiating and preparing all appropriation bills through a single committee . . . as a practical step toward a Budget System." The President's message in December, 1917, did not go beyond this feature.

In December, 1919, the President's regular message expressed the hope that "Congress will bring to a conclusion at this session legislation looking to the establishment of a budget system." It declared that "the burden of preparing the budget must, in the nature of the case, if the work is to be properly done and responsibility concentrated instead of divided, rest upon the executive." The message also approved a single committee in each House. It urged, as not less important, a type of audit that would go beyond questions of mere legality and consider whether the money had been spent wisely, economically, and effectively. "The auditors," said the message, "shall be highly trained officials with permanent tenure in the Treasury Department, free of obligation to or motives of consideration for this or any subsequent administration," reporting their findings to Congress and to the Secretary of the Treasury. Naturally, much of the debate in these years turned on the question of audit as a legislative prerogative.

Meanwhile consideration in Congress had quickened. On February 28, 1919, before the end of the Democratically controlled Congress, the House approved a provision for a joint commission on financial methods.[61] It was adopted as an amendment to a deficiency bill that did not pass the Senate. The upper chamber had been considering a joint resolution for a commission to report a budget plan. This measure

[60] *Public Papers,* III, 215, 222–23.
[61] *Congressional Record,* 65th Cong., 3d sess., H. R. 16187, p. 4623.

passed on February 28, 1919,[62] but was not acted on in the House. It is interesting that some proponents were still saying that cabinet members should defend the budget before Congress. Later in 1919 a budget bill was worked out by select committees in both chambers. It was vetoed by the President on Houston's recommendation because the provision permitting the removal of the comptroller-general only by concurrent resolution was deemed to be an unconstitutional invasion of executive power. The attempt to pass the bill over the veto failed.[63]

Thus did Woodrow Wilson lose the chance to claim as an achievement of his Presidency the statute that laid the basis for the modern Executive Office of the President.

Never again could the Presidency shrink enough to fit a lesser man. Only by degrees would the institutional elements of the office grow to fit its tasks. Amid the machinery, Woodrow Wilson's record remains a reminder of the stature needed in expressing the authorized purpose of a people.

[62] *Congressional Record,* 65th Cong., S. J. Res. 121, p. 4532.

[63] Houston, *op. cit.,* II, 85.

CHAPTER SEVEN

Wilson's Monetary Reform*

By
Lester V. Chandler

In his first inaugural address, in March, 1913, Wilson expressed in the following words his general strategy for economic reform: "We shall restore, not destroy. We shall deal with our economic system as it is and as it may be modified, not as it might be if we had a clean sheet of paper to write upon; and step by step we shall make it what it should be. . . ." Wilson was determined that there should be economic reform, that it should be constructive and not merely restrictive and negative, that it should be both gradual and persistent.

For many reasons it is appropriate that Wilson's words quoted above should be inscribed, as they are, at the main entrance of the Federal Reserve Board building in Washington. The Federal Reserve System was one of the major achievements of the Wilson administration during its first year. The Federal Reserve Board in Washington was first suggested and then insisted upon by Wilson himself. And the Federal Reserve Act and the System resulting from it represent perhaps the most outstanding example of Wilson's gradualist approach—his willingness (in his words) "to deal with the economic system as it is and as it may be modified, not as it might be if we had a clean sheet of paper to write upon." The original Federal Reserve Act, which was Wilson's principal vehicle for monetary reform, certainly made many concessions to the existing financial system and to the whole complex of existing prejudices, vested interests, and pressure groups. But it was an important start toward monetary and banking reform, and from that start has gradually evolved the powerful Federal Reserve System that we know today. In 1913 neither Wilson nor anyone else could foresee that the Federal Reserve System would become the most powerful financial institution in the world and that it would become the principal manager

* Lecture given at Fordham University, April 26, 1956, at the Wilson Centennial.

of the dollar and of the value of gold throughout the world. Wilson's objectives in 1913 as he urged monetary reform were quite different and in general far less ambitious.

For an understanding of both the nature and scope of Wilson's monetary reform it will be useful to review the monetary situation in 1913. By that time the long and bitter controversy over our monetary standard had ended. Faded into the past were the struggles over green-backs and free silver. Bryan's defeat in 1896 had marked the doom of bimetallism, and the Gold Standard Act of 1900 had committed the United States to a gold standard. Perhaps more important, very large gold inflows made it possible for us to enjoy both the virtue of "sound money" and the pleasant exhilaration of a mild inflation. Gold discoveries in the Rand and the Klondike-Yukon area together with the discovery of cheaper processes of refining gold tripled the rate of gold output during the first years of this century. Even Bryan was satisfied; he is reported to have said that he would not have urged the free coinage of silver if he had foreseen that Providence would supply gold so generously. Wilson, never favorable to bimetallism or "unsound" money schemes in general, was quite content with the gold standard and had no wish to change it. But the banking system and the paper currency were different matters. Wilson was determined that banking and currency reform should receive high priority in his program.

Wilson was by no means the only one, or even among the first, to see the need for banking and currency reform or to promote reform schemes. Agitation for such reforms had begun well before 1900, and since 1907 even bankers had admitted that weaknesses existed and should somehow be remedied. All sorts of epithets were directed to the American banking system both at home and abroad. Some of the more polite ones were "the Great American Nuisance," "the most barbarous system on earth," and "breeder of panics."

Though a great majority agreed that something was wrong, there were wide differences in diagnoses of the patient's disease or diseases and in the remedies proposed. Virtually all agreed that the worst defect was the system's repetitive generation of crises and panics. The great panic of 1907 was but the latest of a long series of panics that had done serious damage not only to bank depositors but also to workers who lost their jobs, to farmers who suffered from credit restriction and falling prices, and to virtually all classes of businessmen. In addition to the major panics there had also been a number of minor crises and seasonal credit stringencies.

Experts in the field also noted many other shortcomings of the American banking system, including inadequate and ineffective supervision of state-chartered banks; clumsy, slow, and expensive methods of clearing and collecting checks; inadequate facilities for financing international trade; unsatisfactory fiscal arrangements for the federal Treasury; competitive disadvantages for national banks which imperiled their position relative to state-chartered banks and trust companies. The Federal Reserve Act as it finally emerged was omnibus legislation, aimed at remedying a multitude of real or alleged evils and shortcomings of the pre-1914 system.

In many of these shortcomings Wilson was not interested, and many he probably did not understand. Wilson was not, in any technical sense, an economist or a financial expert. He had no intimate knowledge of banking techniques, and was not qualified either to diagnose technical difficulties or to prescribe technical remedies. But if Wilson lacked technical knowledge he brought to the task of monetary reform other important qualities: the perspective of a historian, a deep interest in the relation between economic and political power and freedom, a religious zeal to broaden economic freedoms, and a great skill in political leadership.

For Wilson, monetary reform had but two important objectives; all others were tangential. One objective was to prevent crises and panics. Time and again he criticized the existing banking system, which he described as "a banking and currency system based upon the necessity of the government to sell its bonds fifty years ago and perfectly adapted to concentrating cash and restricting credits." The other major objective was to break the private monopoly of credit, thereby making credit available to all—and especially to farmers and smaller businesses —on more nearly equal terms and thereby weakening business monopoly in general. Perhaps the major difference between Wilson's attitude on this topic and that of the business and financial community is to be found in Wilson's insistence on the necessity of abolishing the concentration of private control over credit.

Wilson looked upon monetary reform as only a part, but an essential part, of his comprehensive program to bring New Freedom to the American people. Precisely what Wilson meant by the New Freedom is still difficult to define. But the general objective of the New Freedom was fairly clear: it was to free the American people from control by those who wielded concentrated economic power, whether that power was wielded through the government or in the market place. Wilson was convinced that those in whom economic power was concentrated had seized control of the government itself. Writing in February, 1913, before assuming the office of President, he said:

The masters of the government of the United States are the combined capitalists and manufacturers of the United States. . . . The Government of the United States at present is a foster child of the special interests. . . . I will not live under trustees if I can help it. No group of men less than the majority has a right to tell me how I have got to live in America. . . .[1]

He found concentrated private control exercised through the market place no more palatable.

Of all the types of concentration of economic power, Wilson found concentration of private control over credit most dangerous and most objectionable. In *The New Freedom* he expresses his views forcefully:

Take any investment of an industrial character by a great bank. It is known that the directorate of that bank interlaces in personnel with ten, twenty, forty, fifty, sixty boards of directors of all sorts, of railroads which handle commodities, of great groups of manufacturers which manufacture commodities, and of great merchants who distribute commodities; and the result is that every great bank is under suspicion with regard to the motive of its investment. It is at least considered possible that it is playing the game of somebody who has nothing to do with banking, but with whom some of its directors are connected and joined in interest . . . by certain processes, now well known, and perhaps natural in themselves, there has come about an extraordinary and very sinister concentration in the control of business in the country.

However it has come about, it is more important still that the control of credit also has become dangerously centralized. It is the mere truth to say that the financial resources of the country are not at the command of those who do not submit to the direction and domination of small groups of capitalists who wish to keep the economic development of the country under their own eye and guidance. The great monopoly in this country is the monopoly of big credits. So long as that exists, our old variety and freedom and individual energy of development are out of the question. A great industrial nation is controlled by its system of credit. Our system of credit is privately concentrated. The growth of the nation, therefore, and all our activities, are in the hands of a few men who, even if their action be honest and intended for the public interest, are necessarily concentrated upon the great undertakings in which their own money is involved and who necessarily, by very

[1] *The New Freedom* (Garden City: Doubleday, 1913), pp. 57, 58, 64.

reason of their own limitations, chill and check and destroy genuine economic freedom. This is the greatest question of all, and to this statesmen must address themselves with an earnest determination to serve the long future and the true liberties of men.

This money trust, or as it should be more properly called, this credit trust, of which Congress has begun an investigation, is no myth; it is no imaginary thing. . . . I have seen men squeezed by it; I have seen men who, as they themselves expressed it, were put out of business by Wall Street because Wall Street found them inconvenient and didn't want their competition. . . . Are we going to settle the currency question so long as the government listens only to the counsel of those who command the banking situation?[2]

During the preceding Republican administration Senator Aldrich, one of the most influential Republican senators, had introduced a bill for banking reform. This bill provided for a single central bank to be located in New York and to have the power to lend to commercial banks and to issue an elastic currency. This single central bank was to be owned by private commercial banks and controlled by a board of bankers selected by bankers. It was described by its opponents as an institution "of the banks, by the banks, and for the banks." Perhaps this appellation was a bit unfair, but it carried much truth; for the banking community, which strongly supported the Aldrich plan, looked upon the proposed institution not primarily as a regulatory agency but as a sort of mutual aid society which would assist the banks and, through them, the broader community. It is almost needless to say that Wilson vigorously opposed the Aldrich plan. He did not bother to deny that the proposed Aldrich central bank would be effective as a lender of additional reserves to banks and as an issuer of an elastic currency. He could not agree to the creation of any institution that would be located in Wall Street, controlled by bankers—and probably Wall Street bankers at that—and used to increase the concentration of private control over credit. Wilson could approve no plan that did not promise to deconcentrate private control and protect the public interest.

After Wilson had won the election in November, 1912, he went to Bermuda for a rest, but soon after his return in December he began to map out his reform program, on which monetary reform had a high priority. Carter Glass, chairman of a subcommittee of the House Banking and Currency Committee, conferred with Wilson several times in

[2] Quoted in Carter Glass, *An Adventure in Constructive Finance* (Garden City: Doubleday, 1927), pp. 77 ff.

Princeton and Trenton, working out the main features of a new plan for banking and currency reform. Well before Wilson's inauguration in March he had agreed upon two major features of the new system. The first was that the new system should be divided into several regions or districts, each with its own "Reserve Bank" capable of lending to commercial banks in its district and of issuing an elastic type of currency. By this device it was hoped to build up new money markets around each of the regional banks, to reduce the flow of credit from the hinterland into New York, and to decentralize and deconcentrate the control of credit. The second feature agreed upon was first suggested by Wilson himself: the establishment of an altruistic board in Washington to supervise the regional reserve banks, to co-ordinate their policies to the necessary degree, and to protect the public interest. Thus, even before he became President, Wilson had given his approval to a new reserve banking system to be composed of several regional reserve banks, each with a considerable degree of autonomy, but with a board in Washington to act as a capstone, to supervise, to co-ordinate, and to represent the public.

Almost immediately after his inauguration Wilson began to put into operation his theory of the strong executive—that the President must assume leadership in proposing legislation and in helping to push it through. He called an extra session of Congress in April and insisted that tariff reduction should be the first item of business—a reduction of tariffs to remove these "shackles" from business. The next item of business was banking reform. On June 23 he appeared before Congress to urge that tariff reduction be followed by monetary reform. He said, in part:

It is absolutely imperative that we should give the businessmen of this country a banking and currency system by means of which they can make use of the freedom of enterprise and of individual initiative which we are about to bestow on them. . . . The principles upon which we should act are also clear. . . . We must have a currency, not rigid as now, but readily, elastically responsive to sound credit, the expanding and contracting credits of everyday transactions, the normal ebb and flow of personal and corporate dealings. Our banking laws must mobilize its reserves; must not permit the concentration anywhere in a few hands of the monetary resources of the country nor permit their use for speculative purposes in such volume as to hinder or impede or stand in the way of other more legitimate, more fruitful uses. And the control of the system of banking and of issue which our new laws are to set up must be public, not private, must be vested in the government itself, so that the banks may be the instruments, not the masters, of business and of individual enterprise and initiative.

128

Wilson's Monetary Reform

In response to Wilson's request, Congress soon turned its attention to the subject of banking and currency reform, working on it through the hot summer, a long autumn, and the early winter. It was not an easy task. Almost every aspect of the proposed bill was controversial, and there were many currents and crosscurrents of opinion and interest. On several occasions it appeared that the legislation would fail, being opposed by the conservatives because it was too radical and by radicals because it conceded too much to private financial interests. Wilson himself arranged two key compromises without which the legislation probably would have been defeated.

Most of the banking community, and many other conservatives as well, insisted that the new legislation would be acceptable to them only if it met at least the following conditions: first, bankers should control the new system, or at least have a strong voice in it. They argued that only bankers had the expert knowledge and experience necessary to operate such a system soundly and efficiently. Politicians, lacking experience and subject to partisan political pressures, would wreck it. Moreover, the banks were to contribute most of the resources of the reserve banks; they were to subscribe to the stock of these banks and hold deposits there. To require commercial banks to provide the resources of the Reserve Banks and then to deny them control would be nothing short of socialism. Therefore, bankers should control the regional reserve banks and also have at least a strong hold on the central Federal Reserve Board. In the second place, bankers and other conservatives insisted that the new currency to be issued should be a liability of the Federal Reserve Banks alone and should not under any circumstances be a liability of the federal government. Government issues would be fiat money, and everyone knew that fiat money was unsound.

Such views were completely unacceptable to William Jennings Bryan, Wilson's Secretary of State, and to Bryan's many followers in both houses of Congress. And Wilson knew that the reform legislation would almost certainly fail without the support of the Bryanites. Bryan and his followers insisted that the issue of money and monetary regulation were federal functions, conferred by the Constitution and necessary for the proper protection of the public. They therefore insisted that the new reserve system should be controlled by the federal government and that its currency issues should be government liabilities.

On these issues Wilson arranged key compromises which gained the support of Bryan and his followers and assured the successful passage of the Federal Reserve Act. It was provided that the new currency would be an obligation of the United States Treasury but that the first claim would be against all the assets of the new Federal Reserve Banks, individually and collectively. Wilson fully realized that this would be relatively unimportant in practice, for the assets of the Reserve Banks would be adequate to cover their note liabilities. But the provision did preserve the principle that currency issue is in the last analysis a responsibility of the federal government.

Wilson also effected a compromise on the issue of control. The central Federal Reserve Board was to be composed exclusively of members appointed by the President, and bankers were denied representation on it. However, bankers were permitted to select a majority of the members of the boards of directors of the various Federal Reserve Banks and to elect an advisory council to confer with the Federal Reserve Board at least four times a year. Carter Glass has told of the dramatic conference in the White House at which Wilson denied banker representation on the Federal Reserve Board. After a delegation of distinguished bankers had argued their case for appointing at least a part of the membership of the board, Wilson asked them: "Will one of you gentlemen tell me in what civilized country of the earth there are important government boards of control on which private interests are represented? Which of you gentlemen thinks the railroads should select members of the Interstate Commerce Commission?" Wilson had made it clear that the new system was not merely to serve banks; it was also to be an agency for regulating them in the public interest.

Just before Christmas, Congress passed the Federal Reserve Act, and on the day after Christmas in 1913 Wilson signed it into law. Almost a year later, in November, 1914, the Federal Reserve opened for business. Wilson's banking and currency reform became a reality.

Even if I had unlimited time at my disposal I would find it difficult to offer a well-balanced evaluation of either Wilson's ideas on monetary reform or the vehicle that was to carry it. It is easy to be either hypercritical or overlaudatory. Neither Wilson nor the others who originated the Federal Reserve Act were sophisticated in monetary and financial matters. The original Federal Reserve Act itself was far from a model piece of legislation. On many important issues it was silent. It was weakened by compromises. Its drafting was vague, ambiguous, and in places even contradictory. It was not capable of achieving some of the purposes for which it was designed. But to dwell upon these shortcomings would be to hide outstanding achievements. Wilson and his administration did, after all, succeed in establishing a central banking system—the first this country had had since another Democratic President, Andrew Jackson, had abolished the Second Bank of the United States more than seventy-five years earlier. This new legislation did recapture for the federal government a degree of control over money and credit and did establish the principle that this control should be exercised in the general public interest and not merely for the benefit of the banking community. And it did establish a new system which, despite all its original weaknesses and shortcomings, has proved capable of evolution and adaptability to the constantly changing conditions and aspirations of our people.

CHAPTER EIGHT

Woodrow Wilson's Contribution to Antitrust Policy*

By
John Perry Miller

It is fitting on this occasion of the centennial of Woodrow Wilson's birth to assess his contribution to the development of our antitrust policies. These policies, unique to the United States, are perhaps the most distinctive contribution which this country has made to the art of political economy in modern times. The Sherman Act had been the law of the land some twenty-three years before Wilson assumed the Presidency. Although he cannot be credited with the initiation of antitrust, his leadership did much to build a solid basis of public support for a policy of competition at a time when many, despairing of the Sherman Act, were prone to move either to the Scylla of laissez faire or the Charybdis of regulated monopoly.

The first Wilson administration marked the end of the long period of rapid industrialization and economic growth between the Civil War and World War I. Although Woodrow Wilson is often remembered for his leadership in war and in the shaping of the peace, the program upon which he sought the Presidency was concerned predominantly with the economic problems of a rapidly growing society. He came to power on a platform of domestic reform designed to harness the financial and industrial forces of our society so that they might become more effective and humane instruments of public well-being.

The growth of the American economy between the Civil War and the Wilson administration was impressive. From 1870 to 1913 population had increased by about 142 per cent. In the same period national income in constant dollars had increased approximately fivefold, and per capita national income one and a half times. But this growth of the economy had not been an unalloyed blessing. Growth had been un-

* Lecture given at Fordham University, April 26, 1956, at the Wilson Centennial.

even; periods of great prosperity had been interspersed with periods of financial panic, monetary disorder, and depression. Others in this volume have indicated the contribution of the Wilson administration to the solution of these monetary and financial disorders. But there were likewise serious problems in industry. There had been a substantial change in the nature of employment, in the structure of industrial organization, and in the relations of man to man and of man to his work.

From 1870 to 1914 there was a dramatic shift in the character of gainful employment. The proportion of the population engaged in agriculture declined, while the proportion in industrial and related pursuits increased. In 1870 about 52 per cent of the population was engaged in agriculture, but by 1910 the proportion had declined to 30 per cent. As a matter of fact, 1910 marked the high point in total agricultural employment in the country. This relative decline in agriculture was associated with a movement of the gainfully occupied into manufacturing, transportation and public utility industries, trade, finance, and service industries. This shift in occupational employment caused considerable hardship, partly upon the farms but also in the urban-industrial centers to which the workers were flocking.

There was also a change in the structure of industry. This was the era of high finance and the formation of "trusts." Our information on the extent of concentration of control of industry into the hands of a few and of its significance is unsatisfactory. But it is clear that, in recurrent waves of combination, one industry after another became concentrated in the hands of one or a few firms, often by tactics which would not stand the light of public scrutiny. While the Interstate Commerce Commission Act of 1887 had apparently eliminated many of the worst abuses in the field of railroads, the Sherman Antitrust Act had not been as effective in curbing the abuses of concentrated power in industry. In fact, during the period 1897 to 1904 there was a new wave of mergers despite the Sherman Antitrust Act.

The change in the attitudes and behavior of industrial leaders over the last fifty years is impressive. This development is suggested by the change in the image of the business leader from that of "the robber baron" to that of "the man in the grey flannel suit"; but it can also be documented by more scientific literature. There are some who believe that the change is primarily one in the outward forms. They argue that the earlier evils of concentration and monopoly persist today, but in more subtle forms. But I reject this view. I believe there has been a significant change in industrial attitudes and behavior over the last fifty years. There has been a substantial decline in the grosser forms of behavior with respect to labor, competitors, and customers alike. There has also been a decline in the predatory tactics which shocked the public conscience and did so much to undermine respect for free enterprise and competition as instruments of social control. This is an important social and economic gain, one which has strengthened the claims to respect of the traditional American system of free private enterprise. Moreover, conservative estimates of the trends in concentration and monopoly during this century suggest that things are, to say the least, no worse today than at the beginning of the century. And more optimistic views, which I share, suggest that the competitive forces are stronger.

It is interesting to speculate about the factors that have been at work. They must have been many. But surely among the important factors has been the change in the ideological, social, and political climate in which recent industrial leaders have been reared—and in the legal framework in which they have carried on their business affairs. It is in precisely these matters that Woodrow Wilson's leadership and the accomplishments of his first administration have made a difference.

Wilson dramatized the monopoly issue and proposed a conservative solution based on the American traditions of freedom and opportunity. He phrased this program in terms which appealed to the moral conscience of the American people and called for the institutionalization of a code of fair competitive behavior. It has been fashionable to minimize the significance of American antitrust policy and above all the significance of the legislation of 1914. But while the hopes of 1914 have not been completely fulfilled, the choices made by the Wilson administration have been, and still are, the basis of our industrial policy.

When one reads Wilson's campaign speeches, subsequently published under the title *The New Freedom*, one is struck with the prominent position that he gave to the need for reform in the area of large corporate enterprise. Wilson was, of course, not alone in this concern. He was, in many ways, a late-comer to the crusade. There was a long record of agitation against the growth and abuses of corporate enterprise extending from the Granger movement of the 1870's down to the campaign of 1912.

This concern with big business had many facets. One aspect of concern was the increasing impersonalization of relations between management and employees as plants and firms grew in size. As control over industry drifted to the financial centers, the local problems of decision had to be referred to these centers. As a result there was a sense of decline in responsibility of the local community and of its citizens for the well-being of the local economy. The local manager became simply an employee subject to the control of absentee owners. The range of local initiative and responsibility in economic matters was narrowed. At the same time the absentee owners seemed to hide behind the corporate veil, thereby avoiding or denying individual responsibility. These developments caused widespread concern, not only among employees and others specifically injured, but also among the industrial and professional leaders of the local community, whose own status and prestige had depended upon their previous responsibility for decision.

Associated with this resentment of the shift in responsibility away from the local community was resentment at the apparent shift in responsibility from industrialists to financiers. It appeared that decisions were often based on purely financial considerations at the expense of considerations of economic and industrial well-being. The practices of high finance—particularly in industrial and railroad concerns—were widely dramatized. Excessive capitalization, watered stock, financial manipulation, promoters' profits, dishonesty by corporate executives in dealing with their own concerns—these and similar problems led many to urge that finance and industry should be divorced and that corporate directors and executives should be prohibited from assuming roles where their self-interest might conflict with the corporate interest. The sense of personal responsibility in the relations of man to man in their daily work, a responsibility which had been so important in the conduct of smaller local industry, seemed to be lacking in the conduct of the newer corporate enterprises. There was a demand for the development of a moral code of behavior to be applicable in these new circumstances.

Finally, there was concern about the decline in competition and the rise of monopoly in the narrow economic sense, i.e., concentration of market control in the hands of one or a few firms in an industry with power to determine prices or outputs. Moreover, the public conscience had been shocked by the revelation of the tactics used by many of the early trusts in acquiring and defending their dominant market positions. The tactics of the Standard Oil, Tobacco, and Cash Register trusts were only extreme examples among many which had been thoroughly documented and widely publicized. The plight of the owners and employees of firms which had been crushed in the process was felt deeply. And the plight of the customers of the trusts and the consumers of their products also weighed heavily in public discussion. The behavior of the executives of the large corporation did violence to the American ideologies of equal opportunity, wide dispersal of political and economic power, and the doctrine of checks and balances.

It is evident that the problem of large corporate enterprise, the so-called monopoly problem, was a multifaceted one. It had been widely discussed by the economists and political scientists, by the politicians, by the publicists, and by novelists of the era. It was the genius of Woodrow Wilson that he saw the various facets of the problem, called for a change in the moral climate of industrial behavior, and polarized thinking in favor of a policy of competition. Wilson's decision to choose a positive policy of fair competition represented an important turning point in American thought and policy. While the country was, for the most part, agreed that something must be done to curb the trusts, there was division on the crucial issue of what to do. The Sherman Antitrust Act had been on the books for twenty years, but the history of its interpretation and enforcement had not been encouraging. Justice Taft had established a precedent in the Addyston Pipe decision which was to outlaw all agreements between independent business firms with respect to price, production, and sales. In retrospect, when one compares the evolution of policy with respect to restrictive practices in Britain and other countries on the continent of Europe with that in the United States, the importance of this precedent is apparent. But in the area of close combinations or concentrated industry, in contrast with the area of loose combinations or cartel arrangements, the evolution of policy had been less impressive. There had been some victories for the government. But there were justifiable complaints: from industry, about the uncertainties of the law; from the reformers, about the ineffectiveness of the law. It was not until the court decisions breaking up the Standard Oil and Tobacco trusts in 1911 that the teeth of the Sherman Act became apparent.

There was consensus that the legal processes of the Sherman Act were slow and cumbersome and that an administrative commission should be established with both regulatory and investigatory functions. But here the proponents of reform parted company. Theodore Roosevelt and his Progressive supporters urged a policy of regulated monopoly. It was their view that the old world of small competing firms had disappeared and could not be recaptured. Innovations in technology and administrative techniques made the development of large and often dominant business firms inevitable and desirable. They agreed that it was appropriate to use the Sherman Act to break up companies which had gained their size by unconscionable means such as had the Standard Oil and Tobacco trusts. But to quote Theodore Roosevelt:

> The Anti-Trust Law cannot meet the whole situation, nor can any modification of the principle of the Anti-Trust Law avail to meet the whole situation.... Many ... believe that it is possible by strengthening the Anti-Trust Law to restore business to the competitive conditions of the middle of the last century. Any such effort is foredoomed to end in failure, and, if successful would be mischievous to the last degree....
>
> This nation should definitely adopt the policy of attacking, not the mere fact of combination, but the evils and wrong-doing which so frequently accompany combination.... We should enter upon a course of supervision, control, and regulation of these great corporations—a regulation which we should not fear, if necessary, to bring to the point of control of monopoly prices....[1]

Theodore Roosevelt proposed, then, to distinguish between bad monopolies and good. The former might be broken up under the Sherman Act, but the latter were to be regulated in the public interest.

The Wilsonian concept was quite different. Wilson, guided in part by Louis Brandeis, had faith in our ability to preserve a workably competitive industrial society. He had no illusions about returning to a society of small business firms operating under conditions of intense rivalry. In this sense he, like Theodore Roosevelt, implicitly rejected the alternative of return to the eighteenth century. But he proposed a solution which called neither for the fragmentation of industry nor for the regulation of monopoly. It was his belief that we had nothing to fear from a business firm whatever its size, provided it did not conduct its affairs by unfair methods of competition. The trusts had gained their positions more often than not by unconscionable competitive practices. The essence of the problem was to prohibit a list of unfair practices and to establish an administrative agency which would enforce the rules. The objective was to establish the rules of the game, to establish the New Freedom in enterprise by requiring that competition be in a fair field with no favors.

Such a system of regulated competition, Wilson believed, would

[1] "The Trusts, the People, and the Square Deal," *Outlook*, XCIX, No. 12 (November 18, 1911), 649.

prevent the emergence of monopolies. He had no fear of large firms which had acquired their size by such fair means as superior efficiency, better products, superior service, or lower prices. It is doubtful whether he would support the dictum that if a choice must be made between efficiency and the maintenance of several competitors in the market, antitrust policies do and should favor sacrificing efficiency. Neither size nor concentration per se was the issue. In terms of the modern discussion of the monopoly problem, his emphasis was on controlling corporate behavior rather than market structure or the number and size of firms. His concern was with the dynamics of change in market structures and the practices which brought about such change.

The results of Wilson's program were embodied in the Federal Trade Commission and Clayton acts of 1914. These undertook to define the list of unfair practices which are likely to lead to monopoly. The former act also established the Federal Trade Commission, an independent, bipartisan commission to enforce the rules. The task of defining the list of unfair competitive practices proved more difficult than had been anticipated. In the end Congress, in the Clayton Act, specified and legislated against four classes of practices in those circumstances where they might have the effect of lessening competition substantially or of tending to promote monopoly. The four practices included discrimination, tying and exclusive dealing arrangements, mergers and interlocking directors. In addition, Section 5 of the Federal Trade Commission Act included a general prohibition of unfair methods of competition, leaving it to the commission and the courts to give more explicit meaning to the phrase.

Congress in effect abandoned the attempt to specify a list of per se violations and gave the task to the commission and the courts. Upon them devolved the problem of developing standards for determining when one of the specified practices under the Clayton Act would lead to a substantial lessening of competition or tendency to monopoly and when a practice became an unfair method of competition. It was anticipated that Section 5 in particular would not only permit the Federal Trade Commission to proceed against those practices which were clearly illegal but also provide a vehicle by which the commission as an expert body could extend the range of unlawful practices as its understanding increased, or as new practices and conditions might develop.

The prevailing view is that the Federal Trade Commission has proved a great disappointment and that Section 5 and the Clayton Act are inadequate to the task of preserving competition. There is some merit to this view. But it can be exaggerated.

The basic accomplishment of the commission, and one not to be minimized, was the codification of a series of practices illegal under common law or under the Sherman Act and the provision of an administrative mechanism for their eradication. The courts early sustained the commission's view that Section 5 covered two classes of practices: those practices enjoined under the Sherman Act as in restraint of trade; and those prohibited under the common law of unfair competition. The commission has proceeded time and again against various types of restraints of trade including price-fixing, control of production, allocation of orders, and collusive boycotts. The elimination of these practices is, of course, germane to the monopoly problem. Although this task might have been handled by the Department of Justice and is in many cases, there is real advantage in having an administrative agency equipped to deal with such clear-cut, per se violations of the law by less formal procedures. The same can be said of the various forms of unfair competition including misrepresentation, espionage, industrial bribery, defamation of competitors, etc., which had long been offenses under the common law. These practices are not particularly germane to the problem of monopoly. They are today more often than not the practices of small firms rather than of large. But their eradication constitutes an important step in the maintenance of effective or workably competitive markets. The commission has succeeded, then, in codifying a group of competitive practices in restraint of trade which are per se violations of the law.

But the commission has been less successful in interpreting conditions under which Clayton Act practices are in violation of the law and in defining new practices which contravene the law. The history of the emasculation of the Clayton Act is well known. The courts subjected this act to a narrow interpretation to the point where the sections on discrimination and mergers have required amendment. It is to the credit of the commission that it has played an important part in the move for the amendment of Section 7 with respect to mergers. How successful the Celler Anti-Merger Act of 1950 will be in retarding the rate of industrial concentration remains to be seen. The Robinson-Patman Act, which amended Section 2 of the Clayton Act on discrimination, was passed in part as a result of the pressures from the commission in view of the narrow interpretation by the Supreme Court in several cases and in part at the insistence of Congress, which was concerned with the inroads that the chain stores and depression were making upon the more traditional channels of distribution.

But the commission has shown something less than imagination and energy. In defining the conditions under which the various practices prescribed by the Clayton Act would lead to a substantial lessening of competition or tendency toward monopoly, the commission has shown little ingenuity. And the effort of the commission to expand the list of unfair practices under Section 5 into new fields has not been very impressive. It did succeed in banning lottery devices in the sale of penny candy to children, which constituted something of an innovation over the state of the common law of unfair competition. Perhaps its most impressive accomplishment has been its efforts to clarify the legal status of the basing-point system of pricing as used in the steel, cement, and other industries. It has been concerned with this problem since the early twenties and was finally supported by the courts in a series of decisions between 1945 and 1948.

But as one surveys the development of antitrust policy in the last twenty years, one cannot but be impressed by the fact that it has been the Antitrust Division of the Department of Justice rather than the Federal Trade Commission which has made the greatest contribution to clarifying the line between legal and illegal behavior. The cases against Alcoa and against the cigarette manufacturers have clarified the law with respect to dominant firms in several respects and laid the basis on which an imaginative agency might hope to make further progress. The motion-picture cases have clarified the problems of vertical integration. Several cases have clarified the relation between patent policy and antitrust laws. These and other examples of initiative in the clarification of the antitrust laws in the light of changing conditions and practices are to the credit of the Antitrust Division of the Department of Justice rather than of the Federal Trade Commission. The executive agency seems to have proved more effective than the administrative commission in leading antitrust policy in new directions.

It would be interesting to explore the various reasons for the limited success of Wilson's program. The explanations are many. World War I diverted the Federal Trade Commission from its main tasks in its early years. During the 1920's and early 1930's, the commission lacked the financial and moral support of both the legislative and the executive branches of government. Some of its problems have arisen from the unsympathetic treatment of the commission by the courts. Moreover, the commission has tended to become bogged down in the control of a wide variety of unfair and deceptive practices which are mainly characteristic of highly competitive rather than monopolistic industries. Finally, many critics have pointed to the unnecessarily complicated internal structure and procedure of the commission and to deficiencies in personnel in both the commission and the staff.

But one can overemphasize the commission's deficiencies. And it would be most unfortunate if we should fail to recognize its genuine accomplishments in the codification of the per se violations and in its investigatory functions.

Progress in antitrust policy has been fitful and frequently disappointing. But the trend since 1890 has been toward greater clarification and more effective enforcement. The antitrust process can be understood only if viewed against the background of the broad political and social context out of which it grew and in which it continues to flourish. Antitrust policy has roots deep in the moral, political, and social fabric of American life. It reflects the American preference for dispersal of power of all sorts and the pervasive desire to insure equal opportunity to all on the basis of merit. It reflects also the American respect for property and freedom of use of property subject to the rules of fair play. The American ideology as interpreted and revitalized by Wilson has played an important part along with self-interest in welding together a coalition in favor of antitrust policy.

The political, administrative, and legislative processes by which antitrust policy is made and interpreted are crucial to an understanding of that policy. Congressional legislation in this area has necessarily been cast in quite general terms. Ultimate responsibility for determining the meaning of the legislation lies with the federal courts, although they may give weight to congressional debates and documents as evidence of congressional intent. And, if Congress should be dissatisfied with the courts' interpretation, it may enact new legislation. Between the Congress and the courts are the administrative agencies, which must exercise much discretion. It is with these agencies, in large part, that responsibility lies for initiating action to clarify the meaning of the legislation and to enforce it.

But administrative initiative can be either stimulated or retarded in many ways by the Congress and indirectly by interested parties. The administrative agencies depend upon Congress for their appropriations. The appointment of the Assistant Attorney-General in charge of antitrust and of the Federal Trade Commissioners depends upon approval by the Senate. There is consequently considerable opportunity for

Congress to influence indirectly the direction and the extent of enforcement. The influence of public opinion and of interested parties may consequently be brought to bear on the administrative process through the Congress as well as through direct contact with the executive branch of the government.

The courts fortunately would appear to be relatively immune from such influences. Not that the political and economic philosophies are unimportant in interpreting legislation, but judges are appointed for life and their attitudes on antitrust matters will generally be at the most one of several factors influencing their selection.

We find then, on the one hand, a legislative-administrative process which provides a degree of flexibility in the face of changing public attitudes and of the pressures of interested parties and, on the other, a judicial process which provides continuity and stability. In this process an executive agency, such as the Department of Justice, appears often to show more initiative than the independent regulatory commission.

What shall we say of the antitrust policy of Woodrow Wilson in perspective? Consider first Wilson's decision to favor a positive policy of competition rather than a policy of laissez faire or of regulated monopoly. The history of the regulatory commission in this country, our experience with NRA, and observation of cartel policies abroad indicate the wisdom of Wilson's general orientation. Most careful observers of the American scene agree that our antitrust policies have been important in stimulating the spirit of enterprise and in diverting business energies into fair but aggressive competition rather than into pacts of mutual security. It would, of course, be difficult to document this conclusion. But Wilson must be credited with leading us, at a crucial turning point in our industrial history, down the path which has encouraged rather than thwarted industrial enterprise. He reinforced the restless, aggressive climate of American industry at a time when the industrialized nations of Europe were turning to defensive tactics.

But what shall we say of Wilson's assumption that the problem of promoting competition is primarily one of controlling business behavior rather than one of regulating industrial structure? On this issue there is less agreement. The codification of a series of unfair competitive practices by the Federal Trade Commission has reduced the magnitude of the problem of economic concentration and monopoly. Such studies as we have on the trends in industrial concentration in the

United States indicate that there has been little, if any, increase in concentration since the beginning of the century. But when it came to drawing up a list of unfair practices, practices which should be enjoined because of their tendency to lead to strong market positions based on factors other than superior efficiency, it became clear that many practices which might have this tendency under some circumstances were in other circumstances quite harmless. And the fact remains that neither the commission nor the courts have succeeded in developing clear criteria which would distinguish one circumstance from another.

Wilson's policies were based on the prevailing economic thought of the day, which made a sharp distinction between monopoly and competition. More recent developments in economic thought have emphasized the wide variety of market conditions ranging from perfect monopoly at one end of the spectrum through oligopoly and various blends of imperfect and monopolistic competition to pure and perfect competition at the other. We see today that the problem is economically more complicated than that visualized by Woodrow Wilson and his contemporaries. But while economists may talk of various degrees and blends of monopoly and competition, in the field of antitrust policy the problem becomes one of distinguishing between the legal and the illegal. There is today no consensus on what further restrictions it is feasible and desirable to place upon competitive practices or market structure in the interest of a positive policy of competition. The problem remains, today as in 1914, one of developing operationally meaningful tests which will distinguish between practices promoting competition and practices leading to monopoly. Wilson and his associates had expected that the Federal Trade Commission would be the useful vehicle for accomplishing this task. This hope has not been fulfilled.

During the years 1911–14 Woodrow Wilson, faced with the realities of the trusts and concentration, mobilized public opinion in favor of a constructive and conservative solution consistent with the traditional values of the American ideology. The problems of monopoly and concentration are still with us. No one would maintain that the legislation of 1914 has fulfilled the promise with which it was enacted. However, it is a measure of the genius of Woodrow Wilson's conception that, despite many vicissitudes in economic matters, his concepts in the field of monopoly and concentration still dominate American policy and are attracting increasing attention abroad.

PART THREE

WILSON

AND FOREIGN POLICY

CHAPTER NINE

Wilson the Diplomatist*

By
Arthur S. Link

There is considerable revelation in the nature of Wilson's training as a diplomatist, which was, in so far as it went, exclusively theoretical. Few men have come to the White House better equipped in the philosophy or more adequately trained in the techniques of domestic leadership than Woodrow Wilson. He is saved from the reverse generalization—that few men have ever begun the Presidency with less experience and training in the field of foreign affairs than he had had—only because of the naïveté of most beginners in the White House in this field. "It would be the irony of fate if my administration had to deal chiefly with foreign affairs," Wilson remarked to a Princeton friend a few days before he went to Washington in 1913. It was a frank acknowledgment of the fact that, as a scholar and analyst, he had been almost exclusively concerned with domestic politics in the Anglo-American tradition and interested only casually in the mechanisms and history of foreign relations.

To be sure, in the late nineteenth century, when Wilson did most of his scholarly writing, the average American was caught up in great political and economic movements at home and knew next to nothing about affairs abroad. But Wilson was not an average American; he was a distinguished writer and teacher in the fields of government, history, and international law. Yet at least before the turn of the century he wrote and spoke almost as if foreign policy were a minor concern of great powers.

In his first book, *Congressional Government*, an inquiry into the practical functioning of the federal government published in 1885, Wilson made only a passing reference to foreign affairs, and that in

* Reprinted by permission of the Johns Hopkins Press from *Woodrow Wilson: A Look at His Major Foreign Policies* (Baltimore: Johns Hopkins Press, 1957), pp. 4–28.

connection with the Senate's treaty-making power.[1] Four years later Wilson published *The State*, an excellent pioneer text in comparative government. Out of a total of more than one hundred pages devoted to the development of law and legal institutions, he gave a page and a half to international law. In his analysis of the administrative structures of modern governments, he described the machinery of the foreign relations of the British Empire in five words but devoted twenty-six pages to local government in England; and he gave thirteen times as much space to the work of the Interior Department as to the Department of State in the American government. Finally, in his summary chapters on the functions and objects of government, he put foreign relations at the bottom of his list of what he called the "constituent functions" and then went on to elaborate the functions and objects of government without even mentioning the conduct of external affairs![2]

Wilson began to evince more than casual interest in foreign affairs for the first time in the late 1890's and early 1900's. In part he was reacting to disturbing new shifts in international power and in American thinking about the future role of the United States in the world as a consequence of the Venezuelan controversy, the war with Spain, the extension of American interests to the Far East, and the acquisition of an overseas empire. Thus Wilson approved President Cleveland's assertion, made during the Venezuelan boundary dispute with Great Britain, of the right of the United States to compel a European state to arbitrate a territorial controversy anywhere in the Western Hemisphere.[3] After some earlier doubts about the wisdom of the war with Spain and of acquiring overseas possessions, he concluded that the war was the natural outgrowth of American industrial might and that it was America's duty to retain the Philippines and teach the Filipinos order and self-government, even if the effort required the use of force.[4] To cite a final example, he echoed the propaganda of imperialists like Alfred T. Mahan and Albert J. Beveridge in declaring that the flag must follow trade and that the United States must acquire colonies and markets abroad.[5]

---

1 (Boston: Houghton Mifflin Co.), pp. 232–34.

2 *The State: Elements of Historical and Practical Politics* (Boston: D. C. Heath & Co., 1889), *passim*.

3 "Mr. Cleveland as President," *Atlantic Monthly*, LXXIX (March, 1897), 298.

4 "The Ideals of America," *ibid.*, XC (December, 1902), 727–30.

5 *History of the American People* (5 vols.; New York: Harper & Bros., 1902), V, 296.

Wilson, however, did more than merely react to the epochal developments at home and abroad around the turn of the century; he also thought seriously about their future impact upon American policies and institutions. The war with Spain, he asserted with growing conviction, had been only one sign of a more important underlying development—the end of American isolation and the inevitable beginning of a new era in which the United States would have to play an ever widening role in world politics. "Of a sudden, as it seemed, and without premeditation," he wrote in the concluding pages of his *History of the American People,*

the United States had turned away from their long-time, deliberate absorption in their own domestic development, from the policy professed by every generation of their statesmen from the first, of separation from the embarrassing entanglements of foreign affairs; had given themselves a colonial empire, and taken their place of power in the field of international politics. No one who justly studied the courses of their life could reasonably wonder at the thing that had happened. . . . A quick instinct apprised American statesmen that they had come to a turning point in the progress of the nation, which would have disclosed itself in some other way if not in this, had the war for Cuba not made it plain. It had turned from developing its own resources to make conquest of the markets of the world.[6]

It followed inexorably, Wilson added in a revealing essay in 1901, that Americans were living in a new and more perilous age, in which changed circumstances had rendered meaningless and dangerous the time-honored traditions of self-sufficiency and of security through isolation. "There is no masking or concealing the new order of the world," he warned. "It is not the world of the eighteenth century, nor yet of the nineteenth." There were radically new forces at work which would determine the future of mankind; there were shifts in the balance of power that portended new rivalries and threatened the peace. The American people, he concluded, were now neighbors to the world, whether they liked it or not; they could not escape the coming challenges by ignoring them; they had, perforce, to devise new foreign policies and to become efficient in executing them.[7]

Wilson also saw clearly that the sudden emergence of the United States to world power would have a profound and enduring impact upon the location of authority and the system of leadership in the federal government. "Much the most important change to be noticed," he

[6] *Ibid.,* pp. 294–96.

[7] "Democracy and Efficiency," *Atlantic Monthly,* LXXXVII (March, 1901), 292.

wrote in the preface to the fifteenth edition of *Congressional Government* in 1900,

is the result of the war with Spain upon the lodgment and exercise of power within our federal system: the greatly increased power and opportunity for constructive statesmanship given the President, by the plunge into international politics and into the administration of distant dependencies, which has been that war's most striking and momentous consequence.[8]

"The war with Spain again changed the balance of parts," Wilson asserted in 1907.

Foreign questions became leading questions again, as they had been in the first days of the government, and in them the President was of necessity leader. Our new place in the affairs of the world has since that year of transformation kept him at the front of our government, where our own thoughts and the attention of men everywhere is centred upon him. . . . The President can never again be the mere domestic figure he has been throughout so large a part of our history. The nation has risen to the first rank in power and resources. . . . Our President must always, henceforth, be one of the great powers of the world, whether he act greatly and wisely or not. . . . We have but begun to see the presidential office in this light; but it is the light which will more and more beat upon it, and more and more determine its character and its effect upon the politics of the nation.[9]

There is the temptation to conclude from this analysis of Wilson's observations during the decade 1898–1907, that, as one authority has said, he had demonstrated an understanding of the foreign relations of his country and considerable preparation for their conduct by the time he entered the White House.[10] Much, of course, depends upon the criteria that one applies. Compared with a Grant or a Harding, Wilson does indeed seem an eminent authority. On the other hand, to compare Wilson with a Jefferson or a John Quincy Adams is to point up some of the deficiencies in the latter-day President's intellectual and practical training for the difficult business of managing the foreign affairs of a great power.

The strengths and weaknesses in Wilson's unconscious preparation as a diplomatist will, I trust, become more fully evident as we proceed in this analysis, but it might be well to summarize them at this point. There was to his advantage the fact that he had done much serious

[8] P. xi.

[9] *Constitutional Government in the United States* (New York: Columbia University Press, 1908), pp. 59, 78.

[10] Harley Notter, *The Origins of the Foreign Policy of Woodrow Wilson* (Baltimore: Johns Hopkins Press, 1937), p. 145.

thinking about general principles of politics and national ideals that transcended geographical boundaries. That is to say, Wilson came to the Presidency equipped with a coherent and deeply rooted philosophy about the nature and ends of government, a philosophy that could be readily translated into the basis of a foreign policy. Also to his advantage was the fact of his awareness of the larger dimensions of the diplomatic revolution of the period and the impact of that revolution upon American political institutions.

Balanced on the debit side were certain obvious deficiencies in Wilson's thought and training in foreign affairs. The most serious of these was his failure before 1913 to do any systematic thinking about the nature, complexity, and difficulties of foreign policy and his assumption that the main task of diplomacy was the simple one of translating national ideals into a larger program of action.

Second, there was Wilson's apparent ignorance of, or unconcern with, the elementary facts about the main thrusts of American diplomacy from 1901 to 1913 and about the tensions that were impelling Europe toward a general war during the same period. Even about those events on the international scene in which he evidenced a keen interest —the war with Spain and its immediate aftermath—much of Wilson's thinking was superficial and reflected more the faddish thought of the time than an astute understanding of what was taking place. Indeed, after the thrill of the war and of empire had quickly passed, Wilson apparently lost virtually all interest in affairs abroad. There were tremendous new developments in American foreign policy and furious partisan debates at home between 1901 and 1913. There were recurrent crises in Europe during the prolonged prelude to the war that would break out in 1914. Yet throughout this period, during which Wilson emerged as a pre-eminent political leader, he spoke and acted as if foreign problems did not exist. For example, during a brilliant campaign for the Democratic presidential nomination and for the Presidency from 1911 to 1912, he never once mentioned a foreign issue that was not primarily a domestic concern.

A good argument can be made to the effect that Wilson was so absorbed in plans for Princeton from 1902 to 1910 and so engrossed in his political apprenticeship from 1910 to 1913 that he had neither time nor energy for a serious study of foreign policy. The argument has some merit, but we must also conclude that Wilson did not concern himself seriously with affairs abroad during the period 1901 to 1913 both because he was not interested and because he did not think that they were important enough to warrant any diversion from the main stream of his thought. Therefore, Wilson was not being unduly self-deprecatory when he remarked before he went to Washington how ironical it would be if his administration had to deal chiefly with foreign affairs. He was simply recognizing the obvious fact of his primary concern with domestic issues and his superior training for leadership in solving them.

Regardless of the adequacy or inadequacy of his preparation, Wilson after 1913 faced foreign problems of greater magnitude than any President had confronted since the early years of the nineteenth century. Whether he responded wisely or unwisely to the mounting international challenges of the years from 1913 to 1920, he executed policies that were on the whole firmly grounded upon a consistent body of principles and assumptions that supplied motive power and shaped and governed policy in the fields of action. These principles and assumptions were deeply rooted in Wilson's general thinking before 1913 about cosmology, ethics, the nature and ends of government, and the role of his own country in the creative development of mankind; they were in turn enlarged and refined as Wilson sought to apply them in practical affairs after his inauguration. Determining and controlling, they gave both strength and weakness to the diplomatist in action.

The foundations of all of Wilson's political thinking were the religious and ethical beliefs and values that he inherited from the Christian tradition and from his own Presbyterian theology. In matters of basic Christian faith, Wilson was like a little child, never doubting, always believing, and drawing spiritual sustenance from Bible reading, church attendance, and prayer. Having derived his beliefs from the Shorter Catechism, his father's sermons, and the Presbyterian scholastics, Wilson was Calvinistic in theology. He believed in a sovereign God, just and stern as well as loving; in a moral universe, the laws of which ruled nations as well as men; in the supreme revelation and redemption of Jesus Christ; and in the Bible as the incomparable word of God and the rule of life. He was a predestinarian, no so much in his apparent belief in election as in his conviction that God controlled history and used men and nations in the unfolding of His plan according to His purposes. Few ministers of the gospel gave more eloquent voice to these beliefs than did Wilson in his day; to point out that there was nothing unique about them is not to detract from their underlying and pervasive importance.[11]

From such spiritual roots grew a sturdy tree of character, integrity, and concern for first principles in political action—in brief, all the components of the idealism that was the unifying force in Wilson's life. In the conduct of foreign affairs this idealism meant for him the subordination of immediate goals and material interests to superior ethical standards and the exaltation of moral and spiritual purposes. This is not to say that he ignored the existence and powerful operation of economic forces in international life. Indeed, for a brief period following the Spanish-American War he seemed almost to verge upon an economic determinism in his analysis of developments, both past and present, upon the international scene. As President, moreover, he was not unmindful of the necessities of a viable international economic life, of the material interests of Americans abroad, or of the economic rivalries that helped to produce conflict among nations. Even so, idealism was the main drive of Wilson's thinking about international relations. As he put it, foreign policy must not be defined in "terms of material interest" but should be "more concerned about human rights than about property rights."[12]

A second main theme in Wilson's political thinking with large consequences for his foreign policy was his belief in democracy as the most humane and Christian form of government. From the beginning to the end of his adult career he studied, wrote about, and put into practice the essential aspects of democratic government, and it would be superfluous here to review his splendid synthesis of the Anglo-American democratic theories and traditions. More important for our purposes is an understanding of the way in which these assumptions helped to form his objectives and to determine his actions in the field of foreign affairs.

Much, of course, depended upon Wilson's view of the nature and capacities of man. There is in his thinking an implicit if never an out-

[11] For examples of Wilson's religious addresses and writings, see "The Ministry and the Individual" and "The Bible and Progress," printed in R. S. Baker and W. E. Dodd (eds.), *The Public Papers of Woodrow Wilson: College and State* (2 vols.; New York: Harper & Bros., 1925), II, 178–87, 291–302. For a description and analysis, see Arthur S. Link, *Wilson: The New Freedom* (Princeton: Princeton University Press, 1956), pp. 64–65.

[12] For a rewarding amplification of the foregoing generalizations, see William Diamond, *The Economic Thought of Woodrow Wilson* (Baltimore: Johns Hopkins Press, 1943), pp. 131–61.

right repudiation of the classical Presbyterian emphasis upon original sin, and a strong strain of nineteenth-century Christian optimism and social Darwinism. To be sure, he never completely lost sight of man's capacity for evil, but he seems often to have forgotten it, so strong was his faith in man's inherent goodness and in the possibility of progress.

These were the controlling assumptions. It followed in Wilson's mind that all people were capable of self-government because all were endowed with inherent character and a capacity for growth. He was no visionary in these beliefs; following his master Burke, he repudiated and condemned utopianism and taught that people learned democracy only by long years of disciplined experience. The fact remained, nonetheless, that he thought that all people, whether Mexican peons or Russian peasants, whites or Orientals, were capable of being trained in the habits of democracy. "When properly directed," he once declared, "there is no people not fitted for self-government."[13]

These assumptions inevitably had profound implications for Wilson's thought about the development and relationships of nations. His belief in the inherent goodness of man, in progress as the law of organic life and the working out of the divine plan in history, and in democracy as the highest form of government led him straight to the conclusion that democracy must some day be the universal rule of political life. It ultimately led him even further, to the belief that a peaceful world community, governed by a universal public opinion and united for mutual advancement, could exist only when democracy was itself triumphant everywhere. This conviction was more than an assumption underlying Wilson's foreign policy; it was also an imperative force that propelled him into bold plans for Mexico, the Caribbean region, and, afterward, the entire world.

The final main assumptions of Wilson's thought about international relations grew out of his attempt to define America's role in world affairs within the context of his general principles and in light of the contribution that the United States could make. The American people, he believed, had a peculiar role to play, indeed a mission to execute in history precisely because they were in so many ways unique among the peoples of the world. They were unique politically, not because they alone possessed democratic institutions but because they had succeeded in organizing diverse sections and a hundred million people into

[13] Samuel G. Blythe, "Mexico: The Record of a Conversation with President Wilson," *Saturday Evening Post*, CLXXXVI (May 23, 1914), 4.

a federal system such as one day (he at last conceived) must provide a structure for a world organization. The American people were unique socially, first, because of their radical affirmation of equality and their historic repudiation of everything for which the caste- and class-ridden societies of Europe and Asia stood and, second, because they were in fact a new people, the product of the mixing of all the nationalities of Europe. Finally and most importantly, they were unique morally and spiritually. America, Wilson believed, had been born that men might be free; Americans had done more than any other people to advance the cause of human welfare; Americans, above all other peoples, were "custodians of the spirit of righteousness, of the spirit of equal-handed justice, of the spirit of hope which believes in the perfectibility of the law with the perfectibility of human life itself."

Thus America's mission in the world was not to attain wealth and power, but to fulfil the divine plan by service to mankind, by leadership in moral purposes, and above all by advancing peace and world brotherhood. As one scholar has written in summary of Wilson's view:

[America's] mission was to realize an ideal of liberty, provide a model of democracy, vindicate moral principles, give examples of action and ideals of government and righteousness to an interdependent world, uphold the rights of man, work for humanity and the happiness of men everywhere, lead the thinking of the world, promote peace—in sum, to serve mankind and progress.[14]

These assumptions and ideals bore so heavily upon the formation of Wilson's foreign policies that we cannot be content with a mere description of them. We must also attempt to see the way in which they equipped or unfitted the President for the needs of practical statesmanship during a critical period.

Only a confirmed cynic would fail to recognize that a large measure of Wilson's strength as a diplomatist and much of his contribution in the field of international relations derived in the first instance from his spiritual resources. To begin with, there were certain practical advantages in idealism. By rejecting narrow nationalism and materialism as bases for foreign policy and by articulating the noblest traditions of Western culture, Wilson could and did speak as with universal authority, whether in pleading with the imperial German government to respect human life in using the submarine, in proclaiming a people's war for justice as much to the vanquished as to the victors,

14 Notter, *op. cit.*, p. 653.

or in appealing for a world organization based upon the ideals of peace and co-operation. That is to say, ideals are a dynamic force in cultures that acknowledge their validity, and Wilson was a more effective war leader, a more fearful antagonist of the German military dictators on the ideological battlefield, and a more indomitable fighter for a just peace settlement because he stood for what most men in the Western world (including his opponents) were willing to acknowledge were their own best ideals. Besides, on several occasions, particularly in his relations with Mexico, he was able to escape the consequences of a blundering policy only because he had made his real, that is, his ideal, purposes clear.

We should not measure the significance of Wilson's idealism in practical terms alone. Men violate or more often simply ignore the ideals by which they profess to live; but without ideals to recall lost visions and to give guidance for the present and future, societies degenerate into tyrannies of individuals, classes, or ideologies. It was Wilson's great contribution that while hatreds and passions threatened to wreck Western civilization, he held high the traditions of humanity and the ideal of justice, and by so doing he helped to salvage them for a future generation.

It does not detract from the significance of the foregoing to point out that Wilson's assumptions and principles also impaired in some degree his leadership in the mundane affairs of state. This was true in the first place because his philosophy and thought, even more about foreign than about domestic matters, failed to take sufficient account of what theologians call "original sin" or what diplomatic specialists call "realities." The qualifying adjective *sufficient* has a key importance here. Wilson was never a fool or a visionary incapable of facing reality; he was keenly intelligent and often shrewd. And yet his faith in the goodness and rationality of men, in the miraculous potentialities of democracy, and in the inevitable triumph of righteousness sometimes caused him to make illusory appraisals of the situations at hand and to devise quixotic or unworkable solutions.

In executing foreign policy generally, Wilson assumed that foreign relations among the great powers consisted of intercourse between civilized gentlemen controlled by an enlightened public opinion and common moral standards, and that decency, good will, and free discussion sufficed to settle all international disputes. This assumption in turn led him to rely mainly upon enlightened instruments of diplomacy—conciliation treaties, the invocation of universal principles in diplomatic correspondence, and displays of friendship—and, conversely, almost to refuse to think in terms of threat or violence. His dependence upon moral suasion in the protracted controversy with Germany over the submarine is one example of his nearly invetcrate reliance upon the spirit rather than the sword in foreign relations.

In the second place, Wilson's uncommon concern with the fundamental principles of national and international life sometimes led him to oversimplify the vast complexities of international politics. This deficiency stemmed from his methods of thinking and arriving at conclusions—methods that were as much intuitive as rational and deductive rather than inductive; it stemmed also from his tendency to invoke analogies between domestic and international politics without taking sufficient account of the enormous differences between the two.

There is a good example of the danger of an almost exclusive reliance upon general principles in the formation of foreign policy in the manner in which Wilson dealt with an important Far Eastern question in 1913, the issue of American participation in the Six-Power Consortium, which had been formed in 1911 to supply capital to the Chinese government. The full records of his discussions about this matter reveal clearly how Wilson's mind worked in making policy. First he set up the general propositions that the European and Japanese governments involved in the Consortium were scheming in the usual imperialistic manner to impair Chinese sovereignty and to gain control over the internal affairs of a democracy struggling to be born. Reasoning deductively, Wilson quickly concluded what the American government should do in these circumstances. Since imperialism and such an attempt to subvert a democracy in its birth were morally wrong, the United States should withdraw from the Consortium and should help the Chinese people in other and more honorable ways.

It was a "moral" decision, based upon reasoning not altogether unsound as far as it went. The trouble was that the Chinese situation in 1913, domestic and external, could not be encompassed by a few moralizations that ignored the unpleasant realities—the fact that Chinese sovereignty was well nigh a fiction, that there was no Chinese "democracy," and that China desperately needed capital to survive. The consequences of Wilson's "moral" decision were soon obvious: the American withdrawal caused the virtual collapse of the Consortium, and the failure of the Western powers to extend financial assistance weakened the Chinese government precisely at the time when the Japanese were beginning their first great drive to control their continental neighbor.[15]

An even more important example of the consequences of oversimplification through too much reliance upon obvious moral principles was Wilson's response to the situation created in Mexico in 1913 when a military usurper, General Victoriano Huerta, overthrew a constitutional government headed by Francisco Madero. To Wilson the issues were as plain as daylight, and he refused on moral grounds to recognize the Huerta government even though it controlled most of Mexico and was constitutional in form. More than this, Wilson went on to devise a new test of recognition for Mexico, which he later applied to the Bolshevik regime in Russia. It was a test of constitutional legitimacy, which involved going behind the exterior to determine whether a government was legitimate, or politically moral, as well as constitutional in form or *de facto* in authority.[16] It was "moral" diplomacy, but it soon involved Wilson and the American government in far-reaching meddling in the internal affairs of Mexico, and this in turn led to consequences nearly disastrous for both countries.[17]

But let us return to my analysis of the way in which Wilson's assumptions and principles impaired his statesmanship in the field of foreign relations. I have already mentioned his tendency to take insufficient account of hard realities and to oversimplify the complexities of international life. A third point was the unreal quality of some of his thought and policy that resulted from his almost romantic faith in the sufficiency of democratic solutions. This was revealed in his attempts to apply constitutional and democratic criteria to Central America and the Caribbean states,[18] to the revolutionary upheaval in Mexico led by Madero's successors, the Constitutionalists, and finally to the revolutionary situation in Russia between the fall of the tsarist

[15] For an extended discussion, see the excellent study by Tien-yi Li, *Woodrow Wilson's China Policy, 1913–1917* (New York: Twayne Publishers, 1952).

[16] Howard F. Cline, *The United States and Mexico* (Cambridge: Harvard University Press, 1953), p. 142, has an illuminating discussion of this point.

[17] I have told this story at length elsewhere, in *Wilson: The New Freedom*, pp. 347–416, and in *Woodrow Wilson and the Progressive Era, 1910–1917* (New York: Harper & Bros., 1954), pp. 107–44.

[18] As Samuel Flagg Bemis has pointed out in a telling way in "Woodrow Wilson and Latin America," MS in possession of the present writer.

government and the triumph of the Bolsheviks.[19] In all these situations ordinary democratic concepts simply did not apply; yet Wilson insisted upon believing that solutions lay in the establishment of enlightened and responsible governments through free elections.

The fourth and final peril of an excessive concern for ideals and principles in foreign policy was in Wilson's case particularly acute. It was the danger of pharisaism, which often results from too much introspective concern about the standards of right conduct. It was revealed, among other things, in Wilson's assumption that his motives and purposes were purer than those of the men with whom he happened to be contending. Even though they were actually often well grounded, such convictions left little room for a saving humility and gave Wilson the appearance of the Pharisee who thanked God that he was better than other men.

In the final reckoning, Wilson will be judged not so much by what he thought about foreign policy as by what he did, and I conclude this chapter with a word about his techniques and methods as a diplomatist. They stemmed in an all-pervasive way from his temperament, and we can ease some of the problems that puzzle the biographer if we begin by frankly confronting those aspects of his personality that bore directly upon his practice of leadership. Endowed with an intense nervous and emotional constitution, Wilson was in temperament an extreme activist, never satisfied with mere speculation or willing to apply slow-working remedies, but driven as if by demons to almost frenzied efforts to achieve immediate and ideal solutions.

Was the challenge one of transforming Princeton into a leading institution of higher learning in the United States? Then the task had to be done thoroughly and at once, and no vested social interest or obstreperous individuals could be permitted to stand in the way. As Wilson put it, all had to be "digested in the processes of the university." Did the job at hand encompass the reform of federal economic policies? Then Congress must be driven and public opinion must be maintained at a high pitch of excitement in order that all might be finished during a single congressional session. Were the tasks those of reconstructing the world order and of propelling the American people

[19] George F. Kennan, *Soviet-American Relations, 1917–1920: Russia Leaves the War* (Princeton: Princeton University Press, 1956), particularly pp. 140–48.

into an international leadership? Then nothing less than total reconstruction and a total commitment would suffice. This driving force,
relentless energy, and striving for the whole achievement characterized
all of Wilson's major efforts in the field of foreign affairs; they were
at once sources of power and of danger.

Two other aspects of personality or temperament had an equal impact. One was Wilson's egotism, manifested in his remarkable conviction that he was an instrument of divine purpose, or his sense of destiny,
in his awareness of his own intellectual superiority over most of his
associates, and, above all, in his urge to dominate. The other was a
driving ambition, fired as much by a longing for personal distinction
as by a desire to serve God and mankind. Egotism and ambition combined with a compelling activism to produce in Woodrow Wilson a
leader of extraordinary strength and daring, one who would play not
merely an active but the dominant role in foreign affairs while he
was President.

Mature conviction from scholarly study concerning the role that
the President should play also helped to determine Wilson's methods
as a diplomatist. Even during that period in his scholarly writing when
he emphasized congressional government, Wilson recognized the President's wide latitude in the conduct of affairs abroad. That recognition
had grown into a sweeping affirmation of presidential sovereignty by
the time that Wilson had reached maturity in his thought about the
American constitutional system.

"One of the greatest of the President's powers," he said in 1907,

I have not yet spoken of at all: his control, which is very absolute, of the
foreign relations of the nation. The initiative in foreign affairs, which the
President possesses without any restriction whatever, is virtually the power
to control them absolutely. The President cannot conclude a treaty with a
foreign power without the consent of the Senate, but he may guide every
step of diplomacy, and to guide diplomacy is to determine what treaties must
be made, if the faith and prestige of the government are to be maintained.
He need disclose no step of negotiation until it is complete, and when in any
critical matter it is completed the government is virtually committed. Whatever its disinclination, the Senate may feel itself committed also.[20]

It was a striking characterization of Wilson's own management of
foreign affairs a few years after these words were spoken. In the areas
that he considered vitally important—Mexico, relations with the European belligerents, wartime relations with the Allied powers, and the

[20] *Constitutional Government,* pp. 77–78.

writing of a peace settlement—Wilson took absolute personal control. He wrote most of the important notes on his own typewriter, bypassed the State Department by using his own private agents, ignored his secretaries of state by conducting important negotiations behind their backs, and acted like a divine-right monarch in the general conduct of affairs.

Perhaps as good an example of Wilson's personal diplomacy as any I could choose was his handling of the Mexican problem during the period of Huerta's tenure in Mexico City from March, 1913, to August, 1914. Ignoring the men in the State Department who knew anything about the subject, the American ambassador and the chargé in the Mexican capital, and the consuls in the field, Wilson proceeded to make a Mexican policy in his own way, as follows: He first sent a journalist whom he trusted, but who knew nothing about Mexican affairs, to Mexico City to investigate. Accepting this reporter's recommendations, Wilson next sent a former governor of Minnesota, who had neither experience in diplomacy nor any knowledge about Mexico, to present certain proposals for a solution to Huerta. Then, after the dictator had repudiated the President's right to interfere, Wilson pursued a relentless personal campaign to depose Huerta, one that culminated in armed intervention and Huerta's downfall. Time and again Wilson used the same methods and almost always with the same results: the formation of faulty policy through sheer ignorance, men working at cross-purposes, confusion in the State Department and in the embassies and legations, and the like.

To be sure, there were some extenuating circumstances. Wilson often ignored the professionals in the State Department and the Foreign Service because he genuinely distrusted them, because he thought that they, or many of them, were either aristocrats, the products of exclusive schools and a snobbish society, or else sycophantic imitators of the wealthy classes. "We find," he explained in 1913,

that those who have been occupying the legations and embassies have been habituated to a point of view which is very different, indeed, from the point of view of the present administration. They have had the material interests of individuals in the United States very much more in mind than the moral and public considerations which it seems to us ought to control. They have been so bred in a different school that we have found, in several instances, that it was difficult for them to comprehend our point of view and purpose.[21]

21 Wilson to C. W. Eliot, September 17, 1913, Papers of Woodrow Wilson, Library of Congress.

There was also the fact that many of the men through whom Wilson would normally have worked in the conduct of foreign relations *were*, to a varying degree, incompetent, and this because of the necessities of politics and the paucity of Democrats with any experience. Simply and solely because he had to have William J. Bryan's support for domestic policies, Wilson appointed the "Great Commoner" Secretary of State. Because he did not trust Bryan in delicate matters, Wilson turned more and more away from regular channels and leaned increasingly upon unofficial advisers like Colonel Edward M. House.

In the selection of ambassadors for important stations, moreover, Wilson tried desperately to find the best men and to break the custom of using ambassadorships as rewards for party service. Except in a few cases the "best" men would not accept appointment, and Wilson had to yield to pressure and name party hacks to places like Berlin, St. Petersburg, Rome, and Madrid. The classic example was James W. Gerard, a generous contributor to the Democratic treasury and an active Tammany politician, whom Wilson named ambassador to Germany after vowing that he would never stoop so low. Thus it happened that during a period of extreme tension in German-American relations Wilson had as his spokesman in Berlin a man for whom he had no respect and not a little contempt. The President's opinion of Gerard is rather pungently revealed in the following examples of the comments that he penciled on copies of dispatches from the ambassador:

10 Sept. [1915]

Ordinarily our Ambassador ought to be backed up as of course, but—this ass? It is hard to take it seriously. W.

11 Sept. [1915]

Who can fathom this? I wish they would hand this idiot his passports! W.

As he had not much more confidence in most of his other ambassadors, it was little wonder that Wilson used them only as messenger boys.

Thus circumstances that he could not control were in part responsible for Wilson's extreme individualism in conducting foreign affairs. Yet they were not entirely responsible, and the conviction remains that the chief causes of his exercise of an exclusive personal control were his urge to dominate, his egotism, and his reasoned jealousy of the presidential power, that is, his belief that it would be constitutionally dangerous to delegate essential power for national good or ill to men, even to able men, not directly responsible to the people.

The essential validity of this conclusion is to some degree revealed in the nature of Wilson's relations with two men of considerable talents, Robert Lansing and Walter H. Page. Lansing, who served as counselor of the State Department from 1914 to 1915 and as Secretary of State from 1915 to 1920, was thoroughly trained in international law and practice, keenly intelligent, and completely loyal to the President. Yet Wilson never really trusted Lansing's mental processes (once he remarked that Lansing "was so stupid that he was constantly afraid he would commit some serious blunder"), never thought of him as much more than a dignified clerk, and consequently never took full advantage of the resources that Lansing had to offer.

The reasons for this lack of confidence shed an important light upon the Wilsonian character. To begin with, the two men were fundamentally different in their thought processes: where Wilson was intuitive and idealistic, Lansing was inductive in reasoning, coldly analytical, and realistic. But the chief cause of Wilson's distrust was Lansing's refusal to give the kind of loyalty that his chief demanded, which was intellectual submission and agreement as well as understanding. Lansing was a little too strong in mind and character thus to subordinate himself or even to pretend that he did. He survived in office as long as he did only because he became fairly adept in handling the President and only because it was usually inexpedient for Wilson to dismiss him.

Unlike Lansing, Page had no special preparation for his tasks as ambassador to Great Britain, but he had an abundance of natural ability and was soon the master of his functions. So long as he reported what the President wanted to hear, Page was Wilson's intimate friend and best source of opinion abroad, but he soon lost all standing at the White House once he began to offer unwanted advice, to criticize, and to report opinions that disturbed his superior.

Wilson maintained his personal control over foreign policy, finally, by applying the same techniques of leadership of public opinion and of Congress that he used with such spectacular success in domestic struggles. His instruments of public leadership were public papers, statements to the press, and speeches, by means of which he established direct communication with the people and spoke for them in articulating American ideals in foreign policy. Wilson was a spellbinder of immense power during an era when Americans admired oratory above all other political skills, and he was irresistible in leadership so long as he voiced the dominant national sentiments.

The Philosophy and Policies of Woodrow Wilson

In the business of controlling Congress, Wilson's methods were influenced by his conception of the President as the unifying force in the federal government. Believing as he did that the President alone was responsible for the conduct of foreign relations, he had no thought of a genuine collaboration with the legislative branch in the formulation of policies abroad. Believing as he did in party government and responsibility, Wilson never seriously considered a bipartisan approach to foreign policy. To be sure, he took careful pains to render periodic accountings to the members of the House and Senate foreign affairs committees. On several occasions he even asked Congress to approve policies that he had already decided to pursue. Yet one has the suspicion that on all these occasions he was simply observing certain forms in order to buy congressional support cheaply.

The most revealing examples of Wilson's methods of dealing with Congress on matters of foreign policy arose, after all, not during periods of quietude and agreement but during times of sharp controversy with the legislative branch. Wilson's leadership was challenged by a threatened or an actual revolt in Congress on three occasions—in 1914, during the debate over the repeal of a provision in the Panama Canal Act of 1912 exempting American coastwise shipping from the payment of tolls; in 1916, over the issue of the right of Americans to travel in safety on belligerent, armed merchant vessels; and in 1919 and 1920, over ratification of the Treaty of Versailles. To all these challenges Wilson replied with incredible vigor and boldness. In these important tests Wilson revealed his conviction that in foreign affairs the President should lead and the Congress should follow.

CHAPTER TEN

Woodrow Wilson: His Education in World Affairs*

By
William L. Langer

Few statesmen of modern times were in their own day raised so high in the public esteem as Woodrow Wilson or cast down so deeply into disrepute. Less than two score years ago, during the American participation in World War I, he was hailed as the leader in the crusade for democracy—the man to whom millions in the enemy countries as well as in the Allied nations looked as the champion of the just peace and the harbinger of a new and better international order. Yet when he died five years later Wilson was a broken man whose passing aroused a measure of public sympathy but little more. America's crusading days were forgotten, and the country was delighted to return to normalcy, which was equated with isolation and material prosperity. Peace and the new world order were relegated to the realm of dreams, while Wilson's attempted world leadership was widely regarded as an ill-advised, not to say dangerous, aberration.

Within yet another decade compassion had turned into active hostility. As the world sank into the Great Depression, as totalitarianism made gigantic strides in Europe, as collective action for peace became enfeebled and the threat of Fascist-Nazi aggression became immediate, Wilson appeared to more and more of his countrymen as the man who had foolishly abandoned blessed isolation and had purposively involved his people in all the tribulations of world politics. Others went so far as to stamp him a hypocrite who, having secured a re-election in November, 1916, on a platform of continued neutrality, straightway took the country into war against the Central Powers. Many welcomed the

---

* Address delivered at the Harvard Commemoration of the Birth of Woodrow Wilson, March 7, 1956. This is an abridgment of two lectures given at Bryn Mawr College, January 5 and 6, 1956, and is printed by courtesy of the University of Pennsylvania Press.

supposed "findings" of the Nye Committee, which pictured Wilson as a simple-minded professor, easily misled by British propaganda and unwittingly victimized by powerful banking and munitions interests intent on driving the country into war so as to safeguard their huge investment in the Allied cause. Even the more charitable could see in Wilson little more than a starry-eyed idealist who, overlooking or ignoring the real interests of the United States, staked all on an impossible program for peace, only to be completely outmaneuvered by slick European politicians. All he got for his pains, it was said, was a paper scheme for a League of Nations, and even this he could not prevail upon the Senate to ratify without reservations, on which, again, he was too inept or too obstinate to accept a reasonable compromise.

The years that have elapsed since the outbreak of World War II have taught the American people many painful lessons, and with this learning there has come a revival of interest in, and appreciation of, Wilson's aims and policies. It is now easy to see how desperate in the 1930's was the need for collective action to forestall totalitarian aggression and how ineffectual League action was bound to be, failing the full participation or support of the United States. The experience of 1939–41, in turn, revealed the weakness if not the hopelessness of traditional neutrality, to say nothing of isolation. The American people, albeit haltingly and reluctantly, were driven by events to recognize their immense stake in the security of the Atlantic sea-lanes and consequently in the continued independence and integrity of the United Kingdom. The genuine and wholehearted participation of the United States in the establishment of the United Nations and the strong American initiative in the Korean crisis of June, 1950, are eloquent proofs of the now general acceptance of Wilson's doctrine. The main features of his foreign policy are no longer controversial, and it would therefore hardly be worth the time and effort necessary to refute the preposterous charges brought against him twenty years ago. Most of his principles and policies have, indeed, become integral parts of American thinking on world problems. If the world of today, instead of living in peace and harmony, is racked by cold war and plagued by the nightmare of atomic annihilation, the explanation is clearly not to be sought in too much, but rather in too little, of Wilsonism.

Wilson, like many great men, was patently in advance of his time. In one of his early addresses he remarked of Edmund Burke, whom he admired greatly, that he had been not only wise too soon but wise too much, for "he went on from the wisdom of today to the wisdom of tomorrow, to the wisdom which is for all time," and it was impossible that ordinary mortals should have followed him so far. The same might surely be said with equal justice of Wilson, the grandeur of whose principles, the strength of whose convictions, and the depth of whose faith tended to blind him to the meanness of human nature and the realities of political life. But, this having been said, it should be realized that Wilson did not arrive at his program solely by way of inspiration but also by way of harsh experience.

On his advent to the Presidency he was still living in a cloud of misapprehension about international affairs. Only under the steady pressure of events did he gradually fight free of illusion and face up to even the most unpleasant aspects of reality. The lessons he learned were those that the American people were ultimately also to learn, but Wilson was forced by circumstances and by the requirements of his own personality to apprehend in three years what it took most Americans thirty years to grasp. To review some of these lessons will not only clarify his statesmanship but will also illuminate some of the basic issues which have determined and still do determine the action of the United States on the world stage.

Long before the onset of World War I, Wilson had, like a small minority of American statesmen and writers, come to the conclusion that isolation, however desirable, was rapidly becoming impossible for the United States. The passing of the frontier, the ever developing domestic pressures, the constant multiplication and acceleration of communications, and many other factors were making it imperative that the country assume its fair share of responsibility in world affairs just as it was demanding its fair share of opportunity. But Wilson did not pursue this idea to anything like the point eventually reached by such as Admiral Alfred Thayer Mahan or even President Theodore Roosevelt. For him participation in world affairs continued to mean little more than the use of American influence and power in behalf of arbitration, mediation, and, in general, organization and action for international peace. He was interested primarily in domestic politics, and he went abroad merely for short pleasure tours in Britain or possibly France. There is no evidence that he ever studied the details of any foreign issue, and it is hard to escape the harsh conclusion that the breaking of the storm in Europe in 1914 found the President of the United States woefully ignorant of, and still utterly indifferent to, the origins and issues of the cataclysm. As late as 1916 and even 1917 he could refer to the European war as "a drunken brawl in a public house" and could expose himself to obloquy by stating publicly that Americans had no concern with the causes and objects of the conflict.

The fact of the matter was that the President regarded the war as merely the latest manifestation of the ruthless ambition and political amorality of the European states, the details of which were as unimportant as they were unedifying. In these circumstances it was the sole mission of the United States to offer mediation and to use its influence and power to put an end to hostilities and to see that peace, when concluded, was so reasonable and just as to make future conflict unlikely. This mission he attempted to fulfil when the war was only a few days old. In the sequel he was to renew his effort repeatedly, each time with greater insistency. He found, however, that the belligerents had no desire for American intervention; that, on the contrary, they were determined to avoid it at all costs.

Nothing is more instructive in this connection than the story of the second mission of Colonel House to Europe in the early months of 1916. The purpose of his mission was to arrange for a conference of the belligerents under American auspices in the hope of putting an end to the hostilities and in this way forestalling the growing danger of American involvement. Knowing from past experience that the British and French were, if anything, even more opposed to American interference than were the Germans, the President was willing to make substantial concessions to secure the concurrence of the London government. Through House he offered to leave the date for the convocation of the conference to the British, which meant that they could fight on until their cause appeared hopeless, at which time they could count on American intervention. Furthermore, Mr. Wilson was prepared to promise that at the prospective conference he would use his best efforts to insure that the peace terms were "not unfavorable" to the Allied side. In the event of German refusal to attend the conference, the President stated through House, the United States would probably enter the war on the Allied side.

This extraordinary proposal was agreed to by the British Foreign Secretary, Sir Edward Grey, but the British government made no move to take advantage of what was tantamount to an American offer to intervene in the conflict unless the Germans agreed to come to the conference table and accept terms "not unfavorable" to the Allies. Mr.

Wilson and Colonel House were surprised and deeply disappointed that nothing came of their plan. From this time on they became more and more intolerant of the highhanded British treatment of neutral trade and even more suspicious of the war aims of the Entente Powers.

The point is that the experience of the years of American neutrality taught the President not only that continued neutrality was impossible if one or another of the belligerents chose to violate it in the hope of early victory but also that great nations, once they are locked in mortal combat, consider that they must fight on until their vital interests and particularly their national security is fully assured. They will not, if they possibly can help it, accept foreign mediation which means, to all intents and purposes, decision by an outside power with respect to the basic interests of the nation. The British desired American participation in the war against Germany, certainly, but not if it involved acceptance of American direction in the making of the peace. Even so liberal and well-disposed a person as Sir Edward Grey would have none of American mediation if it could in any way be avoided. The lesson which Mr. Wilson had drummed into his mind in these years was that the European powers were fighting not out of mere cussedness but out of the deep conviction that their independence, security, and prosperity depended upon victory. They would accept outside interference only if backed by overwhelming military and economic power. In short, he was brought to realize that the nation that desires to play a leading role in international affairs must have the knowledge to act intelligently and understandingly; it must have the power necessary to reinforce its policies and decisions; and it must be willing to assume an appropriate share of responsibility for the consequences of its acts.

The President's abortive attempts to engineer peace on American terms soon dispelled whatever illusions he may have had about the ultimate aims of the belligerents. "The fight," said Mr. Lloyd George in the autumn of 1916, "must be to the finish—to a knock-out." To this Sir Edward Grey, in a secret memorandum to the cabinet at the same time, added: "As long as the naval and military authorities believe that Germany can be defeated and satisfactory terms of peace can eventually be dictated to her, peace is premature, and to contemplate it is to betray the interests of this country and of the Allies." In a word, not even the monstrous losses of human life suffered by both sides would bring them to yield. All the belligerents were set on a total victory that would permit them to impose their terms on their enemies. They were equally decided that those terms should not only insure substantial territorial and economic gains but should also leave the vanquished helpless to wage another major war in the foreseeable future.

Mr. Wilson was quick to see that under these conditions the outlook for durable peace was dim indeed. His espousal of the program for a League of Nations (May, 1916) no doubt reflected his realization that nations could be dissuaded from imposing Draconian terms on their vanquished enemy only if their security could be guaranteed through an international organization providing for collective action against aggression. At any rate when, on the very eve of American involvement in the conflict, the President addressed the Senate on January 22, 1917, his thought had taken full form and he unflinchingly presented a program of "peace without victory." Though this program was anathema to the activists of that day, the experiences of the next generation were to be such as to make it worthy of further reflection. "Victory would mean peace forced upon the loser, a victor's terms imposed upon the vanquished," Mr. Wilson warned. "It would be accepted in humiliation, under duress, at an intolerable sacrifice, and would have a sting, a resentment, a bitter memory upon which terms of peace would rest, not permanently, but only as upon quicksand." A durable peace could not be based on a victor's terms but could be only a peace without victory: "Only a peace between equals can last. Only a peace the very principle of which is equality and a common participation in a common benefit. The right state of mind, the right feeling between nations, is as necessary for a lasting peace as is the just settlement of vexed questions of territory or of racial and national allegiance."

When, after the entry of the United States into the war, the President learned of the secret treaties between the Allied governments, he must have felt that his worst apprehensions had proved well founded. During the summer of 1917 he had Colonel House organize a group of scholars to study the various issues to come before the future peace conference and above all to make policy recommendations with respect to them. The publication of the secret treaties by the Bolsheviks in November, 1917, obliged the Western Powers to pronounce themselves publicly on their war and peace aims. It was this situation that produced the Fourteen Points (January 8, 1918), which at once became basic to the American position. It may be remembered that the President's programmatic address to Congress was anticipated by the British Prime Minister's speech to the British Trade Union Congress on January 5. A comparison of the Wilson and Lloyd George programs leaves no room for doubt that by this time the two statesmen were openly competing for control of the prospective peace negotiations.

Fate decreed that the Germans should put greater trust in the President than in the Prime Minister. When the time came for the imperial government to sue for an armistice, it turned to Mr. Wilson with the request that he arrange peace negotiations on the basis of the Fourteen Points. For three weeks the President discussed the details of this matter with the Germans without even consulting the Allied governments. Only after he had secured German acceptance of his conditions did he lay his proposal before the Allies to either take it or leave it. Colonel House, sent to Europe to secure official acceptance of the Fourteen Points, met with such resistance that he found it necessary to suggest the possibility of a separate peace between the United States and Germany if the Allies refused to conclude an armistice and negotiate a settlement based on the principles and terms already accepted by the Germans.

To the President the distinction between a victor's peace and a just peace was crucial. He had learned from his dealings with European governments what a punitive, dictated peace might involve, and he knew that only a just peace, resting on an international organization to provide security, could endure. In a speech on the eve of his negotiations with the Germans he had stressed that "the impartial justice meted out must involve no discrimination between those to whom we wish to be just and those to whom we do not wish to be just. It must be a justice that plays no favorites and knows no standard but the equal rights of the several peoples concerned." The record leaves no doubt that he was determined to prevent Germany's being ground under foot or even condemned without a hearing. It was his full intent that the vanquished should have a chance to state their case and that the peace should be a negotiated, not a dictated, one. Furthermore, the Germans were to be members of the League of Nations from the outset and free to appeal to the League for the revision of any injustices that might appear in the settlement. Unfortunately, developments took a very different turn. The peace that was ruthlessly imposed at Versailles was far harsher than what the Fourteen Points envisaged. Had the President's principles and plans prevailed, the world would undoubtedly have been spared much later woe.

Opinion has always been much divided with respect to the President's decision to attend the Peace Conference in person. Obviously his doing so had many disadvantages, especially with respect to the domestic political situation. But it is hard to see how he could have done otherwise if one bears in mind the situation as he saw it. Expecting serious conflict with Allied statesmen over peace terms, he considered it indispensable to be on the scene himself at least for a few weeks while the League of Nations was being organized. And in this connection, too, Mr. Wilson learned fundamental lessons. Originally he had thought of the League as a very loose organization, hardly more than a covenant between states committing them to peace and to collective action against peace-breakers. To the very eve of the peace negotiations he had resisted commitment to any of the quite numerous detailed schemes for international organization and had stuck by his conviction that nothing more than an ambassadorial conference was needed to serve as supreme tribunal and executive organ. But, once the issue came under debate, he soon realized that without much more detailed organization effective action would be difficult if not impossible, that the rights and responsibilities of member states would have to be scrupulously defined, and that the preservation of peace involved so many factors as to make fairly elaborate administrative machinery imperative.

With respect to the actual terms of the Treaty of Versailles, the idea has become well established that Mr. Wilson was so wrapped up in the drafting of the League Covenant and so intent on securing its approval by his European colleagues that he unwittingly permitted Lloyd George, Clemenceau, and other statesmen to work out a highly punitive settlement fundamentally at variance with the Fourteen Points. This is certainly an oversimplified statement, for it can be shown that the harshness of the Versailles Treaty was due to many factors, most of them complex. Among other things the President's lack of information and understanding of concrete questions had much to do with some of the objectionable decisions. President Emeritus Seymour of Yale has recorded the fact that Mr. Wilson was surprised to learn that millions of Germans lived in the territory assigned to the new Czechoslovakia. "Why!" he exclaimed, "Masaryk did not tell me that." His hasty recognition of the Italian claim to the Brenner frontier was clearly another instance of action taken in ignorance of basic facts. His staff experts were, to be sure, well equipped with statistical and other factual data. On technical matters, such as reparations, their judgment, too, was remarkably sound. On the other hand, they lacked the politi-

cal experience and judgment to sense the errors inherent in many decisions. Were this not so, it would be hard to explain the readiness of
both the experts and the President to assume what soon proved to have
been fantastically heavy and even dangerous commitments in the Middle East. Surely the American experience at Paris demonstrated to the
hilt the need for deep knowledge as a prerequisite of effective leadership in international affairs.

The President must furthermore have learned that too much reliance
must not be put upon public opinion, for it would seem that he made
his greatest error in this connection. It is generally agreed that during
the war Mr. Wilson had proved himself a master propagandist and that,
through his speeches and diplomatic notes, he had succeeded in under-
mining the morale of the enemy peoples as much as in firing the imagination and war spirit of the Allied populations. The ovations with
which he was received in Europe in December, 1918, were so enthusiastic as to warrant his thinking that his program had the support of the
peoples of the world and that therefore he would, in any crisis, be able
to prevail against the old-fashioned politicians. This proved very definitely not to be the case. Europeans were undoubtedly sincere in hailing Wilson for his and his country's contribution to victory, but the
elections held in both Britain and France that same December left not
a shadow of doubt that there was strong and widespread sentiment for
a "tough" peace. The spring of 1919 demonstrated with equal clarity
that people everywhere were intent on providing for their future security and attaining their national aspirations. Wilson's attempt to
appeal to the Italians over the heads of their leaders was a pathetic
failure. Other examples could be cited to prove how strong was the
popular pressure for a "realistic" settlement. It is well known that the
French were profoundly disappointed by the failure of their statesmen
to secure the detachment of the Rhineland from Germany. And it
should be remembered that the allegedly "idealistic" American people
were no less implacable. For the most part they were opposed to an
armistice in November, 1918, and shared Pershing's desire to annihilate
the German armies and dictate peace in Berlin. In the sequel little objection was raised in the United States to the harsh Versailles Treaty
itself. On the contrary, opposition was directed almost entirely at the
well-intentioned Covenant of the League of Nations, which had been
made an integral part of the treaty.

Experience, then, showed and in fact proved that Mr. Wilson was wrong in his effort to draw a distinction between governments and peoples and in thinking that the common man would support his program in preference to the search for security in traditional terms. Speaking of the senatorial opposition to the League, the President once remarked that his adversaries did not know what the people were thinking: "They are as far from the people, the great mass of the people, as I am from Mars." On another occasion he declared that he was not obeying the mandate of party or politics but the mandate of mankind, "the great compulsion of the Common Conscience." When his breakdown came in September, 1919, he was off stumping the country because he would not believe that the people, if they knew the full facts, would not insist on ratification of the Covenant of the League. It is by no means certain that Mr. Wilson himself was ever prepared to admit his mistake in relying too simply on public opinion. But his speaking tour in the West shows that at least belatedly he saw the need for much greater information and instruction of the public mind. The common man may by instinct favor what is good and noble, but one can hardly escape the conviction that modern, total war involves such an effort and requires such incitation of aggressive impulses and hostile sentiments that, in the hour of victory, it is hardly possible to gear down and create a climate in which a just and reasonable settlement would find popular support. If indeed Mr. Wilson could never bring himself to acknowledge this, it is nonetheless essential that mankind understand that modern war, from its very nature, precludes any improvement in international relationships. On the contrary, its legacy promises always to be the heightening of old, and the creation of new, antagonisms.

CHAPTER ELEVEN

Woodrow Wilson in Perspective*

By
Charles Seymour

Toward the close of Woodrow Wilson's campaign for re-election to the Presidency of the United States, at a moment when prospects seemed unpromising, he remarked: "As compared with the verdict of the next twenty-five years, I do not care a peppercorn about the verdict of 1916." When those twenty-five years had passed, the verdict, if taken, would have been blurred by our intervention in World War II. How far has the situation been clarified at the present moment, thirty-two years after Wilson's death, one hundred years after his birth? In the case of Abraham Lincoln, the perspective of far less elapsed time authorized his admission to the Valhalla of American greatness. The same is true, with varying emphasis, of the founding fathers of the Republic. But since the death of Lincoln, no clear-cut agreement on immortal greatness in the case of any American President has been achieved.

The claims of Wilson to inclusion in the select group cannot be summarily brushed aside. The significance of the reforms he advocated in vital phases of American life is hardly disputed. The nation has soberly accepted the purposes and the policies which at the time that he first urged them aroused a spirit of bitter controversy. This is true of his educational leadership and of the legislative program of his first term as President of the United States. The tide of history has made it true of the last phase, Wilson's heroic effort to bring the United States into a system of international co-operation. With little dissent, Americans have come to take it for granted that the counterpart of the League, the United Nations, is to be what Allen Dulles has called "our workshop of peace." Whatever the rebuffs at Princeton and in the

* Reprinted by special permission from *Foreign Affairs*, XXXIV (January, 1956), 175–86. Copyright by Council on Foreign Relations, Inc., New York.

United States Senate, succeeding years have vindicated his vision and his policy.

Thus it is eminently fitting that as political passions have cooled and personal prejudice softened, fresh consideration should be given to the position in American history that belongs to Woodrow Wilson. The verdict of public opinion as well as of the historian has not yet been rendered in unmistakable form. In what category and at what level is he finally to be placed?

The importance of Wilson as educational leader has become definitely established with the passing of the years. That leadership has not attracted the public attention in like degree with his direction of the movement for international organization. But in itself, and if he had never entered politics, it would have assured him permanent distinction. He brought an educational ideal to the college world at a moment when Princeton and the nation most needed it. It was not original with him, but there was no one who expressed it so clearly and persuasively. His courage in the rejection of the free elective system was matched by his insistence upon teaching quality which would stimulate the student to sincere interest in and positive enjoyment of study. Thus the main circus was to regain its dominance over the extracurricular sideshows. His preceptorial plan was only one of various methods by which the curiosity and intellectual effort of the student might be aroused. But it caught the imagination of the academic world. The enthusiasm of the young perceptors aroused their colleagues in other institutions. The power of Wilson's provocative arguments for the serious values of college life was infectious. Hence the influence of the Princeton experience served impressively in the general recrudescence of literary and intellectual interest on the American campus.

The controversies which Wilson encountered at Princeton would doubtless have been accepted by most college executives as an inevitable irritation incidental to the office. What seemed to him as defeat, however, coincided with the opportunity to enter politics, his early dream. Thus began, with his success in New Jersey and his astounding advance to the Presidency of the United States, the second phase of his public service. As at Princeton, the earlier aspects of his national political leadership were characterized by almost unbroken success. Indeed, no period of his career since his teaching days has aroused so little controversy and so much praise among historians. They are agreed upon the courage and skill with which he translated an ambitious program of reform into legislation.

In his formulation of the principles of the New Freedom, as well as in his successful demand upon Congress for their immediate political application, Wilson closely approached his own ideals of leadership as laid down in his essay of 1890. His sensitive ear caught the tone of national needs and the trend of popular hopes, which were given form and direction by his persuasive rhetoric. The program was progressive in its farewell to laissez faire; it was conservative in its antisocialistic insistence that the authority of government should be used not for the operation but for the liberation of business. Adlai Stevenson points out that "he taught us to distinguish between governmental action that takes over the functions formerly discharged by individuals and governmental action that restores opportunity for individual action." Hence the significant subtitle of his collected campaign speeches, *A Call for the Emancipation of the Generous Energies of a People*. He sought in the national arena the equality of opportunity which he had enjoined upon Princeton, the enlargement of the frontiers of freedom which was to be the watchword of his international crusade.

The legislation of the first two years of his Presidency dealt with crucial and contentious issues: the tariff, currency reform, the establishment of the Federal Trade Commission, the Clayton Antitrust Act. Wilson's success in achievement in the face of bitter opposition astounded his contemporaries. "This man who was regarded as a pedagogue, a theorist," said Chauncey Depew, "is accomplishing the most astounding practical results."

Of greater historical importance than any contemporary estimate is the almost complete indorsement, over the years, of Wilson's reform program, one that went far toward creating a new social and economic atmosphere. The Federal Reserve is universally taken for granted as the pediment of our national financial structure. The use of federal authority to assure competitive conditions in trade has become a permanent aspect of our economic life. Public opinion has come to accept emancipation of labor, in its organization for the betterment of working conditions, from the restrictions designed to control monopolistic tendencies of capital. The solid permanence of Wilson's legislative achievement is impressive.

The march of events has brought it about that Wilson's position in history would be determined not by the contribution he made to

American legislation, important as that was, but rather by the role he played on the international stage. There were three well-defined acts in the drama which began with the outbreak of the European war in August, 1914. The first covered the period of American neutrality, the second that of the active participation of the United States in the war, the third that of the Peace Conference and its aftermath. Wilson's attitude and tactics underwent considerable change during the course of these three periods. But from beginning to end his main purpose was not altered. He was determined to bring the conscience and the power of America into a co-operative effort that would everywhere secure the liberty of all peoples. Whether as a neutral or belligerent or a peace commissioner, Wilson looked upon himself as leader in a crusade for international freedom.

A sense of responsibility to the rest of the world underlay his policy of determined neutrality. His emotions boiled with protest at the suggestion that he chose neutrality merely as the road to safety. It was imposed upon us, rather, in fulfilment of our duty as the only great neutral at peace, "the one people holding itself ready to play a part of impartial mediation and speak the counsels of peace and accommodation, not as a partisan, but as a friend." His insistence was constant, and today it is recognized as sincere, that we would serve better by remaining outside the conflict. His determination to protect the rights of America against the attacks of the German submarines and the infringements of the British blockade led him finally to espouse the movement for national preparedness. But his call for military armament stressed not merely our rights but our responsibility for the salvation of the equipoise of the world and "the redemption of the affairs of mankind."

Hence his persistent eagerness in the search for effective methods of mediation, and his constant encouragement to Colonel House in the effort to discover some basis for a compromise peace. Wilson's personal sympathy for the cause of the Entente Allies did not at any time during the period of our neutrality disturb his conviction that such a peace would prove the only sure basis of a permanent settlement. This conviction was at its firmest and clearest as he came to discuss specifically conditions essential to international security, immediately before the break with Germany, in January of 1917. His public suggestion of a "peace without victory" proved offensive to the belligerents and a diplomatic impossibility. But Wilson was quite right in maintaining that a victor's terms imposed upon the vanquished would be "accepted in humiliation, under duress . . . and would leave a sting, a resentment, a bitter memory upon which terms of peace would rest, not permanently, but only as upon quicksand." The quality of Wilson's foresight was amply borne out in the years that followed the Peace Conference and led to the Hitler regime.

There are few who would suggest today that our interests called for intervention in the war previous to the declaration of the intensive German submarine campaign. On the other hand, the band of critics who in later years assailed Wilson as responsible for unnecessary and ultimately disastrous participation in the war has diminished to the vanishing point. That criticism was most strident twenty years ago. It was stimulated by the sense of betrayal that captured American liberals after the Peace Conference as well as by the ill-documented propaganda emanating from the Nye Committee and culminating in the neutrality legislation of the mid-thirties. But it was short-lived. Even those who today believe that only a compromise peace would have provided the base for a permanent settlement admit that Wilson's hand was forced and that the Germans left him no alternative but to enter the war.

Contemporary criticism of the process by which a peaceful, ill-prepared nation was transformed into a fighting machine has been replaced by enthusiastic recognition of the quality of Wilson's leadership in the war. The unity of national effort which he inspired made possible the astounding contribution of American manpower, finance, and supplies which turned the tide of battle in Europe. But his outstanding demonstration of leadership lay in the war of ideas. Inevitably the attitude of the President toward the belligerents was radically altered by our own belligerency. He could no longer imply that the war aims on either side were the same. It was not difficult for him to frame his indictment against Germany as an international criminal since he had been profoundly shocked, in a personal sense, by the declaration of submarine warfare. Against such a criminal it was necessary to use force without stint or limit. Henceforth he was unwilling to accept any peace except one based upon the absolute defeat of German militarism.

While Wilson as war leader cast his denunciatory and destructive thunderbolts against the German government, he did not fail to stress constructively the ideals of his crusade for freedom, which he inherited from the period of neutrality and which he led on behalf of all peoples. In his Flag Day address of June 14, 1917, perhaps in itself the outstanding example of his wartime rhetoric, he drew the distinction between the "military masters of Germany [who] denied us the right to be neutral" and the German people, "themselves in the grip of the same sinister power that has . . . stretched its ugly talons out and drawn blood from us." He went on to reiterate his ultimate war aims: "This is the People's War, a war for freedom and justice and self-government amongst all the nations of the world, a war to make the world safe for the peoples who live upon it . . . the German peoples themselves included."

So also in his speech of the Fourteen Points, Wilson forged a weapon of psychological warfare at the same time that he drafted a charter of peace. The address failed in its primary purpose of dissuading Russia from negotiations with the enemy. But it drove a deeper wedge between the German government and people, and it presented the latter with the possibilities of an attractive program once their hopes of military victory faded. Germany was offered a place of equality and a guaranty of friendship, "if she is willing to associate herself with us and the other peace-loving nations of the world in covenants of justice and law and fair dealing." Small wonder that, when they were confronted with an imminent military collapse, the Germans turned to Wilson, invoking the Fourteen Points and the succeeding speeches couched in similar terms.

Wilson's program as an instrument of political warfare thus achieved resounding success. It became a determining factor in Allied military victory in 1918. It gave to Wilson himself a moral position of such strength that willy-nilly the British and French leaders in their negotiations with House were compelled to indorse that program. But the Fourteen Points, a powerful weapon of war, were not so well fitted to serve as the design for an international peace settlement. They were at once too general in their statement of abstract principles and too specific in various geographical details. Furthermore, the very success of Wilson's psychological campaign enforced the nationalistic aspirations of the European peoples and thus raised powerful opposition to his international ideals.

Wilson went to the Peace Conference pledged to the fulfilment of a threefold and interlocking concept: the liberation of peoples, justice for all without distinction, the assurance of peace through international organization. In his mind, freedom and justice outweighed in their importance the assurance of peace; he always believed that "the right is more precious than peace." But it was clear that an organized system of security would be essential to the maintenance of a regime of freedom and justice. All three principles must be worked out together in a world-wide association of nations: "A universal dominion of right by such a concert of free peoples as shall bring peace and safety to all nations and make the world itself at last free."

Wilson's chief difficulty lay not so much in the opposition of Allied leaders in Paris, for few would dare openly to oppose such ideals, as in the inherent difficulty of applying general principles to concrete issues. For lack of an explicit program, there was at Paris a high degree of improvisation and of confusion in the effort to solve specific problems in the light of abstractions which were difficult to define.

The recurrent leitmotiv of Wilson's policy lay in his ideal of freedom, whether of the individual or of the national group. But this ideal he found it impossible to formulate at Paris in terms that might find exact expression in an international agreement. The principles of self-government were rather vaguely considered in nineteenth-century concepts, without any clear attempt to reinterpret them in contemporary terms or in the light of political and industrial conditions of central and southeastern Europe. The doctrine of self-determination, expressive of national freedom, Wilson soon discovered to be an untrustworthy guide, incapable of universal application. How was he to decide the validity of conflicting aspirations? Linguistic statistics often proved as unreliable a criterion as the rhetoric of partisan leaders. In various areas he found the principle of self-determination to be in clear conflict with other Wilsonian doctrines. It would seem to justify the separation of the German Sudetenland from Bohemia, an obvious disaster to the Czechoslovak state, itself founded upon the principle of self-determination. Its strict application would have cut in two an economic entity such as the Klagenfurt Basin.

In the approach to these and similar problems Wilson hoped for guidance from the application of the principle of justice, which he had stressed equally as an essential foundation of a liberating and a lasting peace. "It must be a justice that seeks no favors and knows no standards but the equal rights of the several peoples concerned. No special or separate interest of any single nation or any group of nations can be made the basis of any part of the settlement which is not consistent with the common interest of all." As a principle this seemed indisputable.

But when he came to cases at Paris he discovered that there was a conflict of rights as well as of interests. Every government was bound to feel that justice to its own people demanded a protection of national security that often could be achieved only at the expense of another. Even the impartial-minded Americans could not with any confidence apply the principle of justice to specific problems. Crossing to Europe on the "George Washington," Wilson had said to the members of The Inquiry: "Tell me what's right and I'll fight for it. Give me a guaranteed position." But whatever position they might try to guarantee on the basis of justice, a case could be found with which to dispute it. How did the justice of the Polish claim to the Corridor compare with the injustice done to Germany in its establishment? Was the separation of the Saar from the Reich a justifiable reparation for the wanton damage inflicted by German troops on the coal mines of Lens and Valenciennes? As Wilson met Allied leaders day after day, despite the personal irritation of debate, his own attitude toward the strict application of the principle of justice became more fluid.

Wilson's expanding appreciation of the inexorable realities of European politics was manifest in his changed outlook upon the problem of security. This is not to imply that he ever wavered in his conviction that the old system was bankrupt and that the new must be based upon the principle of collective security as expressed in the League of Nations. To that cause he devoted his most impassioned efforts. At the opening of the conference it seemed doubtful whether he could withstand pressure for postponement of the League in favor of the "practical" aspects of the settlement; whether, also, he could secure incorporation of the Covenant as the first and essential portion of the treaty with Germany and the others to follow. His triumph was clear cut. The League became the cornerstone of the treaties. It would serve, Wilson believed, not merely to safeguard the peace but to correct the inequities that were bound to creep into any settlement.

But in the intimate discussions of the Council of Four he came to realize the justified anxiety of the French as to security and the validity of their demand for special guaranties of protection, at least until the League had demonstrated its effective authority. One must read the recently published notes of Professor Mantoux[1] in order to appreciate

---

[1] Paul Mantoux, *Les Délibérations du Conseil des Quatre (24 mars–28 juin 1919)* (2 vols.; Paris: Éditions du Centre National de la Recherche Scientifique, 1955).

the emotional and the logical force of the appeal from Clemenceau. The latter's concept of "strategic security," based upon a demilitarized Rhineland and the fortified bastion of Bohemia in the hands of the Czechs, was recognized by Wilson not as a substitute for but as a regional supplement to collective security. And Wilson was further willing to buttress the defense of France by the agreement that the United States would join with Great Britain, in case of attack by Germany, to defend the French frontier.

These departures from ideological perfection have been pictured as constituting a moral and political surrender by Wilson. But he was indebted to Clemenceau for his acquiescence in the League of Nations, and he had to acknowledge that conditions in Europe went far to justify the latter's policy. Indeed, that policy, properly implemented, might have sufficed to contain Hitler. The same sort of defense can be offered in behalf of various other compromises that Wilson accepted. They were, in his opinion, essential to the completion of the treaties, upon which the revival of the economic as well as the political life of the world depended. Whether Wilson might have salvaged more of his original program is a question still in doubt. On the whole, historical opinion has come to the conclusion that the settlement as agreed upon, had it actually been carried into effect, would have proved practicable and enduring.

The decision of Wilson to adjust to circumstances which he could not alter was made to appear in certain quarters as the bankruptcy of his entire program. The indictment against him was in part the expression of partisan prejudice, but it was chiefly inspired by disappointment. He had aroused hopes that his vision of utopia could obliterate political facts. He now paid the price for the enthusiasm his program had evoked while it was still in the stage of generalities. His position would doubtless have been stronger had he not attempted to rationalize the compromises into such a form that they would fit into the design of his abstract principles. He thereby opened himself to the charge of hypocrisy and to the attack of perfectionists who joined with American isolationists in denunciation of the Versailles Treaty.

But his prestige on the return to Washington in July of 1919 was still sufficient to assure ratification of the treaty and American participation in the League, assuming a reasonably sagacious political approach. At that time Senator Lodge himself, determined that the Republican party should not be split in two, hardly hoped for more than the reservations that would enable him to insist that he and his party had saved American independence from Wilsonian internationalism. But ratification depended upon conciliation of the Republican mild reservationists in such numbers as would compel Lodge to compromise.

The President could not bring himself to make the necessary concessions. His determination was hardened by the psychological effects of his illness and by his isolation from experienced political advisers. When it became clear that a two-thirds vote in the Senate could not be secured except upon the basis of the Lodge reservations, he would have been wise, without indorsing these reservations, to permit his followers to accept them and thus assure ratification. Historical opinion has tended toward the conclusion that since he had compromised in Paris he made a fatal mistake in refusing the compromises in Washington necessary to ratification. It was fatal, at least, in the sense that he thereby destroyed the crowning success of his policies, so nearly achieved, and his own immediate glorification. The action of the Senate, fortified, as it was made to appear, by the election of 1920, kept the United States not merely out of the League but apart from the close participation in European affairs upon which the Versailles Treaty was predicated. The consequences of that withdrawal upon the authority of the League were momentous—no less so upon the relationships of the Great Powers with Germany and among themselves. In the debacle of the thirties, Europe and ultimately the United States paid a heavy price.

Woodrow Wilson completed his term as President in the shadow of political disaster. The indorsement of his program for which he called in the election of 1920 was refused him by an overwhelming vote. The dignity of his attitude in retirement and the pathos of his physical collapse assured him nationwide sympathy. But his dream of American leadership in world organization was dead and in a practical sense forgotten. Comfortably and blindly the United States fell back into the spirit of isolationism.

Abroad, the reputation of Wilson has never recovered from the reaction that followed the Peace Conference and the political disappearance of its leaders. His memory was summarily dismissed by conservative impatience at his attempt to inoculate Europe with his visionary principles and by liberal disappointment consequent upon his readiness to compromise them. Only in Geneva was adequate honor still paid him. The rise and fall of his hold on popular affection may be traced in the streets and squares that were named in tribute to his efforts on behalf of freedom, only to be renamed for some subsequent hero.

Woodrow Wilson in Perspective

On this side of the Atlantic the upswing of opinion in Wilson's favor has been definite. But it has not yet become universal. He has suffered from the clash of contradictory elements in his temperament which affected not only his political career but the later judgment of history. It is by no means easy for the analytical historian to reach clear-cut conclusions in an estimate of Wilson in view of the fact that his political defects proceeded largely and often directly from his personal talents.

His outstanding characteristic as leader was an almost uncanny genius for persuasion, whether by the written or by the spoken word. In both respects Wilson greatly excelled. Through his peculiar and abiding influence upon individuals and upon small groups of high intelligence he exercised unheralded and permanent power in the nation. His outstanding capacity for persuading mankind in the large accounts in chief measure for the emphatic success of his legislative program on behalf of the New Freedom. But there was always the danger that by the very magic of his eloquence he would, like less distinguished evangelists in the religious field, bring his congregation into a process of conversion that was not to prove permanent. Thus he won the enthusiastic support of the people for the League as the chief buttress of American foreign policy; it was a revolutionary but a temporary achievement. Popular devotion to Wilson's great ideal turned out to be merely skin deep and was soon lost in the other issues that beclouded the ill-fated election of 1920.

Another paradox in the public life of Wilson, when one comes to making up the main account, lies in the fact that his noblest attribute, an undeviating faith in principles, became a primary factor in the miscarriage of his plans for establishing those principles as a directive influence in the affairs of the world. No statesman has given to mankind a more cogent and elevated exposition of the infinite power and the enduring righteousness of justice and freedom. But his illusion that such ideals could obliterate the stubborn facts of political life unsettled his policy at Paris and led directly to the disaster which he suffered at the hands of Senator Lodge.

Wilson's reputation has inevitably been heightened by the events of the quarter-century that followed his death. The world received a terrible confirmation of his prophetic vision of the cataclysm which the League of Nations was designed to avert. The establishment of the United Nations consecrated the validity of his leadership, which had been mutilated at Paris and spurned by the United States Senate. Thus the defeat of 1920 became a sacrificial step toward his ultimate justification; and the failure of his League, "a necessary part of the stumbling process," as Secretary Dulles puts it, "by which humanity develops the means for its own self-preservation."

But it would be a grievous error to permit the historical position of Wilson to depend upon the fortunes of any single institution no matter how impressive. It rests rather upon an invincible idea "so greatly conceived and set forth," as Edwin Alderman insisted immediately after Wilson's death, "that it must continue to grow into new and finer form and his fame must grow with it." Entirely apart from his contribution to a tangible instrument of political idealism, whether permanent or fugitive, Wilson is justified by faith. Magnificent in his leadership, he was too far in advance of his time. Men were not ready for the sacrifice of self-interest, the revolution in national outlook which his ideals demanded. But the inspiration of those ideals is permanent, and no one has issued a more compelling call than Wilson's to devotion in their behalf or given a more moving example of undeviating faith in their nobility. Regardless of the ebb and flow of political and historical opinion, he stands forth as among the greatest of all prophets in the cause of international justice and freedom.

Long before entering active politics, in his address on "Leaders of Men," Wilson provided a clue to his own future claim to immortality. "Great reformers," he said, "do not, indeed, observe times and circumstances. Theirs is not a service of opportunity. They have no thought for occasion, no capacity for compromise. They are early vehicles of the Spirit of the Age. They are born of the very times that oppose them . . . theirs to hear the inarticulate voices that stir in the nightwatches, apprising the lonely sentinel of what the day will bring forth."

CHAPTER TWELVE

Woodrow Wilson, Collective Security, and the Lessons of History*

By
Robert E. Osgood

In our foreign relations we have made a revolutionary break with the past; yet we are haunted by the ghosts of history. However dissimilar the two periods may be, we approach the problems of the cold war in the perspective of 1917–41. The events of that momentous quarter-century destroyed America's illusion of isolation and set the stage for its present role as one of the world's two most active interventionists. Through our interpretation of these events we find some meaning and pattern—some historical continuity—in the transformation in our foreign policy. The lessons of history form a bridge between the past and the present. They help us to explain the shattering of our traditional image of the outside world, and they serve as a guide for avoiding the "mistakes" that propelled the nation into its present time of troubles.

Yet precisely because we regard the lessons of history as a bridge between our current adversities and a past with which we are reluctant to break entirely, we seek in these lessons some vindication of our present policies that will establish a bond with our traditional approach to foreign relations. We find this bond, above all, in the lesson of collective security—in the belief that we are now conducting, or should be conducting, our foreign relations according to this principle, which is said to be a true expression of America's mission in the world, but which we failed to live up to after World War I, thereby facilitating a chain of aggression that culminated in World War II.

There is a moral and emotional quality about our belief in collective security that elevates it above a mere historical interpretation to the status of a primary tenet of foreign policy. It is as though we envisioned world affairs as a gigantic morality play, in which every action

* Reprinted by special permission from *Confluence,* V (Winter, 1957), 341–54.

is part of a necessary sequence that punishes national sin and rewards national virtue with perfect justice. The United States, with the burden of history upon its shoulders, is the chief actor in this drama. Because the United States rejected the League of Nations—the story goes—it eventually paid the penalty of involvement in a terrible world war. But now—we repeatedly tell ourselves and the world—we have dedicated American policy to strengthening the system of collective security which we mistakenly rejected in our period of isolation. There is no more prominent theme in American pronouncements on foreign policy throughout the last decade than the affirmation of collective security as the guiding objective of our foreign relations. With a repetitiveness bordering upon incantation, Democratic and Republican spokesmen alike have expounded and justified America's postwar entanglements and interventions in the vocabulary of collective security, as if the god of history could be propitiated by redeeming past errors with declarations of present rectitude.

In this international morality play Woodrow Wilson is, of course, the central figure—a kind of Moses—since it was he who made collective security an American policy, enshrined it in the Covenant of the League of Nations, and then, tragically, failed to gain America's adherence to the instrument he had fashioned. The story of Wilson's vision and the obstruction of that vision is still a poignant episode in our national memory. Today many are doubtful about the wisdom of Wilson's methods in seeking the Senate's consent to the Treaty of Versailles, which incorporated the League Covenant. Robert E. Sherwood has written of Franklin Roosevelt's preoccupation with avoiding Wilson's tactical errors.[1] But the vision of collective security itself remains untarnished in the eyes of the nation as a whole. We regard our present support of the United Nations and our leadership of an anti-Communist coalition as a vindication of Wilson's vision.

No one should begrudge Americans what solace and inspiration they can derive from recanting past errors and pursuing their true historical destiny. The only trouble is that in paying this particular debt to history we are in danger of falsifying Wilson's conception of collective security and—what is much more serious—misconceiving our own.

"Collective security"—a phrase that entered into our vocabulary only

[1] *Roosevelt and Hopkins* (New York: Harper & Bros., 1948), pp. 263, 360, 697, 756–57, 855, 876.

after Wilson's time—can cover a wide range of phenomena, from military alliances to world government; but its significance as a tenet of American foreign policy rests upon the implication it conveys of the moral superiority of organized police action in behalf of the international community over the independent exercise of national power for purely selfish ends. Certainly it was this same moral implication that distinguished Wilson's conception of collective security. Yet a faithful interpretation of Wilson's view of an association of nations reveals how poorly his conception of collective security fits contemporary American practice and how badly the prevailing American conception of collective security is distorted by the efforts to reconcile the two.

President Wilson's conception of collective security posited a system of international organization in which all nations would recognize an obligation to combine against any nation guilty of aggression, as determined by impartial procedures and laws. This conception reflected Wilson's conviction, which emerged in the course of his own futile efforts to uphold America's neutral rights while keeping the nation out of war, that modern war had reached such dimensions that neutrality was no longer possible. Henceforth, he concluded, if peace were to be preserved, all nations would have to subordinate their special, immediate interests to their common, long-run interest in maintaining a system of international law and order. All nations would have to regard aggression upon one nation as aggression upon all, instead of each nation resting its security upon its independent power and the power of allies to counter only those aggressions that happened to threaten its special interests. Just as policemen are obliged to combat crime rather than particular criminals as their private interests may dictate, so sovereign nations would be obliged to oppose aggression as such, not merely particular aggressors under particular circumstances. In short, Wilson envisioned nothing less than a community of power, built upon universal obligations, as the indispensable alternative to the outmoded system of the balance of power. He envisioned a "new and more wholesome diplomacy" based upon general principles of law and justice in place of the old-style diplomacy based upon the selfish pursuit of power politics.

Clearly, Wilson's ideal is a far cry from what we call collective security today. We share his appreciation of the necessity of concerting power in order to deter and resist aggression, and we recognize that aggression anywhere in the world is likely to affect our interests in one degree or another. But neither the United States nor any other nation in its right mind is willing to subordinate its special security interests to a hypothetical general interest in maintaining a stable international order, especially if that subordination would impose a claim upon its armed forces. The United States, like every nation, must choose the aggression it opposes and the method of opposition according to the particular circumstances and the calculated effect of alternative courses of action upon its power position. The government may decide that a particular aggression, even though its immediate effect upon national security is slight, poses an ultimate threat to America's power position that demands an effort of resistance; but rationally it must base this decision on the criteria of *Realpolitik* rather than of international law and universal moral principles, regardless of whether the two kinds of criteria happen to coincide. For otherwise the nation would almost certainly place itself in the anomalous position of having squandered its capacity to resist aggression—even its capacity to defend its most vital interests—for the sake of maintaining a system designed to make aggression in general unprofitable.

We have attached the phrase "collective security" primarily to our policies with respect to two types of international arrangements: (1) regional alliances, such as NATO; and (2) the United Nations. But in neither case have we acted in accordance with the principle of collective security as President Wilson envisioned it.

To be sure, the North Atlantic Treaty prescribes that an attack on one member shall be regarded as an attack upon all; but its membership is confined to a group of nations sharing a common security interest, who combined to form a military alliance against a particular potential aggressor; and the obligations it imposes upon its members are narrowly defined so as to serve only that common security interest. The organization will be viable only so long as its members continue to feel the need of combining against the common threat that brought them together in the first place.

This is precisely the kind of entangling alliance, designed to promote a particular alignment of power, that President Wilson hoped would be replaced by a universal concert of nations. Repeatedly, he contrasted such balance-of-power arrangements with his conception of a community of power, which would *disentangle* nations from the kinds of combinations in which they sought only their own separate interests and based their policies on selfish advantage rather than "the general moral judgment of mankind." "If you do not have this universal concert," he declared, "you have what we have always avoided, necessary alignment of this or that nation with one other nation or with some other group of nations."[2] He maintained that although America, true to its traditional principles, had consistently sought to avoid special alignments of power, a *concert* of nations was the very embodiment of the American mission, because we had always sought to be the impartial mediator of justice and right. To perceive the contradiction between Wilson's conception of collective security and our own, one has but to imagine the disastrous effect which the application of universal obligations would have upon NATO: its members, instead of concentrating their armed strength for the defense of a special strategic area, would have to spread their forces throughout the world in order to be prepared to resist aggression wherever it might occur.

The United Nations Charter, like the League Covenant, purports to affirm the universal moral and legal obligations propounded in Wilson's conception of collective security. Like the Covenant, it is based on the principle that all nations have such a compelling interest in maintaining an international system for peace and order that a unilateral resort to violence against any nation constitutes an offense against all. However, in the United Nations, as in the League, collective action against aggression has not actually depended upon all nations subordinating their immediate interests to the welfare of the organization but rather upon the few nations who possess a preponderance of world power displaying unanimous approval of, or at least common acquiescence in, measures for dealing with the situation at hand. This fact is recognized in the provisions of the Charter and Covenant, in official interpretations of them, and, most conspicuously, in the practice of member-nations. Great-power unanimity or acquiescence have, in turn, depended not upon the dictates of universal legal and moral obligations but rather upon the existence of an alignment of interests and a distribution of power such that these nations have found it to their self-interest to support, or at least not actively to resist, measures taken in the name of the international organization. Manifestly, this necessary political condition has existed only sporadically.

[2] R. S. Baker and W. E. Dodd (eds.), *The Public Papers of Woodrow Wilson* (New York: Harper & Bros., 1925–27), VI, 294 (hereinafter cited as "*Public Papers*").

The fact that the preponderance of world power is currently concentrated in the hands of the United States and the Soviet Union, whose interests and aims are antagonistic, only exacerbates the fundamental political difficulties involved in attempting to put the universal obligations of an international organization into practice in a world of sovereign states. In practice, the legal and moral obligations of the United Nations have resulted in collective action to deter or resist aggression only when the configurations of power and interest among United Nations members—and especially the permanent members of the Security Council—have made it to the political advantage of enough nations and the right nations to carry out these obligations or permit others to carry them out.[3] The Korean War, the only time in history when an international organization met aggression with force, is no exception.[4] Thanks to the absence of the Soviet delegate from the Security Council, the American government was able to gain United Nations sanction for an intervention which it had undertaken unilaterally for the sake of its own long-run political interests. As an agent of the United Nations it directed the military operations and bore the overwhelming burden of the fighting with the political support of fifty-three members whose interests coincided to the extent of indorsing American action, and with the military support of fifteen members whose interests warranted sending token forces. To perceive the power-political basis of this collective action under United Nations auspices one has but to imagine how different the political situation would have been had the Korean War resulted from an attack of the South Korean forces upon North Korea, even though legally the United Nations members would have been bound to oppose one aggression as it opposed the other.

This is not to say that the United Nations has had no influence upon the struggle for power in the pursuit of national security. The truth is, rather, that it has added a new dimension to power politics by establishing new procedures and institutional arrangements through which the

[3] Ernst B, Haas has identified and analyzed three types of collective security which have operated within the framework of the United Nations, but the operation of all three has depended upon special configurations of power and interest. "Types of Collective Security: An Examination of Operational Concepts," *American Political Science Review,* XLIX (March, 1955), 40–62.

[4] See *ibid.,* pp. 47–54; Howard C. Johnson and Gerhart Niemeyer, "Collective Security: The Validity of an Ideal," *International Organization,* VIII (February, 1954), 19–35; Arnold Wolfers, "Collective Security and the War in Korea," *Yale Review,* XLIII (Summer, 1954), 481–96.

traditional struggle for power must operate.[5] The point is simply that the kind of power politics that Wilson abhorred has not been abjured in favor of the New Diplomacy, which he expected to spring up around the universal obligations of a concert of nations. No nation is willing to subordinate its special security interests to the general requirements of a system of law designed to protect a hypothetical international community. This being the case, the decisive factor determining the effectiveness or ineffectiveness of collective security arrangements is not their legal and moral obligations but the accompanying configurations of power and interest. If these are the decisive elements, then the breakdown of international security culminating in World War II may properly be attributed to the failure of the United States to concert its power with the status quo nations in checking the expansion of Fascist power, and not, simply, to the failure of the United States to follow Wilson's leadership by joining the League of Nations. And by the same token, the containment of the Soviet Union will depend primarily upon the way in which we manage our power and prestige in competition with the Communist bloc rather than upon the rights and wrongs of national conduct according to the UN Charter.

Nevertheless, the conception of collective security that Wilson expounded remains a powerful influence upon our minds, since it is infinitely more compatible with our traditional image of America's role in the world than the policies we are compelled to pursue in reality. In order to retain a sense of continuity with our traditional outlook we are tempted to bring conception and reality into closer harmony by two methods, neither of which promotes our recognition of the true state of affairs: on the one hand, we read our contemporary practice of collective security into Wilson's conception; on the other hand, we read Wilson's conception of collective security into our own practice.

The first method is, perhaps, of more interest to historians than to anyone else; but in an era in which history has a pervasive influence upon policy, the interpretation of Wilson's conception of collective security is of more than academic significance. In terms of our own experience it is easy to believe that Woodrow Wilson, despite his high-

[5] See Haas, *op. cit.*, pp. 54–60, on "balancing and collective security"; and Hans J. Morgenthau on the "new United Nations," in *Politics among Nations* (2d ed.; New York: Alfred A. Knopf, 1954), pp. 458–64.

flown rhetoric, made concessions to national self-interest and power politics in his mind similar to the ones we make today in practice; that he was really swayed much more by the imperatives of national security and the balance of power and much less by universal principles than he professed to be or, perhaps, than he even realized. It is hard—for the student of international relations, at least—to believe that Wilson meant what he said or knew what he meant when he propounded his conception of collective security, because his views seem so implausible in the light of our contemporary knowledge of the limited efficacy of universal principles in international politics. Certainly, we reason, he must really have understood that the concert of nations he advocated would rest upon a particular configuration of power and interests, even though he preferred to clothe this fact in the palatable generalities of internationalism.

Yet actually Wilson's views are not at all implausible in terms of America's national experience and the assumptions about international relations then prevalent throughout the Western world. Indeed, it would have been truly implausible for Wilson to have demonstrated a political sophistication which—if one excludes the early years of independence—has only appeared in the United States on a significant scale during the past decade or two, under circumstances he could not have imagined in his relatively placid and secure age.

Wilson's conception of collective security was firmly rooted in nineteenth-century liberalism and twentieth-century progressivism. It was perfectly compatible with ideas commonly propounded by the reformers of his age. These ideas revolved about the assumption that as democratic institutions spread throughout the world and as trade and commerce drew nations together, the peoples of the world would gradually acquire a better knowledge of their naturally harmonious interests and would become increasingly willing to act in accordance with them, until eventually (and in the decade before World War I "eventually" might mean within the same generation) all nations would observe the same standards of reasonableness and good will that existed among individuals. Wilson and the great body of international reformers of his age expected that when this stage of human progress should be reached, international society would constitute a universal legal community in which conflicts would be composed according to legal rules enforced by the enlightened opinion of mankind.

These ideas are quite explicit in Wilson's writings, in his public addresses, and in his private letters. If we are to attribute to Wilson a grasp of *Realpolitik* which is not reflected in his words, we must assume one of two things: either his words are sheer ornamentation, a mere rhetorical style of expression unrelated to substantive thoughts, or else they are a deliberate guise, designed to dissemble thoughts which he dared not present in their nakedness. But even after one has made the normal allowances for self-deception and rhetorical expansiveness in public spokesmen, neither of these assumptions seems tenable. Whatever one may think of the quality of his thoughts, no one can deny that Woodrow Wilson thought long and deliberately. His rhetoric was no mere mannerism tacked on to random cerebrations but an integral extension of intellectual and moral convictions, formulated and expressed with remarkable consistency—both publicly and privately—throughout a lifetime of conscious reflection.[6] From his days as a young scholar through the years of his Presidency, Wilson's whole character, the substance of his thoughts, and the nature of his actions manifest a supreme confidence in the power of moral principles to prevail over selfish and material interests. This confidence was particularly marked and its practical consequences especially significant in the sphere of international relations, where Wilson envisioned the United States fulfilling its God-given mission to establish the reign of law and bring about the standards of conduct among nations that applied among individuals.

Where a man's words are so compatible with assumptions that were prevalent in his time and so consistent with his character, the record of his thoughts and his actions, the burden of proof must lie upon those who contend that Wilson actually held some conception of collective security other than the one he so plainly and frequently avowed. The evidence for this contention is extremely fragmentary and tenuous. For example, Edward H. Buehrig, in an excellent account of President Wilson's vain attempt to escape the drift to war, has suggested that his appeal for a "peace without victory" reflected his concealed view that a working peace under a league of nations had to be based on an equilibrium of national power.[7] However, since Wilson himself never avowed this interpretation but, as Buehrig shows, consistently depreci-

---

[6] See Harley Notter's analysis of the development of Wilson's conception of foreign policy from the 1870's to 1917 in *The Origins of the Foreign Policy of Woodrow Wilson* (Baltimore: Johns Hopkins Press, 1937).

[7] *Woodrow Wilson and the Balance of Power* (Bloomington: Indiana University Press, 1955), pp. 144, 260, 264–65, 274.

ated considerations of power as a basis for a league, it seems more reasonable to suppose that Wilson had no more in mind than what he professed: that "the guarantees of a universal covenant" would have to "win the approval of mankind" and that, therefore, a lasting peace settlement, based on a "community of power," had to be a "peace between equals" rather than a harsh, one-sided peace that would serve only the interests of the victors and create deep resentments in the vanquished.[8]

The idea that the observance of universal legal obligations depends upon a favorable balance of power reflects a contemporary interpretation of international organization which is alien to Wilson's way of thinking.[9] It also has antecedents in the legal theory of the eighteenth century; but the early proponents of international law saw more clearly than we that the balance-of-power system is incompatible with the conception of a universal community of nations in which governments subordinate their separate security interests. Thus the German philosopher Christian Wolff reasoned that the mitigation of war through the imposition of legal rules of national conduct would be facilitated by an equilibrium of power among nations, but he also recognized that the balance-of-power system would be unnecessary if states acted perfectly reasonably and fulfilled the obligations toward each other which the law of nature imposed upon them. Precisely because he believed that people could not attain the state of reasonableness that Wilson envisioned, Wolff sanctioned the ceaseless struggles between ever-shift-

[8] Address on January 22, 1917, *Public Papers,* IV, 407–14. Consistent with his desire to preserve America's role as an impartial mediator above power politics, Wilson also intended his appeal for a peace without victory to counter the views of those who wanted America to align herself squarely with Allied interest. Wilson's fear that the disintegration of Germany might permit the advance of Bolshevism may have been another consideration in his mind.

[9] See, for example, Quincy Wright, "International Law and Power and Politics," *Measure,* II (Spring, 1951), 123–45. Wright makes the point that "The difference between a world regime of law and a world regime of power politics is not that the latter rests on balance of power and the former on union of power, but rather that the latter rests on a simple balance and the former on a complex balance." And he concludes, "If a law-governed world is to develop peacefully from the present situation, statesmen must seek to make the balance more complicated." But the dominant characteristic of Wilson's conception of collective security was his stress upon the moral factor, as opposed to material power, as the foundation for the rule of law. As he said in the plenary session of the Peace Conference, February 14, 1919, in speaking of the Covenant, "Throughout this instrument we are depending primarily and chiefly upon one great force, and that is the moral force of the public opinion of the world, the cleansing and clarifying and compelling influences of publicity." David Hunter Miller, *The Drafting of the Covenant* (New York: G. P. Putnam's Sons, 1928), II, 562.

ing power combinations which characterized the political system of his age. Far from subscribing to Wilson's conception of collective security, Wolff stated that it was neither necessary nor desirable that all states should participate in a war against a disturber of the peace. In order to *mitigate* war he put his faith in the prevailing balance-of-power system, by which states entered war or remained neutral as their special interests dictated, and not in the theoretical system Wilson envisioned, which was designed to *abolish* war by obliging states to employ or withhold force as the impartial application of legal rules might prescribe.[10]

The truth is that Wilson's ideas were a product of *his* age and no other. If we appraise his conception of collective security in terms of his own representation of it, we can better appreciate the extent to which it emerged from idealistic assumptions about international relations which are incompatible with the present realities. To be sure, Wilson was not able to fashion the Versailles peace settlement into a perfect embodiment of his conception of collective security; and had he continued as President and had the United States been a member of the League, he would certainly not have been able to conduct foreign policy on the basis of the universal moral and legal principles which he would undoubtedly have continued to affirm. But it is precisely because the United States had not yet ultimately experienced the sobering difficulties of reconciling power politics and international organization that Wilson could expound his conception of universal obligations with such genuine and unambiguous conviction.

Today our approach to collective security cannot help being ambiguous: on the one hand, we covet the symbols of universality that Wilson exalted; yet, on the other hand, we must recognize that our security depends not upon "the guarantees of a universal covenant" but upon the configurations of power in their relation to our special interests. Although we live and act in the world of power politics, we are reluctant to acknowledge a fact so contrary to our traditional image of America's international role. So we try to get the best of both worlds by talking—and to some extent thinking—in terms of Wilson's conception of collective security, while making concessions to

[10] Christian Wolff, *Jus gentium methodo scientifica pertractatum,* English translation of 1764 ed. by Joseph H. Drake (Washington, D.C.: Carnegie Endowment for International Peace, 1934), pp. 330 ff.

power politics on an *ad hoc* basis. If we must also speak the language of power—"situations of strength," "military shield," "massive retaliation," etc.—this does not keep us from seizing every opportunity, especially when expediency and the obligations of the United Nations Charter coincide, to assure ourselves and the world that the determining objective of our policy is really the impartial support of universal law and justice in behalf of the international community. In this way we read Wilson's pure conception of collective security into our own corrupted practice. We envision the United States as leading the civilized world in establishing the reign of law. We see ourselves recanting the mistakes of the past and taking up the banner of peacemaker, which Wilson had so gallantly offered and we had so meanly rejected. In this image of our contemporary role there is enough truth mixed with historical myth to lend the color of a crusade to policies and actions that are repugnant on straight strategic grounds.

But one may wonder what difference it makes if we console ourselves with a myth as long as we are compelled, in practice, to conduct our policies as the realities dictate. The only answer is that our longing for the myth may inhibit our adjustment to the realities. The problems of the cold war, the problems of containment, cannot be resolved in terms of the general goals of opposing aggression and upholding collective security. They are concrete military and political problems which require the coherent management of national power according to an over-all strategic plan for achieving specific security objectives. Our commitment to the ideal conception of collective security becomes a liability only when it conceals this necessary basis of action and leaves us caught awkwardly between two worlds—the one, a world of aspirations; the other, a world of power politics—bridged only by a succession of pragmatic improvisations to meet a series of unanticipated crises. We shall be in a better position to avoid this liability when we can retain Wilson's conception as an ultimate aspiration but repay our debt to history with a candid acknowledgment that we live in a world he never envisioned.

PART FOUR

THE PERSPECTIVE

OF THREE DECADES

CHAPTER THIRTEEN

Woodrow Wilson's *Congressional Government* Reconsidered*

By
Roland Young

The assessment of Woodrow Wilson's contribution to American public life and scholarship now being carried on in many forums in this, the centennial of Wilson's birth, makes it timely to assess the value and weigh the arguments of one of Wilson's earliest major political writings, *Congressional Government*.[1] This treatise, written more than seventy years ago when Wilson was twenty-eight years old, is still cited by scholars, if not widely read, and the recent publication of an inexpensive popular edition now makes the book available to a broader public. It is pertinent, then, to inquire what significance the volume holds for us now. Is it of interest because of the light it sheds on the development of Wilson's thinking, or because of the clarity and accuracy of the description of Congress in the early 1800's, or because it transcends the period in which it was written by developing a frame of reference generally useful for examining Congress and other legislative bodies? In different degrees, it is of interest for all three reasons. The book was written when Wilson's ideas were still developing, when he was still testing the strength of his own opinions; and the influence of other writings and other ideas is clearly apparent. It is less satisfactory as a description of the Congress of an earlier period, for Wilson makes little attempt to provide an accurate description of how Congress actually works. Its greatest value so far as this paper is concerned lies in Wilson's criticism of the structure of Congress.

Congressional Government may be classified as an extended argumentative essay in which a point of view is developed. Wilson's en-

---

* Paper delivered at the Annual Meeting of the American Political Science Association, Washington, D.C., September, 1956.

[1] References are to the second edition (Boston: Houghton Mifflin Co., 1885).

gaging literary style, his free use of metaphors and figures of speech, and his penchant for sweeping and often acute generalizations (or moralizations) combine to make a provocative volume which holds the reader's attention. One is left with the impression that the author has read widely (especially in American and English political history), that he writes vigorously (if not always convincingly), and that he holds his opinions strongly, unmodified by reservations or doubts caused by lack of sufficient evidence. In the development of his thesis, the argument is made and remade, stated unequivocally, asserted, deduced, and concluded. There is no wavering, no examination of basic assumptions, and the thesis is drummed in by constant repetition. And the thesis, in brief, is that the leadership of Congress is deficient because it is scattered among the chairmen of some forty-seven House committees and twenty-nine Senate committees.

In developing his theory of legislation, Wilson relies on a rather narrow set of concepts, too narrow, in fact, to be the basis for an adequate analysis of the functioning of Congress or for a comparison of the functioning of Congress with that of other legislatures. He assumes, in short, that certain functions can be performed only within the confines of particular political structures of which the British parliamentary system is the model. His concepts, then, are less useful for analyzing, less useful for describing existing legislative behavior, than for advocating a type of legislative structure which will produce the results he wants. Given the structure, an achievement of the desired purposes is assumed. The structure is the thing.

The compelling quality of Wilson's argument owes something to the restricted nature of the material with which he is concerned. Surplus and tedious detail is stripped away, and the legislature is examined from a few selected points of view. This valuable method provides a means by which the whole can be examined without the distractions of less important minutiae. The main argument, always on the surface, never founders under the weight of surplus detail or unproductive meanderings, but particular importance is thereby given to the selection of appropriate, unifying concepts. An examination of the original purpose of the concepts, however, raises some misgivings about their applicability for describing and analyzing congressional behavior.

Wilson borrowed his model of an ideal legislature from Walter Bagehot, who had used it for describing the workings of the British Parliament in his volume *English Constitution*. The Bagehot description of the operation of the House of Commons became, in Wilson's hands, a prescription for the structure of other national legislatures. Without entering into any controversy over the adequacy of Bagehot's intellectual kit for analyzing the British Parliament, it can nevertheless be said that one borrows with peril sets of concepts developed primarily to describe other structures. The period of the Middle Ages, for example, is replete with attempts to make Roman governmental concepts fit vastly different types of institutions, or in our own day we can see (among many possible choices) the often incongruous application of the American constitutional system in the Republic of Liberia.

The adoption of the Bagehot idea of a model legislature made Wilson's task of analyzing Congress easier than it might have been otherwise. Having a legislative model on hand which might be—which should be!—emulated, Wilson was not compelled to carry on independent research concerning the operation of the American legislature or to test empirically some of the hypotheses which are advanced. It became obvious by inspection that Congress was a different and somewhat inferior kind of bird. In preparing the volume, Wilson undertook no special investigation; held no interviews; did not, although he was living in Baltimore, observe the proceedings of the House or Senate or the operation of the party system; and did not read the relevant legislative documents. In describing the actual organization of Congress, he drew heavily on articles from the *North American Review*. This somewhat cavalier neglect of research was possible because Congress so obviously lacked any form of ministerial responsibility, which was Wilson's chief concern. Any precise knowledge of how Congress actually worked, or managed to work at all (or so well), was irrelevant.

I am not complaining about the absence of detail or even the absence, as such, of any obvious research. It is possible that whatever the extent of research, combined with more knowledge and additional experience, it would have confirmed Wilson's judgment and that Wilson would have reached the same conclusions had he himself been a veteran of Congress for twenty years. However this may be, the reader is not given enough material evidence on which to judge the merits of the case, nor does he have full confidence in the accuracy of Wilson's picture of Congress, which is particularly wooden and unconvincing. What is lacking in facts is made up in rhetoric, and the reader is confronted with a kind of legislative charade in which the chief characters appear to be bumblers one minute and tyrants the next. The chairmen of committees are presented as a group of skulking mediocrities, plotting against the public interest and making government distasteful by their very existence. They appear, in short, to be the type of person with whom one should not associate. Curiously enough, however, it seems that, if one of these petty leaders were to be raised above all his colleagues as the chief of the ministers, his character would undergo a metamorphosis. This one person could then speak with an informed and authoritative voice on all subjects and would represent at one and the same time the majority party, the legislature, the government, the people, and the nation. Here we would have eloquence indeed and leadership and responsibility in abundance.

Wilson makes no special analysis of the character or background of the current membership of Congress, although he strongly believes that men of greater ability would be attracted to seek office if they had some reasonable expectation that their career would extend on into the ministry. As it is, the committee system "makes all the prizes of leadership small, and nowhere gathers power into a few hands." This is "a great drawback" in that "it makes legislative service unattractive to minds of the highest order, to whom the offer of really great place and power at the head of the governing assembly, the supreme council of the nation, would be of all things the most attractive." If the Presidency itself "could be won by distinguished congressional service" no one could doubt "that there would be a notable influx of talents into Congress and a significant elevation of tone and betterment of method in its proceedings."[2] Prior membership in the House of Representatives appears to be a handicap for later service in the Senate, Wilson thought. If the membership of the Senate were made up of men "specially trained for its peculiar duties" it would be more effective "in fulfilling the great function of instructive and business-like debate of public questions."[3]

To one familiar with modern political writing, one of the most striking aspects of the Wilson volume is the lack of appreciation of the significance of process. All action seems to be two-dimensional; there is no awareness of what constitutes a system of action, where interrelated events occur at different periods of time. This neglect of the nature of process within a legislature, or the nature of process of any kind, leads Wilson to pose solutions which often fail to take into

[2] *Ibid.*, p. 206.
[3] *Ibid.*, p. 210.

account other significant factors in the total system of action. The most glaring oversight, it seems to me, is Wilson's apparent failure to recognize the special type of process through which the legislature resolves conflict in society. Legislation is not merely a matter of persuasion through eloquent speeches or of taking votes backed by a party majority. It is essentially a matter of making adjustments and regulating action so that anticipated desires may be met. The legislature is concerned with maladjustments occurring in society, where there are conflicts of purpose and competitive wants, and its function is that of establishing patterns of order in which various purposes can be achieved.

Wilson's failure to recognize process in the creation of legislation causes him to overlook the very nature of group conflict and group representation. We get no clear view of the type of conflict which Congress resolves or of the type of special information which it may need to resolve it. The interest of special groups is alluded to inferentially only in connection with appropriations—and then as a type of activity which is probably reprehensible. He speaks of "the power of corrupt lobbyists to turn legislation to their own uses" and to secure subsidies, pensions, and appropriations. These are "evils inherent in the very nature of Congress" for the power of the lobbyist consists "in the facility afforded him by the committee system."[4]

Wilson's tendency to overlook the nature of process is less apparent in the introductory chapter, where he develops something close to what might now be called an equilibrium theory in his careful discussion of the balances found in the American system of government. Here he is on more familiar ground, and he uses to good advantage his knowledge of American constitutional history and of the development of judicial doctrines by the Supreme Court. He is apprehensive about the centralizing tendency of court decisions, about the willingness of states to seek federal support and of the federal government to spend funds for internal improvements. The most dangerous encroachments are to be apprehended from the legislature, not the executive. "Congress must wantonly go very far outside of the plain and unquestionable meaning of the Constitution, must bump its head directly against all right and precedent, must kick against the very pricks of all well-established rulings and interpretations, before the Supreme Court will offer it any distinct rebuke."[5]

4 *Ibid.*, p. 189.

5 *Ibid.*, pp. 36–37.

Political adjustments of one kind or another are continually occurring, and they are by no means confined to the legislative chamber itself. The legislators (including committee chairmen or ministers) are part of this broader process of resolving conflict in different ways at many levels over a period of time. The nature of the total system of resolving conflict has necessarily some relationship to the system of authority created within the legislature. A ministerial type of government might well develop from a strong party system, but such an organization would depend on the structure of political authority in society fully as much as it would depend on the organization of authority within the legislative chamber itself.

Wilson's criticism of Congress is based in part on his preference for a system where the government in power has the continued support of a political party. He in effect assumes—rather than explains the need for—strong party competition, and the nature of party competition which then existed makes the assumption seem tenable. The control of Congress swayed from party to party, and in 1884, the year the book was published, the Democrats gained the Presidency for the first time since the Civil War. Party competition was close and continuous, and the parties were almost evenly matched. Wilson was not against parties but against their failure to assume firmer control over the instruments of government. To him it seemed "unquestionably and in a high degree desirable that all legislation should distinctly represent the action of parties as parties."[6] The British system was found to be "perfected party government," with no effort being made in the House of Commons "to give the minority a share in law-making."[7] Similarly, he would have the committees of the American Congress "composed entirely of members of the majority."[8]

The type of party system actually in effect in Congress during this period is not clearly revealed, and the few oblique references to some of its characteristics are tantalizing but inadequate. The caucus had more control over votes and over party policy than have the present party conferences, and authority in the House came to a head in the Speaker, who among other perquisites had the power to name (and remove) the members of committees, including the chairmen. By modern standards, this was a long advance toward party control, but Wilson claims that the otherwise beneficial effects of party government

[6] *Ibid.*, p. 97.
[7] *Ibid.*, p. 117.
[8] *Ibid.*, p. 97.

were vitiated by the bipartisan nature of the committee system. This extenuation is too lightly made, for it would seem unlikely that partisanship would be completely dropped when a member was assigned to a committee.

In addition to the nature of partisanship within a committee, one would also like to know something of the nature of policy co-ordination which actually existed and would presumably be found in the relations between the Speaker, the chairmen of committees, and the executive officials. We get little more from Wilson, however, than the statement that "the only bond of cohesion is the caucus, which occasionally whips a party together for co-operative action against the time for casting its vote upon some critical question."[9] Nevertheless, Wilson did not approve of the caucus, this "drilling-ground of the party," as one might expect him to do. "Having no Prime Minister to confer with about the policy of government, as they see members of parliament doing," Wilson explains, "our congressmen confer with each other in caucus," where each party "hastens to remove disrupting debate from the floor," "frightened scruples" are reassured, and "every disagreement healed with a salve of compromise or subdued with the whip of political expediency."[10] How, one might ask, does Wilson propose to hold parties together? Where is the institutional device by which a unified policy can be developed and where all legislation will "distinctly represent the action of parties as parties?"[11] There is a curious lack of reference to the standards for an effective party organization either inside or outside the legislature which would develop party policy, control elections, and instruct the legislators how to vote. One is left with the uncomfortable feeling that all this would be left to one man who in some fashion would be raised high above his colleagues.

With some pruning it would have been possible to have transformed the Speaker-committee system as described by Wilson into something closely resembling a ministerial system. This could have been accomplished by divesting the Speaker of the House of the functions of presiding and making him exclusively a legislative and party leader. He would also have had to become articulate and not merely managerial. When a test of preferences came some years after Wilson wrote, however, the House chose to reduce the Speaker's power rather than remove him from office when there was an obvious lack of confidence.

[9] *Ibid.*, p. 99.

[10] *Ibid.*, p. 327.   [11] *Ibid.*, p. 97.

Wilson's estimate of congressional debate is so colored by standards of British expediency that one does not get a clear impression of the type of debate which was actually carried on. Once again the committees are at fault, for if committees reach agreement on legislation in off-the-record discussions, nothing significant remains to be discussed in the chambers. The effectiveness of Congress in resolving conflict is its crowning glory and its chief reason for existence, and indeed, because making legislation is a process, one might well expect (or hope) that a considerable degree of agreement would be reached before the final debate. In the event the adjustment is formulated in terms of law, it is requisite that a record be made of the reasons which entered into the agreement and the nature of the decision which was made. However, it is neither possible nor desirable that all political conflicts reach a climax in a great legislative debate, with party competition fierce at every stage, and in any event there are limits on time which make it necessary to establish some order of precedence and emphasis in legislative deliberations.

Since Wilson's day committee deliberations have been greatly extended by the development of research facilities and public hearings which provide a conduit through which Congress has access to information relating to the technical feasibility of legislation, policy integration, administrative competence, societal needs, and the type and extent of political support (or opposition) which may be expected. The function of committees in accumulating and digesting information gives the committees an importance which they would not have as narrowly constituted bodies, all of whose members belonged to the same political party.

Wilson was critical of and somewhat ungenerous toward debates in the chambers, which he judged from their effectiveness as expressions of partisan competition. He wanted the ministry "subjected to the most determined attacks and the keenest criticisms of the Opposition," where every day of the session the ministers would be "put to the task of vindicating their course and establishing anew their claim to the confidence of their party."[12] The ministers "must look to it, therefore, not only that their policy be defensible, but that it be valiantly defended also."[13] In actual practice, he found that the House of Representatives did not sit for serious discussion "but to sanction the con-

[12] *Ibid.*, p. 119.
[13] *Ibid.*, p. 120.

clusions of its committees as rapidly as possible."[14] The rules governing debate were "customs which baffle and perplex and astound the new member."[15] There is more than a grain of truth in this criticism, for the stringent controls over time may be used primarily to direct the attention of the House toward the point of climax where a decision is made. However, it is not uniformly true that no serious discussion occurs in the House, for debate there can be rigorous, penetrating, and eloquent.

On the other hand, Wilson found the debates of the Senate to be "of a very high order of excellence,"[16] a merit which was at least partially attributed to the inability to close debate by moving the previous question. In weighing the merits and demerits of oratory, Wilson pointed out that representative government may be "often misled by deceitful pleas and swayed by unwise counsels." On the balance, however, he favored political oratory, as the following favorable judgment reveals: "Men can scarcely be orators," he said, "without that force of character, that readiness of resource, that clearness of vision, that grasp of intellect, that courage of conviction, that earnestness of purpose, and that instinct and capacity for leadership which are the eight horses that draw the triumphal chariot of every leader and ruler of free men."[17] Might not this be a description of the type of leader Wilson himself attempted to emulate?

Wilson's description of fiscal procedures reveals clearly the unsatisfactory method of appropriating money which existed before the passage of the Budget and Accounting Act in 1921. Control was scattered among several committees, and there was no centralized consideration of fiscal policy in the executive branch. Raising the necessary revenue was not so onerous a problem, however, and the discussion of the temptation to make imprudent appropriations because of Treasury surpluses not only makes strange reading but also reveals some historic reasons for the separate consideration of revenue and supply.

Despite the recorded inadequacies of fiscal procedures, there is no suggestion for adopting a budgetary system of the type eventually enacted in 1921 (budget legislation passed in 1920 was vetoed by President Wilson because of provisions governing the appointment and removal of the Comptroller-General). Indeed, in the discussion of revenue and supply we have yet another example of Wilson's failure

14 *Ibid.,* p. 79.   16 *Ibid.,* p. 218.
15 *Ibid.,* p. 77.   17 *Ibid.,* p. 209.

to think in terms of a system, where a series of interrelated functional acts are carried on by different groups over a period of time. The discussion of the work of the Committee on Expenditures, for instance, shows no awareness of the part such a committee might play in the fiscal system other than in the random discovery of unwise or illegal expenditures. No satisfactory theory, no adequate procedures, have yet been developed for supplying Congress with pertinent and useful information on the expenditure of funds.

The analysis of Congress as an agency of review is less well developed than the analysis of its function in enacting legislation, and indeed Wilson considered congressional control to be exercised primarily through laws. The secretaries of the departments "are in the leading-strings of statutes," "all their duties look towards a strict obedience to Congress," and "it is to Congress that they must render account for the conduct of administration."[18] It is not clear precisely who, in Congress, Wilson would have examine the information submitted, for if the committees were composed exclusively of members of a majority, themselves controlled by the ministers submitting the reports, the type of oversight actually achieved would be somewhat lacking in vigor.

Wilson did not believe it essential that the chief administrators be partisans, for they had no initiative of their own and were limited to carrying out policy as determined by Congress in the form of law. Congress kept them on a very short leash, and it was belittling for them to be forced to carry out policy which they did not participate in making. In Wilson's opinion, the leaders of the legislature and the chief administrators should be the same men, and the accountability which the ministers owed to Congress would be enforced by making it mandatory for them to retain a majority. Congress would "have the privilege of dismissing them whenever their service became unsatisfactory."[19]

Under procedures then existing, Wilson believed that "the means which Congress has of controlling the departments and of exercising the searching oversight at which it aims are limited and defective."[20] Intercourse with the President was restricted to the executive message and with the departments to private consultations, informal interviews, and written correspondence. "Even the special, irksome, ungracious investigations which Congress from time to time institutes in its

18 *Ibid.*, p. 262.
19 *Ibid.*, p. 274.
20 *Ibid.*, p. 270.

spasmodic endeavors to dispel or confirm suspicions of malfeasance or of wanton corruption do not afford it more than a glimpse of the inside of a small province of federal administration."[21] Any astute administrator could keep Congress at arm's length.

In considering the merits of Wilson's position, we might at this point consider further the nature of accountability. Although Wilson was of course as anxious as anyone could be that government be responsible, he appears to have taken a somewhat narrow view of the elements by which accountability is achieved. Channels of accountability may flow toward various institutions, and they may flow laterally as well as vertically. One need not assume that accountability is limited to a single type of institutional arrangement, however effectively such an arrangement may operate within Great Britain itself. The essence of accountability is the requirement that action be defended (or defensible) before some individual or group whom the person in authority does not control. Types of accountability are built into the bureaucratic hierarchy, but it does not follow that the administrative structure combined with a party system should monopolize all types of accountability. Accountability extends to the courts, to fiscal control organs, to professions, and, in a non-institutionalized sense, to one's own conscience; and congressional committees provide a type of scrutiny over policy which may not be found within the hierarchy of the bureaucracy. Here is an area worthy of further research, but the research need not begin with the assumption that party majorities exercise the only type of control which is effective or desirable. In some cases, it may be neither. As a random criticism it would seem that legislative scrutiny might lead to such concern for detail as to obscure the broader aims on the basis of which general directions are debated and the lines of conduct are clearly laid out in the form of law. In the long run, law is still the most effective control over government, for by this device the type of permissible action can be closely defined and a bureaucratic structure can be created with its own self-correcting mechanisms.

Another justification for the wide supervision exercised by Congress is closely related to the ultimate acceptance of policy by Congress and the public. Policy of whatever variety must be able to mesh with other behavior in the social system as a whole. It is necessary, in other words, to develop an extensive network of communications which interrelates

21 *Ibid.*, p. 271.

the executive, Congress, and the public at large. It is not necessary that access to government agencies or information about government policy be limited to those in the top echelons (either in public or private). It is not only that malefactors might go undetected or that vertical control is insufficient but that the ensuing policy might be less well integrated with the actual scheme of affairs within society.

The role of the President as described here by Wilson the professor gives only the barest hint of the enlarged function of the office as it developed later under Wilson the President. One even gathers that at the time the book was written Wilson might rather have been a senator! In Wilson's view, the President was not the effective leader of the legislature, except in the negative sense of exercising a veto. Administration did not appear to offer any special challenges inasmuch as the departments had little or no discretionary authority in carrying out the law, and there is no hint given of the possible needs for administrative co-ordination, planning, or consultation. Nor is any hint given of the President's position in foreign affairs, or of his possible war powers, or of his function as commander-in-chief of the Army and Navy. In all, the President emerges as a humble figure who is continually embarrassed by being compelled to carry out law which he has had little or no part in making. The golden period of presidential leadership is found in the past. "There can be little doubt that, had the presidential chair always been filled by men of commanding character, of acknowledged ability, and of thorough political training, it would have continued to be a seat of the highest authority and consideration, the true centre of the federal structure, the real throne of administration, and the frequent source of policies."[22]

The picture of the Congress which emerges is, as has been said, judged by the model of the British House of Commons. However much some may deplore the lack of a ministerial system in the American government, note must nevertheless be made of the ability of Congress to operate over a prolonged period of time without the benefits of such a system. The legislature is able to keep on functioning, despite the ups and downs of the fortunes of political parties, and it does not require the development of a disciplined political majority to be effective. Indeed, it can be claimed that the pattern of behavior where consent and consensus are actually developed within the legislature itself is more prevalent than one operated through disciplined political

[22] *Ibid.,* p. 41.

parties, where consensus may be developed outside the chamber. The pattern of Congress, where policy is formulated through discussion, is also found in city councils and state legislatures, in international organizations and numerous public non-governmental assemblies.

Although Wilson makes a strong indictment of congressional leadership and the committee system, some of the criticism may be discounted as literary hyperbole, and the book on the whole is neither anti-Congress nor antilegislature. Wilson plea is that Congress increase its authority by organizing itself differently and by using its increased authority to exercise greater, more constant, and more effective control over those who administer the great governmental departments. This is a plea for congressional supremacy, not presidential supremacy. Some of the deficiencies Wilson found in the organization of Congress have been lessened by the developing function of the President as co-ordinator. The center of the government, though, was clearly to be Congress; it would weave a web of law over all governmental action, and it would be the agency to which government officials would ultimately be responsible.

CHAPTER FOURTEEN

Congressional Reorganization: Unfinished Business[*]

By
George B. Galloway

The youthful Wilson was the first political scientist who, in his words, "examined minutely and at length that internal organization of Congress which determines its methods of legislation, which shapes its means of governing the executive departments, which contains in it the whole mechanism whereby the policy of the country is in all points directed, and which is therefore an essential branch of constitutional study."[1] What were some of his judgments on the organization of Congress as it stood in 1885 and how valid are they today?

On the question of leadership in Congress, which I shall consider first, Wilson's study of our national legislature led him to conclude that "there are in Congress no authoritative leaders who are the recognized spokesmen of their parties. Power is nowhere concentrated; it is rather deliberately and of set policy scattered amongst many small chiefs . . . [and] the more power is divided the more irresponsible it becomes. . . ."[2] And further:

In a country which governs itself by means of a public meeting, a Congress or a Parliament, a country whose political life is representative, the only real leadership in governmental affairs must be legislative leadership. . . . The leaders, if there be any, must be those who suggest the opinions and rule the actions of the representative body. We have in this country, therefore, no real leadership, because no man is allowed to direct the course of Congress, and there is no way of governing the country save through the Congress, which is supreme.[3]

[*] Paper delivered at the Annual Meeting of the American Political Science Association, Washington, D.C., September, 1956.

[1] *Congressional Government* (15th ed.; Boston: Houghton Mifflin Co., 1900), p. 57.

[2] *Ibid.*, pp. 92–93.

[3] *Ibid.*, pp. 204–5.

Congressional Reorganization: Unfinished Business

After analyzing the organization of the House of Representatives, Wilson examined the structure of the Senate and concluded:

[The Senate] has those same radical defects of organization which weaken the House. Its functions also, like those of the House, are segregated in the prerogatives of numerous Standing Committees. In this regard Congress is all of a piece. . . . So far as its organization controls it, the Senate, notwithstanding the one or two special excellences which make it more temperate and often more rational than the House, has no virtue which marks it as of a different nature. Its proceedings bear most of the characteristic features of committee rule. Its conclusions are suggested now by one set of its members, now by another set, and again by a third; an arrangement which is of course quite effective in its case, as in that of the House, in depriving it of that leadership which is valuable in more ways than in imparting distinct purpose to legislative action, because it concentrates party responsibility, attracts the best talents, and fixes public interest.[4]

In short, Wilson then felt that Congress, "though honest and diligent, [was] meddlesome and inefficient . . . because it [was] 'without the guidance of recognized leaders, without adequate information, and destitute of that organization out of which alone a definite policy can come.' "[5]

The conditions of political leadership have been considerably modified during the past seventy years. During the twentieth century the center of initiative and decision in American politics has been shifting from the legislative to the executive branch in which the top command posts, except the Presidency, are held by appointive officials. The position of Congress in the American system of government is not so supreme today as it was when Wilson wrote his little classic on congressional government. Since then, some fifty administrative departments and agencies created by the Congress have been delegated legislative authority; the annual volume of their published rules vastly exceeds the volume of laws enacted by Congress itself and has perhaps a greater impact on the general population.

National leadership is now widely regarded as a presidential, not a legislative, function. Locally elected and locally responsible, congressmen function frequently as brokers of power, as political middlemen mediating between the claims of competing interest groups in their constituencies and the top political directorate in the executive branch of the national government. The modern role of Congress on the do-

[4] *Ibid.*, pp. 212–13.
[5] *Ibid.*, p. 315.

mestic side is to maintain a balance of power among the conflicting economic and sectional interests of American society. Congress performs this role either by making compromises among, or by giving something in the way of subsidies, benefits, and concessions to, potent interests seriatim. Where an interest is strong and coherent enough, for example, the Southern interest in its sustained opposition to civil rights legislation, it can create a legislative stalemate by resort to dilatory tactics. Southern legislators are past masters in the use of the filibuster and the pigeonhole.

The conditions of leadership within the Congress have also been altered somewhat since 1885. In the House of Representatives the powers of the Speaker, after reaching a peak during the Reed and Cannon regimes, were weakened by the "revolution of 1910," while the position of floor leader was strengthened. The floor leader stands today in a place of great influence and prestige, the acknowledged leader of the majority party on the floor of the House and heir apparent to the Speakership.

Meanwhile, since 1883 the Rules Committee has acquired great powers and has become virtually the key committee of the House. After 1937 this powerful committee ceased to function as an agent of the majority leadership and came under the control of a bipartisan coalition which has been able to exercise an effective veto power over measures favored by the majority party and its leadership, subject of course to the discharge petition.

The net effect of the various changes of the past half-century in the power structure of the House of Representatives has been to diffuse the leadership among a numerous body of leaders. The superstructure which has come to control "overhead" strategy now includes the Speaker, the floor leader, the chairman of Rules, and the party whip. At a somewhat lower echelon are the chairmen of the standing committees, those "elders of the assembly," as Wilson called them, who continue to occupy a pre-eminent place in legislative councils.

An effort to focus responsible leadership in the Senate was made in 1947 when majority and minority policy committees were established. These committees may in time become useful devices for co-ordinating legislative policy-making and integrating party leadership. They have not included committee chairmen as a matter of course and have not yet exercised effective leadership. Thus far they appear to have functioned largely as order-of-business committees. In practice, leadership

in the Senate has been weakened by the forces of federalism and localism. In a federal system like ours, senators are chosen by the people of
particular states, and they naturally tend to identify themselves primarily with state and regional interests. They wear party labels, to be
sure, but their first allegiance is to their constituencies which have sent
them to Washington, rather than to national political parties and the
claims of national interest.

Factionalism within both parties has also handicapped the development
of effective party leadership in the Senate in recent years. As often as
not, legislative action has been controlled by shifting bipartisan coalitions in an almost evenly divided chamber rather than by the majority
party. Party caucuses to determine the party stand on legislative issues
are seldom held and are never binding. And party responsibility for
policy-making is weakened by the operation of the seniority system.
During the first session of the Eight-fourth Congress, however, Senator Lyndon Johnson, majority leader of the Senate, demonstrated exceptional talents in uniting the northern and southern wings of the
Democratic party and in obtaining the passage of an impressive list of
major legislative measures.

Wilson's criticism that Congress was "without adequate information" is no longer valid, thanks to the striking gains made in recent
decades in the staffing of Congress and in the supply of information
furnished by executive agencies and private groups. More than $25
million was appropriated for the staffing of Congress in 1956, and a vast
flood of facts and figures is now at the disposal of the inquiring congressman.

In spite of all these twentieth-century developments, however, Wilson's analysis of the internal organization of Congress is still essentially
sound today. Diffusion continues to be the characteristic feature of
legislative leadership. Congress still operates not as a unified institution
but as a collection of autonomous committees that seldom act in concert. The system of autonomous committees and the selection of committee chairmen on the basis of seniority militate against the development of centralized legislative leadership and the adoption of a coherent
legislative program. The function of leadership is scattered in 1956
among the chairmen of more than 230 "little legislatures" of all types,
including subcommittees, that largely control legislative action. Congressional government is still, in a large sense, "government by the
chairmen of the standing committees of Congress."

Wilson's remedy for the "defects" of diffuse leadership and "the rule of irresponsible committees" lay in the establishment of a system of responsible cabinet government. This could be done, he thought, "by making the leaders of the dominant party in Congress the executive officers of the legislative will; by making them also members of the President's Cabinet, and thus at once the executive chiefs of the departments of State and the leaders of their party on the floor of Congress." Although this proposal is still being seriously advocated today by writers like Professor Corwin and Thomas K. Finletter, and by congressmen like Frederic R. Coudert, Jr., it seems impracticable at this late date in American constitutional history, whatever its intrinsic merits.

A more feasible remedy for the "disintegrate" machinery of Congress was embodied in the 1950 report of the Committee on Political Parties of the American Political Science Association. The authors of this report believed that existing handicaps to effective legislative leadership could be corrected by more responsible party organization in Congress. They suggested that this could be developed by tightening up the internal organization of the congressional parties in both houses through the merger of their various leadership groups into genuine party policy committees; the holding of frequent party conferences; the adoption of party standing orders; and the assumption of majority party responsibility for planning and guiding the legislative agenda, making committee assignments, and selecting committee chairmen. Party discipline could be strengthened by reviving the party caucus with binding decisions, the skilful use of patronage and promotions for the faithful and committee demotions for the disloyal, and perhaps the expulsion of serious offenders from the congressional parties.

These proposals assume a degree of party homogeneity and discipline that does not exist in Congress today. Most major legislation is now the product of bipartisan coalitions and compromises. Party realignments in the future may make these proposals more feasible than they appear at present.

For many years, however, the legislative caucus was the effective "drilling-ground" of the parties in Congress. It served as a corrective of the centrifugal forces of the committee system. Each party had its own caucus, and there were separate caucuses for the two houses. The caucus selected the party's candidates for office in the chamber and formulated and enforced the party's will with respect to legislative action. Decisions reached in caucus concerning legislative policy and program were binding upon the entire membership of the party and controlled their votes. Caucus decisions of the majority party determined the action of the chamber itself. Thus, the line of party responsibility ran straight from the electorate through the majority caucus to the party leadership and membership in Congress.

Woodrow Wilson extolled this type of party government in 1885. It supplied the cohesive and disciplinary force now so lacking in legislative halls. It served "to reduce malcontents and mutineers into submission." As Wilson said: "The silvern speech spent in caucus secures the golden silence maintained on the floor of Congress, making each party rich in concord and happy in cooperation."

It is interesting to recall that the machinery Wilson admired in 1885 reached its apex during the first years of his Presidency. Democrats in Congress listened to the eloquent voice of their leader in the White House and enacted the greater part of his legislative program via the caucus route in both houses. Historians have assigned the credit for the establishment of the Federal Reserve System, the Underwood Tariff Act, the currency and other reforms of the New Freedom era to effective use of the legislative caucus in Congress.

I suggest that the remedy for the defects of the committee system is not to abolish it but to reform it. The committee system will be retained both because it is deeply imbedded in congressional practice and because of its undoubted utility in dividing the labor of the legislative business, screening the bills, and educating the members. The objective of committee reform would be to enable the Congress to recover control of its legislative and investigative processes. This could be done (1) by assigning the selection of the chairmen of the legislative committees to secret ballot of the majority party caucus; (2) by converting the Senate Majority Policy Committee and the House Rules Committee into truly representative agents of the majority party in their respective chambers; and (3) by making these committees responsible for planning the legislative program on the basis of the platform promises of the majority party and for scheduling the order of business on the floor.

On the problem of the control of executive action, which I shall consider next, Wilson wrote in 1885 that "quite as important as legislation is vigilant oversight of administration. . . ."[6] But he added that

[6] *Ibid.,* p. 297.

. . . it is quite evident that the means which Congress has of controlling the departments and of exercising the searching oversight at which it aims are limited and defective. Its intercourse with the President is restricted to the executive messages, and its intercourse with the departments has no easier channels than private consultations between executive officials and the committees, informal interviews of the ministers with individual members of Congress, and the written correspondence which the cabinet officers from time to time address to the presiding officers of the two Houses, at stated intervals, or in response to formal resolutions of inquiry. . . .[7]

And then follows this famous passage:

Even the special, irksome, ungracious investigations which it from time to time institutes in its spasmodic endeavors to dispel or confirm suspicions of malfeasance or of wanton corruption do not accord it more than a glimpse of the inside of a small province of federal administration. Hostile or designing officials can always hold it at arm's length by dexterous evasions and concealments. It can violently disturb, but it cannot often fathom, the waters of the sea in which the bigger fish of the civil service swim and feed. Its dragnet stirs without cleansing the bottom. Unless it have at the head of the departments capable, fearless men, altogether in its confidence and entirely in sympathy with its designs, it is clearly helpless to do more than affright those officials whose consciences are their accusers.[8]

Wilson concluded on this question of controlling the administration that "members of Congress ought not to be censured too severely, however, when they fail to check evil courses on the part of the executive. [For] they have been denied the means of doing so promptly and with effect."[9]

Since Woodrow Wilson wrote these words, the problem of effective supervision of administration has been greatly magnified by the steady growth of executive power induced by recurring economic crises, two world wars, the emergence of the United States as a world power, and the perils of the postwar period. Meanwhile, there has also been a notable increase in the means of legislative liaison with the executive and in the techniques of congressional control of administrative action.

Liaison with the President, while still not entirely satisfactory, has been improved by the weekly meetings at the White House with the leaders of Congress; the personal delivery of the State of the Union messages before joint sessions, a practice revived by Wilson himself; and by the designation of a deputy assistant to the President to handle

[7] *Ibid.*, pp. 270–71.

[8] *Ibid.*, p. 271.   [9] *Ibid.*, p. 302.

congressional relations. President Eisenhower's practice of inviting each member of Congress to a meal at the White House has increased the social intercourse between them.

Meanwhile, liaison with the departments has been improved by the appointment in a few cases of assistant secretaries for congressional relations, by the opening of branch departmental offices on Capitol Hill, and by some recent experiments with question periods at the committee stage. In recent years a few committees have developed the practice of holding periodic or sporadic question-and-review sessions with the officials of executive agencies under their jurisdiction. These meetings afford an opportunity for the review of administrative action, the discussion of citizen complaints, and the reaching of informal understandings concerning administrative policies and procedures.

Aside from these steps toward closer liaison between the legislative and executive branches, three major developments of the past half-century have gone far to correct the defects of the "oversight" function to which Wilson referred in 1885. The first development has been the extension of the function of standing committees from the consideration of bills to the study and control of administration. "Committee government," as Wilson described it in the middle 1880's, was a system primarily if not entirely concerned with "digesting schemes of legislation." Occasional investigations of the executive were conducted by select committees. Today "legislative oversight" has become *a*, if not *the*, principal activity of the standing committees of both houses. There has been an extraordinary increase in the exercise of the investigative function of Congress in recent times. Almost as many inquiries have been conducted by each Congress since 1950 as were carried on in the whole nineteenth century. This amazing development has been due, at least in part, to the directive in Section 136 of the Legislative Reorganization Act of 1946 that "each standing committee of the Senate and the House of Representatives shall exercise continuous watchfulness of the execution . . . of any laws" by the administrative agencies within their jurisdiction.

The great expansion of the investigative function has also been facilitated by the increase in standing committee staffs, which have doubled in the Senate and tripled in the House during the past decade. And it has been stimulated by the revival in 1946 of the long moribund committees on expenditures in the executive departments with authority to study the operation of government at all levels, by the creation of the Permanent Investigations Subcommittee in the Senate in 1948 and the standing Committee on Un-American Activities in the House in 1945, and by the establishment of several new joint standing study and "watchdog" committees in the past ten years including those on the economic report, atomic energy, defense production, and immigration and nationality policy.

With a mandate to watch continuously, with large staffs and ample funds, "committee government" in our time has acquired new significance as a system of inspection and review of administrative performance. The Eighty-third Congress alone authorized upwards of $7.5 million for various probes. Various oversight techniques are employed, some of ancient usage, some of recent vintage. They include question periods at the committee stage (already mentioned), field inspection trips at home and abroad, interim supervision of agency activities, and demands for documents and testimony—all of which have been increasingly used in recent years to strengthen the oversight function of Congress. And they have had many far-reaching effects, of which one of the most spectacular was the forced resignation of Secretary of the Air Force Talbott in 1955.

A comparatively novel weapon in the oversight arsenal is the provision, found in several statutes of recent years, vesting in standing committees the power to approve or disapprove proposed actions of executive officials. Prior committee clearance is now required by law for military real estate transactions, contracts for the development of naval petroleum reserves, construction of military public works, erection of veterans' hospitals, the purchase of public buildings, and the allocation of funds among the states for the interstate highway program. In one case the control of administrative action is placed solely in the hands of the chairman of the House Appropriations Committee. A section of the Defense Appropriation Act of 1956 provided that no business enterprises of the armed forces could be closed if the appropriations committee of either house disapproved, but this section was struck from the new defense money bill by a record vote in the House in May, 1956. These instances indicate an apparent gradual trend toward the participation of Congress in the actual administration of the laws.

The second major development, beginning about thirty-five years ago, has been in the field of fiscal control. Woodrow Wilson reported in 1885 that "the financial administration of the country is in the hands of twenty-four committees of Congress."[10] In 1920 jurisdiction over all appropriations was consolidated in a single House Committee on Appropriations, and the Budget and Accounting Act of the following year set up a national budget system and an independent audit of government accounts. Further improvements in financial administration were provided for by the Budget and Accounting Procedures Act of 1950. Beginning coincidentally in the same year that Wilson left the White House, the modern efforts of Congress to control expenditures have been marked by the close, annual scrutiny of departmental estimates and the enactment of specific, itemized appropriation bills.

In 1945 the House Appropriations Committee was authorized to conduct studies and examinations of the organization and operation of executive departments and agencies, and it has made numerous such studies since. The Legislative Reorganization Act of 1946 contained several provisions designed to strengthen the congressional power of the purse. Outstanding among them was that for the creation of a Joint Budget Committee which was to formulate a legislative budget and fix a ceiling on expenditures. But the Joint Budget Committee has failed to function since 1949; and the provision for expenditure analyses by the Comptroller-General has remained inoperative for a decade owing to lack of funds to implement it. A short-lived attempt at co-ordination in the fiscal field was the consolidation of all the general supply bills in a single package in 1950.

Meanwhile, acting under the Government Corporation Control Act of 1945 and the Budget and Accounting Procedures Act of 1950, the General Accounting Office, as an agency of Congress, has been auditing the financial transactions of executive departments and agencies and has submitted to Congress and its committees more than four hundred audit reports, which have been widely used in considering new and amendatory legislation. Despite these gains, the fiscal machinery of Congress is now dispersed among six full committees and thirty subcommittees, compared with the twenty-four that handled financial affairs in 1885.

The third major development in congressional control of administration has been in the field of administrative regulation. Ten regulatory commissions have been created and granted rule-making powers: the first, the Interstate Commerce Commission (1887), the most recent, the Atomic Energy Commission (1946). Congress exercises oversight

10 *Ibid.*, p. 136.

of these "floating ribs of government" through statutes prescribing the terms and qualifications of their members, through the power of the Senate to reject nominees to them, through the annual appropriation hearings and interim amendments of the basic statutes, through sporadic committee question periods and occasional full-dress investigations of their work, and by requiring them to submit periodic and special reports.

Despite the variety of weapons in the armory of congressional oversight of delegated powers, these methods of inspection and review apparently proved inadequate, especially under the emergency conditions of depression and war. Recurring complaints of abuse of the rule-making power finally led, after long study, to the Federal Administrative Procedure Act of 1946. This act laid down a series of procedural safeguards for the guidance of the rule-makers, prescribing the minimum requirements of fair administrative procedure.

The legislative veto procedure is another safeguard of delegated powers that Congress has repeatedly used in latter years in authorizing reorganizations of the executive branch. Under this procedure, resembling the British system of provisional orders, the President is required to submit reorganization plans before a given date; these will take effect after a specified period unless they are rejected meantime by a simple resolution approved by a constitutional majority of either house.

Such control of executive or administrative action by a congressional resolution is a comparatively recent innovation. Since 1939 many federal statutes have provided that a resolution passed by one or both houses of Congress, without the President's signature, may veto, terminate, or compel executive action. Five types of control of administrative action by simple or concurrent resolution of Congress have received statutory sanction in recent years: (1) veto of action proposed by the President or an executive officer pursuant to a statute, as in the Executive Reorganization Acts of 1939, 1945, and 1949, and the alien deportation statute; (2) terminations of statutes or statutory powers, as in the Lend-Lease Act of 1941 and many other statutes; (3) termination of executive action carried on pursuant to statute, as in the foreign aid statutes; (4) direction of executive action pursuant to a statute, as in the Neutrality Act of 1939; and (5) removal of executive officers, as in the Tennessee Valley Authority Act.

From this sketchy review of developments since 1885, it will be seen that Congress has found new means of supervising the administration and that it has been increasingly vigilant in watching and controlling the government. The unfinished business in this area may be briefly itemized.

It has been suggested, first, that exercise of the investigative function could be improved: by adopting and enforcing standards of fair procedure for the guidance of investigating committees; by delegating the conduct of fact-finding inquiries to mixed commissions like the British Royal Commissions and the Hoover Commissions; and by delegating investigations of charges of official corruption, subversion, and disloyalty to agencies like the Tribunals of Inquiry in Great Britain and the Moreland Commissions in New York State. Some writers have little faith in the proposed codes of fair play because such codes are based on the assumption, believed to be erroneous, that a legislative investigating committee can be made to resemble, and operate like, a court. They suggest, instead, that the subpoena power of standing committees be repealed and, further, that the investigative power be enforced and tested, not by criminal prosecutions as at present, but by court order.

It has been suggested, second, that the power of the purse could be reinforced by: creation of a joint committee on fiscal policy to consider the fiscal policies embodied in the President's budget and the economic report and to provide a fiscal policy framework for the work of the revenue and spending committees; establishment of a joint committee on public accounts to receive and examine the reports of the Comptroller-General; the implementation of Section 206 of the Legislative Reorganization Act, providing for a review by the General Accounting Office of the economy and efficiency of public expenditures; and enactment of the Kennedy Bill (S. 3897, Eighty-fourth Congress), which amends the Budget and Accounting Acts of 1921 and 1950 to permit the submission of budgetary requests for appropriations on an annual accrued expenditure basis, etc. (I have spelled out the case for these proposals elsewhere.[11]) Reinforcement of the spending power is a thorny problem to which there is no pat answer. No one can be certain that a particular proposal for improvement is the right course.

It has been suggested, third, that oversight of administrative regulation and delegated powers could be strengthened by: the creation of a joint standing committee on delegated legislation, to scrutinize quasi-legislative administrative rules and regulations, to draw the attention of

---

[11] See George B. Galloway, *The Legislative Process in Congress* (New York: Thomas Y. Crowell Co., 1953), pp. 660 ff.

Congress to any of them, and to advise about their affirmation or annulment; or, alternatively, the establishment of a standing committee on administrative procedure in each house, as Representative Smith of Virginia has proposed (H. Res. 462, 84th Congress, 2d Session). At hearings in May, 1956, on the Smith resolution, witnesses representing the American Bar Association testified that:

> The proposed committee would evaluate the effects of laws enacted to regulate the procedures of administrative agencies. It also would study the procedures and practices of administrative agencies with a view to determining whether they were in accordance with law, adequately protected public and private rights, avoided undue delay and unnecessary expense, and comported with principles of fair play. No standing committee presently appears to be vested with the jurisdiction to inquire into such matters on an over-all basis throughout the entire executive branch.

Supervision of a powerful administration is a formidable task. The combination of popular control with efficient administrative management is not easy to achieve. It requires continuous readjustment to changing conditions. While general review of executive performance is a proper legislative function, congressional surveillance of the details of administration, under normal conditions, is generally impractical and disruptive. In place of detailed tutelage of the departments, Congress might well endeavor to improve the administrative system and strengthen its internal controls. For the satisfactory performance of its oversight function, Congress must rely in the last analysis upon its standing committees to inspect and review policy execution; and upon the over-all supervisory agencies—the Budget Bureau, the Civil Service Commission, and the General Accounting Office—for surveillance of the details of administrative conduct.

What are the prospects for action, you may ask, on the unfinished business of congressional reorganization? My answer is that they are not bright at the present time. There is scattered support in Congress for particular items on the agenda of reform but no sign of such widespread backing as preceded passage of the Legislative Reorganization Act.

The obstacles to reform were well expressed by Woodrow Wilson in his pioneer essay, "The Study of Administration" (1887). "In government, as in virtue," he said, the hardest of hard things is to make progress. . . . Once the advantage of the reformer was that the sovereign's mind had a definite locality, that it was contained in one man's head, and that consequently it could be gotten at. . . . Now, on the contrary, the reformer is bewildered by the fact that the sovereign's mind has no definite locality, but is contained in a voting majority of several million heads. . . .

Wherever regard for public opinion is a first principle of government, practical reform must be slow and all reform must be full of compromises. . . . Whoever would effect a change in a modern constitutional government must first educate his fellow-citizens to want *some* change. That done, he must persuade them to want the particular change he wants. . . .

Institutions which one generation regards as only a make-shift approximation to the realization of a principle, the next generation honors as the nearest possible approximation to that principle, and the next worships as the principle itself. It takes scarcely three generations for the apotheosis.[12]

[12] In R. S. Baker and W. E. Dodd (eds.), *The Public Papers of Woodrow Wilson* (New York: Harper & Bros., 1925–27), I, 142–43.

CHAPTER FIFTEEN

Wilson the Domestic Reformer*

By
Marshall E. Dimock

Wilson was a reformer, but only because he believed in first principles, in the connectedness of all life and institutions, and because he had a deep reverence and respect for all kinds of peoples; he was not a reformer in the sense of being envious of others, attracted to the idea of class struggle, or attached to the idea of power politics and reform for the sake of partisan advantage. He was a statesman, not a politician.

Briefly, I contend that Wilson was better grounded in economics (more strictly "political economy," or a mixture of economics and political science) than any President before or since; that during the time he was able to concentrate on domestic policy, his two administrations accomplished more of permanent value to sound business-government relationships than any other administration in American history; and that the solutions to most, but not all, of our basic politico-economic problems, even today, are found in the program initiated during his regime.

If it is true that in a free-enterprise system the most important duty of government is to help maintain necessary equilibriums, then Wilson institutionalized more of these stabilizers than any other President, and with a consistent philosophy to guide him: he gave us the Federal Reserve System, which is the basis of credit and monetary stabilities; he gave us the Clayton Act and the Federal Trade Commission, the nearest we have come to putting teeth into enforced competition, which is the basis of a free-enterprise system; and, although I do not claim as much distinctiveness for this, he brought America back to a moderate tariff policy which, today even more than formerly, largely controls our own ability to combat monopoly at home and international economic anarchy in the world at large.

* Reprinted by special permission from the *Virginia Quarterly Review*, XXXII (Autumn, 1956), 546–65.

Wilson the Domestic Reformer

This is not the whole of Wilson's domestic program by any means; it is only the part that seems to me most remarkable because it concentrated upon just those areas where today, even more than in Wilson's time, wise public policy is most needed if freedom of choice and the uninhibited allocation of resources are to be dominant characteristics of the American system.

Other significant legislation attributable to Wilson's executive and legislative leadership may be mentioned. In the field of agriculture, for example, there was the extension of credits through the Farm Loan Bank Act, the regulation of speculation in "futures," improvements in warehousing and the standardization of basic crops, and the promotion of the Agricultural Extension Service. In labor legislation there was the Adamson, or eight-hour day, law for the railroads, legislation for seamen which is the Magna Carta in that field, enlargement of the powers of the Bureau of Mines covering one of the nation's most hazardous industries, creation of the National War Labor Board during World War I, and the organization of the United States Department of Labor, established in the final days of the Taft administration. In public utility regulation there was the enactment of the Federal Water Power Act of 1920, the creation of the federal barge lines and other public corporations in 1918, and passage of the Transportation Act of 1920. In international commerce there was the repeal of the toll-free and monopolistic provisions of the Panama Canal Act, ship purchase legislation that helped to strengthen America's merchant marine by a government building program, and the Webb-Pomerene Export Act of 1918. There was also the passage of the basic immigration laws of 1917 and the development of the resources of Alaska involving a government system of railways and the public leasing of coal fields. Finally there was the extension of citizenship to Puerto Ricans, self-government for Hawaii, and the promise of ultimate independence for the Philippines as earnest of America's anticolonialism and preference for economic and moral influence as contrasted with political domination.

Although this is an imposing total, what it signifies in the way of fundamental philosophy and point of view toward a dynamic political economy is even more important. On rereading Wilson's own writings and what others have said about him, I am more convinced than ever that what we need in 1956—and this applies to both major political parties—can be found in a close study of Wilson's views concerning men, economics, and politics; in other words, the guides we need today are to be found in Wilson's over-all view of political economy.

The Philosophy and Policies of Woodrow Wilson

Wilson was an astute legislative strategist, the best, I suspect, of any in the entire history of the Presidency, despite his failure where the League of Nations was concerned. Although with him legislative leadership was probably more a matter of instinct than of consciously developed technique, nevertheless he was so successful that some evaluation of his leadership techniques seems justified.

The more important rules he seems to have followed are these: first, fight only one major legislative battle at a time; if you attempt several, a stalemate is likely to submerge them all. Second, undertake basic policy reforms in a logical order, so far as possible; for example, when you advance legislation imposing a burden on a particular organized group, such as businessmen, and hence cause resentment, follow this, if you can, with a measure that will do something beneficial for the same group. Third, try to determine your own timetable instead of leaving it to pressure groups, logrolling, or the inclinations of individual lawmakers; this will permit you to pick the best battleground and to work out a solution to a particular problem in relation to the larger strategy. Fourth, do not single out any segment of the country as the continual "whipping boy" of political attack; assume that where antisocial activity is indulged in, it is simply the aberration of the few and not the cussedness of the many, and that the majority of right-minded people, even among the affected interest, is bound to agree with you and support you. Fifth, never be vindictive or punitive in your approach to legislation, but, instead, show how your proposal naturally arises from basic considerations of philosophy and public policy, in which human values are central. Sixth, try if possible to justify your legislative proposal by its consistency with and fundamental contribution to the strengthening of American values and traditions, such as equality of opportunity or the discouragement of special interests and unfair advantage. And, finally, when you talk as a philosopher-ruler, do so in words that are homespun, genuine, deeply moving, and poetical. Out of all his many qualifications for political leadership, this last was probably Wilson's greatest gift.

Almost every major legislative battle that Wilson fought in the first three years of his Presidency—the period when the most was accomplished—seems to bear out these interpretations of his methods. Moreover, I have an idea that even though personality varies in the White House as elsewhere and even though there are clearly two or more methods of accomplishing most things, even as regards leadership and legislation, it is still true that these rules of Wilson's have a considerable validity in (i.e., transferability to) other political situations. I have never heard anyone deny that Wilson was canny, even when they do stoutly deny that he was at times politician and not idealist. He had a genuine sense of strategy that in great leaders stems from an agreeable combination of character, philosophy, human qualities, and powerful intellect, making it possible to achieve solutions characterized by Chester Barnard as "intuitive."

To most people, banking sounds like a pretty dull subject except, as you will recall, during Jackson's administration, or later during the New Deal, when President Roosevelt did nothing to discourage the popular picture of the banker as a first-class malefactor. But on so prosaic a question as the Federal Reserve System with its twelve regional banks under government control, Wilson made the subject understandable and interesting, even to the newspaper reader, because of his ability to explain complex systems in terms of homely philosophy.

In his address to a joint session of Congress on June 23, 1913, for example, Wilson explained the need of a Federal Reserve System thus: "It is absolutely imperative that we should give the business men of this country a banking and currency system by means of which they can make use of the freedom of enterprise and of individual initiative which we are about to bestow upon them." His reference was to the protective tariff which many if not most of these same businessmen did not wish to be freed from at all. But even so, Wilson told them that they were getting something they wanted in return; that the reason in both cases was something to which they attached a high value (i.e., freedom of enterprise and individual initiative); that in both cases it was a matter of principle and not of punitive action; and that the government wanted to confer a favor.

Now see how subtly he chides businessmen because they have not been true to their avowed belief in free enterprise:

We are about to set them free; we must not leave them without the tools of action when they are free. We are about to set them free by removing the trammels of the protective tariff. Ever since the Civil War they have waited for this emancipation and for the free opportunities it will bring with it. It has been reserved for us to give it to them. Some fell in love, indeed, with the slothful security of their dependence upon the Government; some took advantage of the shelter of the nursery to set up a mimic mastery of their own within its walls. Now both the tonic and the discipline of liberty and maturity are to ensue.

The Philosophy and Policies of Woodrow Wilson

Woodrow Wilson believed in the creative state. His was not a negative philosophy avowing only that that state governs best which governs least; on the contrary, as an able political economist he realized that government has an indispensable, positive role in the economy. We see this when we read on in the same address to the two houses of Congress:

> It is not enough to strike the shackles from business. The duty of statesmanship is not negative merely. It is constructive also. We must show that we understand what business needs and that we know how to supply it. No man, however casual and superficial his observation of the conditions now prevailing in the country, can fail to see that one of the chief things business needs now, and will need increasingly as it gains in scope and vigor in the years immediately ahead of us, is the proper means by which readily to vitalize its credit, corporate and individual, and its originative brains. What will it profit us to be free if we are not to have the best and most accessible instrumentalities of commerce and enterprise? What will it profit us to be quit of one kind of monopoly if we are to remain in the grip of another and more effective kind? How are we to gain and keep the confidence of the business community unless we show them how both to aid and protect it?

The Federal Reserve Act, passed nine months after Wilson became President, was in many ways the most important single piece of legislation enacted during his entire tenure. Moreover, it was put through Congress in record time despite buffeting from both the Progressive left and the banker right. Something of Wilson's tenacity of purpose and his skill as legislative leader were revealed in this epochal battle. At issue was a decision for either private banking or socialized banking, or a compromise between the two, and Wilson finally secured the compromise. During these bitter debates, both in Congress and in the press, Wilson first was strangely surprised and profoundly disturbed by the dimensions of the struggle; later, serenely unaware of the meaning and seriousness of the revolt among his own supporters; then, entering the thick of the fray to fight, cajole, plead, and promise that a successful compromise would be found; next, faced with the prospect of yielding, which he did not; then, during the summer of 1913, moving from crisis to crisis; and finally, in the face of a torrent of abuse and criticism, remaining immovable and becoming at last successful. As in another major battle involving concentrated private power versus public power, it was Louis Brandeis who seemingly influenced the President as much as anyone. Only the government can be allowed to issue currency, Brandeis insisted. "The conflict between the policies of the Administration and the desires of the financiers and of big business, is an irreconcilable one," he counseled, and the progressive sentiment must be supported. It was this stiffening influence on the President that apparently won over Carter Glass of Virginia and made possible the compromise between him at one extreme and McAdoo and Bryan at the other.

Wilson's characteristics as legislative leader, commented on above, are also clearly demonstrated in the fight he led for the Clayton and Federal Trade Commission Acts in 1914, the year following the Federal Reserve Act. Louis Brandeis and his close friend and associate George L. Rublee had been at work since October, 1913, on antitrust legislation, the main feature of which was a strong trade commission. One of the President's most successful methods was to prepare the country well in advance for his major enactments rather than to "spring" seemingly radical proposals suddenly and run the risk of irrational repulsion. Accordingly, in his first annual address, delivered to a joint session of Congress on December 2, 1913, Wilson planted this idea:

I think it will be easily agreed that we should not let the Sherman antitrust law stand, unaltered, as it is, with its debatable ground about it, but that we should as much as possible reduce the area of that debatable ground by further and more explicit legislation, and should also supplement that great act by legislation which will not only clarify it but also facilitate its administration and make it fairer to all concerned.

Nothing to make the stock market take a nose dive in that utterance— at least the way Wilson put it!

"The best informed men of the business world," said Wilson in a special address to Congress on antitrust legislation, on January 20, 1914, "condemn the methods and processes and consequences of monopoly as we condemn them; and the instinctive judgment of the vast majority of business men everywhere goes with them." We are all agreed, he continued, that "private monopoly is indefensible and intolerable"; nothing hampers business like uncertainty; and the new legislation, which he sketched in broad strokes, "will bring new men, new energies, a new spirit of initiative, new blood, into the management of our great business enterprises." It will open the field of industrial development and origination to scores of men who have been obliged to serve when their abilities entitled them to direct. It will immensely hearten the young men coming on and will greatly enrich the business activities of the whole country.

The Philosophy and Policies of Woodrow Wilson

This was late in January of 1914, and the four Clayton bills were introduced immediately afterward. So successful was Wilson as molder of public opinion and as legislative tactician that the Federal Trade Commission had been created by September of the same year, and the consolidated Clayton Bill, containing new antitrust provisions, had been passed and signed by the middle of October.

One of Woodrow Wilson's great strengths as a political leader was that he avoided alienating whole classes of voters, the business community, for example. He assumed that most people are decent, patriotic, and intelligent, and his appeal was always expressed in the words and sentiments of those whose interests were to be affected by the proposed legislation. He spoke as one of them, not as one opposed to them.

Wilson felt so strongly about the distinction between personal and institutional culpability that in some rare but important instances it probably adversely affected the legislation he succeeded in enacting. Toward the latter part of his special message on monopoly problems, for example, the President enunciated a principle, the effect of which was to be great in subsequent draftsmanship and administration:

Penalties and punishments should fall, not upon business itself, but upon individuals who use the instrumentalities of business to do things which public policy and sound business practice condemn. Every act of business is done at the command or upon the initiative of some ascertainable person or group of persons. These should be held individually responsible and the punishment should fall upon them, not upon the business organization of which they make illegal use. It should be one of the main objects of our legislation to divest such persons of their corporate cloak and deal with them as with those who do not represent their corporations, but merely by deliberate intention break the law. Business men the country through would, I am sure, applaud us if we were to take effectual steps to see that the officers and directors of great business bodies were prevented from bringing them and the business of the country into disrepute and danger.

This is a fine brand of liberalism and of individualism, and we must fight to strengthen it and keep it alive. But in this case, my own belief is that Wilson carried his idea too far. Just as the individual in most cases is held by laws to be responsible for his acts, so likewise should the corporate entity be held reponsible.

What we are to conclude about the living qualities of Wilson's domestic program depends upon the basic assumption with which we begin.

Wilson the Domestic Reformer

If one naïvely asks, "Has all of the legislation of the Wilsonian era withstood the ravages of time?" the answer is, unquestionably, "No." But as has been suggested, this is a thoughtless and unfair question. The reason that new legislation is constantly required is that conditions constantly change, and with every significant change the need exists for amendatory or new legislation. Hence, the fair question concerning Wilson's legislation is, "Has the pattern of legislation remained pretty much the same, and did his legislation provide a solid formulation on which to build?" When the question is so formulated, the answer is an unequivocal "Yes."

At the time Wilson came into power, about the only major regulations of the economy were through the Interstate Commerce Commission (1887) and the Sherman Antitrust Act (1890). There had been a good deal of assistance to business enterprises and little outright government ownership. Wilson continued, but strengthened, this tradition. And with remarkably little change—considering the fact that we have weathered a major depression and two world wars—this is still the balance of private-public power in the United States today. That we have succeeded in maintaining this distinctive method of public control, which is so unlike that of most countries, stressing regulation and control and minimizing outright public ownership, is due, I think, not only to the vigor and individualism of inherited forces in the United States but also to the economic statesmanship of the Wilsonian era.

To the Interstate Commerce Commission Wilson added two great, new regulatory bodies: the Federal Trade Commission and the Federal Water Power Commission. To the departments of Commerce and Agriculture he added another, representing labor, the third member of the triumvirate. To the strictly judicial method of enforcing the antitrust laws he added an administrative arm, growing out of the old Bureau of Corporations; this was one of the first moves toward what has since become so widespread, that is, the substitution of administration for strictly judicial methods in major areas of economic regulation because administration, being continuous and flexible, is so much more effective. And finally, underlying the entire edifice was the Federal Reserve System, the first major development in banking since the Civil War, with its built-in stabilizers that have led to the parallel device of the President's Council of Economic Advisers, created under the provisions of the Employment Act of 1946 to help formulate fiscal controls.

The Philosophy and Policies of Woodrow Wilson

Judged by our criteria, the most successful of Wilson's major laws has been, I suppose, the Federal Reserve Act of 1913. Although subsequently amended and improved, it has passed the test of time so well that there is remarkably little criticism of its major features, and proposals for a drastic replacement of it, as by creating a central bank under government ownership and control, are seldom heard. Supplementing it, of course, are now such valuable adjuncts as the Federal Deposit Insurance Corporation, the Securities and Exchange Commission, and the holding company legislation of the Roosevelt administration. Still, it is no exaggeration to say that the Federal Reserve System is basic to all these.

The verdict concerning the antitrust legislation of 1914 is not, unfortunately, nearly so clear. Among those who can be counted upon to take an impartial view of this subject, the tendency seems to be to divide into a right and left wing, with a consequent weakening of the solid center. The right wing wants to abolish the antitrust laws entirely and rely upon the self-regulation of industry (incidentally this group was strong and vocal even in Wilson's time), or, alternatively, greatly to reduce the punitive provisions and to provide for advance consultation and trade practice conferences. The left wing, in contrast, holds that the antitrust laws now serve no useful purpose except to give the farmer, laborer, and consumer a false sense of security; in short, that the laws themselves are a false front for monopoly. The left wing usually advocates the partial or complete socialization of monopolies and government coercion to secure more effective competition where that is still possible.

I often wonder what Woodrow Wilson would say and do about the antitrust laws if he were alive today. Of one thing I am sure: for a different condition or magnitude he would not hesitate to propose a new and appropriate remedy, because his ultimate test was human welfare, not intellectual preferences. Would he think that the laws could be made to work? I think he would—but not without much overhauling and strengthening. He might start by consolidating and codifying the separate laws; to this codification he would probably add new and stronger provisions defining what, both structurally and behaviorally, constitutes monopoly and restraint of trade. I would expect him to differentiate between size per se and size that is technologically justified; to propose limits beyond which corporations would not be allowed to trespass through consolidations and mergers; and to attempt

236

to determine what constitutes optimum size in terms of public welfare. Although I am not sure of all these things, of this I am convinced: he would take the case to the people and see to it that the antitrust agencies got the kind of financial support from Congress that Franklin D. Roosevelt secured for the first time during the latter part of his administration. And I feel equally sure that he would sit down with labor and farm leaders and find out why so many of them are either lukewarm or secretly hostile to the antitrust laws, because he would realize that without the spirited and constant support of these groups the antitrust laws might become what their critics say they already are—a mask for privilege.

Arthur Link, in dealing with Wilson's handling of the monopoly problem, points out two things that are admittedly damaging to the sanguine view just expressed. Link refers to Senator James A. Reed's statement that when the Clayton Bill was first drafted: "It was a raging lion with a mouth full of teeth. It has degenerated to a tabby cat with soft gums, a plaintive mew, and an anaemic appearance. It is a sort of legislative apology to the trusts, delivered hat in hand, and accompanied by assurances that no discourtesy is intended." Link then adds, "Of course, this was largely true, but it was true because the administration had put all faith in the trade commission plan and had given up its effort to prohibit restraints of trade by statutory action."[1] I am a little suspicious of this statement as a fair conclusion from the facts. Rather, I think Wilson did get some statutory definitions of monopolistic practices, though clearly (in today's perspective) not nearly enough. Second, I think it quite likely that Wilson got as much, or nearly as much, as he could have got at the time. And finally, I think the real difficulty has been that presidential leaders have shirked their duty in not amending the laws in a bold and thoroughgoing way as Wilson did in 1914. From 1890 to 1914 was a matter of twenty-four years. Twenty-four years later, 1938, might have been a good time to undertake a second overhaul of the monopoly laws because the weaknesses were then crystal clear, and enforcement, within existing limitations, had reached its zenith. But, of course, World War II interfered, and the job has still not been done. And it will not be done, it seems apparent, unless a national leader such as Wilson is able to penetrate the brooding lethargy behind which lingers the American's traditional belief in competition and free entry into markets.

[1] *Woodrow Wilson and the Progressive Era* (New York: Harper & Bros., 1954), pp. 72–73.

The Philosophy and Policies of Woodrow Wilson

Wilson, being steeped in history and political philosophy, would clearly not countenance today's roseate complacency, such as that expressed by John K. Galbraith, that countervailing powers inherent in the system will take care of everything if we but bide our time patiently. Nor would he have much confidence, I believe, except as a matter of expediency, in the modern idea of monopolistic competition. He would most certainly agree with the points made by Adolf Berle in *The Twentieth Century Capitalist Revolution*, that economic power is no different from political power and that rulers from time immemorial have always tried to rationalize their excessive powers by merely avowing, "You can trust me, even if history proves otherwise." And he would conclude, I think, that the greater the mass of power in labor, corporations, agriculture, and government, the greater become the dangers of eventual abuse and either domination or violence. This conclusion is fully borne out in all his private and public utterances on this crucial subject. But, at the same time, it seems likely that he would be prepared to make a distinction, as most scholars are prone to do today, between technological advances that require size and produce efficiencies and those that are due to financially inspired mergers resulting in conglomerate industrial empires and a holding-company type of variegated but concentrated control.

To substantiate this thesis we have but to turn to the record of Wilson's own writings. He had a positive approach to competition, one resembling that of the late Henry Simons; he did not merely pay lip service to an abstract idea. In his opening message to the Sixty-third Congress, for example, Wilson said:

We must abolish everything that bears the semblance of privilege or of any kind of artificial advantage, and put our business men and producers under the stimulation of a constant necessity to be efficient, economical, and enterprising—masters of competitive supremacy, better workers and merchants than any in the world.

In Wilson's writings there are many references to the difference between good and bad big businesses, and I bring you one that indicates the general tenor of his thinking:

A trust is an arrangement to get rid of competition, and a big business is a business that has survived competition by conquering in the field of intelligence and economy. A trust does not bring efficiency to the aid of business: it *buys efficiency out of business*. I am for big business, and I am against the trust.

And in the next paragraph of *The New Freedom* he explains why this is so:

You know perfectly well that a trust business staggering under a capitalization many times too big is not a business that can afford to admit competitors into the field; because the minute an economical business, a business with its capital down to hard pan, with every ounce of its capital working, comes into the field against such an over-loaded corporation, it will inevitably beat it and undersell it; therefore it is to the interest of these gentlemen that monopoly be maintained. They cannot rule the markets of the world in any way but monopoly. It is not surprising to find them helping to found a new party with a fine program of benevolence, but also with a tolerant acceptance of monopoly.[2]

Wilson's pithy observations concerning overcapitalization were borne out during the giant power investigations of the late 1920's and in the various railway reorganizations this country has gone through. An even more trenchant criticism of the inherent evils of intrenched power, however, is found in his reference to freedom or restriction of entry to competition:

American industry is not free, as once it was free; American enterprise is not free; the man with only a little capital is finding it harder to get into the field, more and more impossible to compete with the big fellow. Why? Because the laws of the country do not prevent the strong from crushing the weak.[3]

Freedom is in inverse ratio to size. Only the small can afford to be left completely free because they can harm no one; but if a similar freedom is accorded the Gargantuas, the danger is that they will strip the small of their non-defendable freedom and that they will eventually lose even their own.

The reason Wilson was so successful a domestic reformer that his ideas and his accomplishments are as timely today as they were forty years ago is, I believe, attributable not merely to his personal traits but also to the fact that he was trained equally in history, economics, and political science; and from this concentration, plus his spiritual heritage, he developed what the British have long called (and still do, though not so frequently) a "moral philosophy."

Wilson's basic tenets, as I read them in his private and public writings, provide a remarkably clear concept of his values, his institutional beliefs, and his theory of the political economy. He stressed justice as

[2] (Garden City: Doubleday, 1913), p. 180. [3] *Ibid.*, p. 15.

the cement of human relationships, a belief in human values and human perfectibility, an insistence on equality of opportunity, a belief that strength and wisdom come from the soil and from the common people, and a fierce championing of liberty as the condition precedent to all orderly growth and change. He was in the tradition of Jefferson, Jackson, Lincoln, and Cleveland. But, as I have previously indicated, he probably excelled all of these in his conscious attention to economics.

In his first inaugural address he stressed the theme of justice:

> The firm basis of government is justice, not pity. These [his proposed reforms] are matters of justice. There can be no equality of opportunity, the first essential of justice in the body politic, if men and women and children be not shielded in their lives, their very vitality, from the consequences of great industrial processes which they cannot alter, control, or singly cope with.

And in his first annual address to Congress he called for an effective employers' liability act and then added, "We ought to devote ourselves to meeting pressing demands of plain justice like this as earnestly as to the accomplishment of political and economic reforms. Social justice comes first. Law is the machinery for its realization and is vital only as it expresses and embodies it."

Woodrow Wilson, although an intellectual, understood the minds and aspirations of the common people as few political leaders ever have, before or since. A few quotations from *The New Freedom* will make that point abundantly clear: "I believe, as I believe in nothing else, in the average integrity and the average intelligence of the American people, and I do not believe that the intelligence of America can be put into commission anywhere. I do not believe that there is any group of men of any kind to whom we can afford to give that kind of trusteeship." "What this country needs above everything else," said Wilson at another point, "is a body of laws which will look after the men who are on the make rather than the men who are already made. Because the men who are already made are not going to live indefinitely, and they are not always kind enough to leave sons as honest as they were." No country, he continued, can afford to have its prosperity originated by a small controlling class. Every country is renewed out of the ranks of the unknown, not out of the ranks of those already famous and powerful and in control. And then, speaking of the monopoly question, he observed, "For my part, I want the pigmy to have a chance to come out. And I foresee when the pigmies will be so much more athletic, so much more astute, so much more active, than the giants, that it will be a case of Jack the giant-killer."[4]

But before there can be justice or an assured chance for those with ability to rise, there must be equality of opportunity. In a ringing statement, full of pathos and hope, Wilson stated:

There has come over the land that un-American set of conditions which enables a small number of men who control the government to get favors from the government; by those favors to exclude their fellows from equal business opportunity; by those favors to extend a network of control which will presently dominate every industry in the country, and so make men forget the ancient time when America lay in every hamlet, when America was seen in every fair valley, when America displayed her great forces on the broad prairies, ran her fine fires of enterprise up over the mountainsides and down into the bowels of the earth, and eager men were everywhere captains of industry, not employees; not looking to a distant city to find out what they might do, but looking about among their neighbors, finding credit according to their character, not according to their connections, finding credit in proportion to what was known to be in them and behind them, not in proportion to the securities they held that were approved where they were not known. . . . Is that freedom? That is dependence, not freedom.[5]

"We must abolish everything that bears even the semblance of privilege or of any kind of artificial advantage," thundered Wilson in one of his early addresses to Congress.

Two of the most beautiful chapters in Wilson's *The New Freedom*— "Life Comes from the Soil" and "The Liberation of a People's Vital Energies"—together reveal a good deal concerning Wilson's philosophical assumptions. In a passage from "Life Comes from the Soil," Wilson says:

When I look back on the processes of history, when I survey the genesis of America, I see this written over every page: that the nations are renewed from the bottom, not from the top; that the genius which springs up from the ranks of the unknown men is the genius which renews the youth and energy of the people. Everything I know about history, every bit of experience and observation that has contributed to my thought, has confirmed me in the conviction that the real wisdom of human life is compounded out of the experiences of the common men. The utility, the vitality, the fruitage of life does not come from the top to the bottom; it comes, like the natural growth of a great tree, from the soil, up through the trunk into the branches to the foliage and the fruit. The great struggling unknown masses of the men who are at the base of everything are the dynamic force that is lifting the levels of society. A nation is as great, and only as great, as her rank and file.[6]

[4] Pp. 64, 17, 169.   [5] Pp. 18–19.   [6] Pp. 79–80.

The Philosophy and Policies of Woodrow Wilson

Freedom, Wilson once told Congress, is like clearing the decks, removing the shackles, allowing the energies of those with initiative to flow forth spontaneously. Wilson's concept of liberty was not a negative one; it was a positive one. It was to be free to do something, not merely the right to be left alone. On another occasion, speaking at Independence Hall in Philadelphia, the President said: "Liberty does not consist, my fellow citizens, in mere general declarations of the rights of man. It consists in the translation of those declarations into definite action."

It was one of the sources of Wilson's strength that he would never allow a label to be attached to his philosophy, be it liberal, progressive, democratic, or independent. He was all of these things because at base he was great humanitarian. That he was an independent, because he put humanity and principles above personal and party advantage, Wilson said again and again. In one of his major political speeches, for example, he insisted:

I am not an independent voter, but I hope I can claim to be an independent person, and I want to say this distinctly: I do not love any party any longer than it continues to serve the immediate and pressing needs of America. I have been bred in the Democratic party; I love the Democratic party; but I love America a great deal more than I love the Democratic party; and when the Democratic party thinks that it is an end in itself, then I rise up and dissent.[7]

He did not hesitate to call himself a progressive or a radical, but he was always careful to define what he meant by these terms. In *The New Freedom* he said this about being a progressive: "I am, therefore, forced to be a progressive, if for no other reason, because we have not kept up with our changes of conditions, either in the economic field or in the political field. We have not kept up as well as other nations have." Or, again, "All that progressives ask or desire is permission—in an era when 'development,' 'evolution,' is the scientific word—to interpret the Constitution according to the Darwinian principle; all they ask is recognition that a nation is a living thing and not a machine."

And here is his definition of an American radical:

I tell you, the so-called radicalism of our times is simply the effort of nature to release the generous energies of our people. This great American people is at bottom just, virtuous, and hopeful; the roots of its being are in the soil

[7] *Messages and Papers of the Presidents* (Bureau of National Literature edition, 1917), p. 8333.

of what is lovely, pure, and of good report, and the need of the hour is just that radicalism that will clear a way for the realization of the aspirations of a sturdy race.[8]

But most of all, Wilson was a true humanitarian whose dream of America was the dream of all peoples. He once said in a speech at Pittsburgh: "Life, gentlemen—the life of society, the life of the world— has constantly to be fed from the bottom. It has to be fed by those great sources of strength which are constantly rising in new generations. Red blood has to be pumped into it. New fiber to be supplied. That is the reason I have always believed in popular institutions."

Finally, Wilson said two things that to me express the interdependence of domestic and foreign policy better than anything I have read in a long time. The first is from *The New Freedom:*

The reason America was set up was that she might be different from all the nations of the world in this: that the strong could not put the weak to the wall, that the strong could not prevent the weak from entering the race. America stands for opportunity. America stands for a free field and no favor. America stands for a government responsive to the interests of all. And until America recovers those ideals in practice, she will not have the right to hold her head high again amidst the nations as she used to hold it.[9]

The second is from a speech delivered in New York. Insisting that America's aims and those of the world ought to be one and the same, Wilson said:

The interesting and inspiring thing about America, gentlemen, is that she asks nothing for herself except what she has a right to ask for humanity itself. We want no nation's property. We mean to question no nation's honor. We do not wish to stand selfishly in the way of the development of any nation. We want nothing that we cannot get by our own legitimate enterprise and by the inspiration of our own example; and, standing for these things, it is not pretension on our part to say that we are privileged to stand for what every nation would wish to stand for, and speak for those things which all humanity must desire.[10]

For all these reasons—and as I said at the outset—Woodrow Wilson's ideas are as changeless and as timeless as when first he expressed them.

[8] Pp. 34, 48, 89.

[9] P. 221.

[10] *Messages and Papers of the Presidents,* pp. 8069–70.

CHAPTER SIXTEEN

Woodrow Wilson: An Appraisal and Recapitulation*

By
August Heckscher

The centennial celebration for Woodrow Wilson has helped us to see this American President in a fresh light. A generation of younger students and scholars has found itself for the first time brought face to face with a figure who had been dim in their consciousness. The mists have cleared, mists caused by passing time and old controversies; and he stands there "clearly seen and heroic"—not quite the same person his contemporaries loved or hated, but still a great leader, summoning us to causes which have not yet been won.

"We meet him wherever we turn." So Thoreau said of the martyred John Brown. During the centennial year we have met Wilson in many guises—as party chief, administrator, world prophet, scholar, President, philosopher. We have seen his shortcomings along with his virtues, his failures along with the triumph which no passing defeat could obscure. I would like to think that he emerges from this reappraisal at the same time more commanding and more human. For at this distance it is not necessary to gloss over the man's weaknesses; and it is not possible to conceal from ourselves his greatness.

I cannot claim to be an "old Wilsonian." I never knew the man, never heard him speak. Yet I remember as if it were yesterday the moment when, as a schoolboy, I first took down from the shelf in my school library a biography of Wilson—it was William Allen White's biography, still worth reading for the wizardry of Emporia's journalistic sage. At that time Wilson had been dead for more than half a decade. Yet he lived for me; and afterward as I read his collected

* Paper delivered at the Annual Meeting of the American Political Science Association, Washington, D.C., September, 1956.

speeches I felt that in no small part my interests had been wakened and given form by that encounter.

Wilson liked to feel that his career would in the end be rightly judged; for as a historian he knew that the verdict of the day would ultimately be set straight, that its distortions would be corrected and its passions cooled. He spoke of the quiet men, sitting in their studies apart, who would have the last word. For them, he believed, the purity of a man's motives and the rectitude of his purposes would weigh more heavily in the scales than the cries of the contemporary market place. Yet it was Wilson's misfortune to fare rather poorly with the scholars who first returned to him. When the violent partisanship of his own day subsided, the New Deal was engaging the attention of the country; it seemed in many of its aspects to represent a tradition directly contrary to that of the Wilsonian New Freedom. World War II found the students of diplomacy more intent on avoiding the errors of the former President than on profiting from his example.

More recently, Wilson scholars and biographers have seemed in many cases not really to like the man to whom they devoted such prodigies of detailed research. Even where they tried to be fair, it was the kind of fairness which balanced a favorable judgment with an unfavorable one, and in the process they missed the scale of the man, the essence of his spirit, and the heroic dimensions of the stage on which his greatest battles were fought.

Yet the tale, rightly seen, is extraordinary enough to capture the imagination of subsequent generations. We could search the records of free government everywhere without coming upon anything quite like the story of this scholar and dreamer, projected suddenly into affairs and casting across the world scene a shadow of godlike proportions. No man, in our history at least, has been elected to the Presidency who had brooded so long upon the nature of government. Had Wilson been defeated in his 1912 campaign, we should have gone on to the end of time wondering what would have been the outcome if the philosopher had really been made king. But Wilson was not defeated—at least not then; and in terms of drama and tragedy the result surpasses what the most daring imagination could have conceived. We know the end of the story—the idealist made a prisoner of his ideals, the proud man brought to a fall. Yet Wilson was never a prisoner really; some glint of the man's spirit went out to illumine causes still unborn. And even in his fall there was a quality of faith that turned darkness into a kind of light.

The movie of Wilson which the Woodrow Wilson Foundation has recently completed contains one scene which I can never view without emotion. In an old newsreel shot, the defeated warrior is at the window of the house on S Street, Washington, where he lived in retirement. A crowd of well-wishers has gathered below. Wilson's words are spoken: "That we shall prevail is as sure as that God reigns." Then the stricken man lifts his arm to close the window. Three times he tries, unable to muster sufficient strength, and the arm falls limp at his side. There is the grim epilogue of the Wilson story—the defiant spirit in the shattered body, the immortal ideal embodied in a frail and doomed institution.

Yet it is not my purpose to dwell on these final scenes. That is the Wilson too easily remembered. We recall the dour figure with the drawn visage and set jaw, the man who faced implacable enemies and went down before a physical stroke. But by comparison how seldom do we see in the mind's eye that other Wilson, the young college professor repeatedly voted by his students the most popular teacher on the campus; the scholar who quit his study as one born to lead and filled politics with the zest of righteous battle! In thinking of this lecture I took down Bliss Perry's charming autobiography, *And Gladly Teach*; there one finds that younger Wilson. The gay Irish streak was later to grow dim, but the affection, the gentle gallantry which Perry notes, endured through the fire of searing battles to cast its glow around the circle of his trusted friends. Perry came to Princeton in the nineties; he left before Wilson became president of the university. He knew only the happy years: "We were all in Arcadia then," he says. That Wilson was cold, that he did not listen to those who disagreed with him, were inventions, he adds, of subsequent times.

One is tempted to see the Wilson of this period in terms which he applied to his own hero, Burke. We must remember what extraordinary success had come to him as a young scholar, how already he was being offered the presidencies of several universities, how his fame as a speaker had spread. "It was pleasing and indeed touching"—so the young Wilson writes of Burke—"to see how his companions thus freely accorded him the immunities and privileges of a prince among them. No one failed to perceive how large and imperial he was, alike in natural gifts and in the wonderful range of his varied accomplishments." Yet even Perry, it is interesting to observe, did not foresee the future in store for his colleague. He supposed that in this success, surrounded by so many marks of affectionate esteem, Wilson had attained what his heart desired.

It was characteristic of Wilson that he should burn with an inner resolve, never fully persuaded that he was performing the work he had been called to do. In the successive stages of his career he stepped repeatedly into new fields, acting as if he had always been fated for the change. As president of Princeton, with no previous experience in administration, he took up the reins of government with a sure hand. In New Jersey politics he showed the bosses a thing or two about their own game. The nation's liberal leader seemed in 1912 to have been made for the great work waiting to be done, and even foreign policy became in due course an element he moved in naturally. This variousness has been a source of some of the misunderstanding about Wilson; it is assumed that he could not have been quite serious in any single stage, when he could pass with such consummate mastery into the next.

Wilson himself was conscious of the difficulties. He complained of the sense of uprooting, of lost anchorages, as he was driven forward into the new life of action and politics. Yet he had walked confidently from the start. "Who shall show us the way to this place?" he asked at the climax of his Princeton Sesquicentennial address, after describing the "perfect place of learning." He must have known that the charge would fall to none other than himself. "I wish there were some great orator," he declared, "who could go about and make men drunk with this spirit of self-sacrifice . . . [in] accents which would ring like tones of reassurance around the whole circle of the globe." He was to be that orator, in days when the foundations of the civilized world seemed to be falling.

The more we know of Wilson, indeed, the more we have the feeling that he was all of a piece, as if everything were within this extraordinary man, destined to unfold in season. Wilson himself would have thought it was a divine plan which he fulfilled, and that faith was the secret of his strength as it was the cause of many of the qualities which turned men against him.

I shall come back to this matter of Wilson's faith, but I would first like to speak of another factor which has sometimes set him apart from the present generation. I mean his being a deliberate and artful stylist. Wilson set out in youth to become a practiced writer and speaker. He learned by heart passages from the great English orators, and we have glimpses of the young man declaiming in the woods or in his father's deserted church at night. His early writings are often mannered and artificial, the self-conscious experiments of a man trying to find his voice and accent. Robert Louis Stevenson, it will be remembered, confessed to a similar course as a young man. He had played "the sedulous ape," he said, to the masters of English prose; and his critics have never quite forgiven him the indiscretion. Yet with such men the process does not stop with imitation; they go on to a style unmistakably their own. One can take up Wilson anywhere and his tone is in the words. As he matured, and as the great tasks fell to him, the tone deepens. The straining after effect ceases, until the ultimate achievement is long passages that stand with Lincoln or with Churchill (as these stand with Burke) in the anthology of English political prose.

One authority on Wilson has spoken of "character as statecraft." Here I would speak briefly of "style as statecraft." For the point about Wilson as a stylist was that he conceived the accomplishment to be not a mere ornament, a crown upon other gifts and qualities; he thought of it, rather, as the very essence of leadership. Style, he believed, lifted men and women to the level where action in great causes was possible, brought issues to life and lighted the whole political stage. Excellence in speaking and writing has been considered desirable in all free countries except possibly of late in our own; but too often it has been as a graceful instrument or a means to a secondary career in seasons of political exile. Wilson made it the basis of his power. "Words have cut as deep as the sword," he said in the course of his triumphant European tour at the close of the war. This was not an exaggeration. And the words had been very largely his own—the fruit of arduous training.

As a writer Wilson first sought to extend his reach, then as a teacher. The classroom gave him a forum which he felt could be used to greater advantage than most teachers realized. Eloquence touched and awakened the student, spoke straight to the spirit as facts by themselves could never do. Imagination, he wrote characteristically, was quite as important as scholarship, and the good lecture was "a thing of conviction, of insight." By all accounts his own lectures were supremely good. There are men alive today for whom the experience of sitting in Wilson's classroom was one of the shaping events of their careers.

Still untested lay Wilson's ability to move men in the mass. Here, as he conceived it, was the real challenge. This scholar and intellectual felt within himself the power to communicate directly with men, to put fire to their visions and ideals. And nothing less, he believed, was adequate to the task of statesmanship. While still an undergraduate he had written of the elder Pitt that "His imagination was powerful enough to invest all plans of national policy with poetic charm." I repeat the words "poetic charm," for that is a quality one ordinarily expects national policy to be devoid of. Yet Wilson himself, when he emerged on the national scene, did indeed give to politics a sense of meaning and even of beauty—overtones of that divine provenance which can make victory in a cause ennobling and make even defeat seem not wholly vain. He had to do this, he realized well enough, amid the expediencies which politics inevitably exacts. The leader must wear "the harness of compromise"—so he wrote as a young man still waiting in the wings for destiny's call. But there comes a moment when that harness falls away, when the nation's soul is ready for the great cause to possess and transform it. Then the true orator speaks his faith without dissimulation or timidity. In the hour of ultimate revelation something, however, remains hidden, some intimation of powers too vast for words. And in that silence, a silence heavy with meaning, the orator becomes one with the prophet and with the poet.

In discussing style we have passed from the written to the spoken word. That is a dangerous transition. For oratory is of all forms of art the most treacherous, the most easily doomed to transience. The word conceived to be spoken before the crowd has rhythms of its own; if it performs its task it is different from that born merely to be read and to be remembered for its own sake, apart from the circumstances of its delivery. Wilson's speaking style had about it evident touches of incantation; men were to complain that they could not recall precisely what he had said, once the light of his utterance had been extinguished. These dangers to the purity and elegance of a man's style are doubled when speaking must be extemporaneous. In the volumes of Wilson's collected works the greater part is speaking of this kind—compositions forged by the mind at the moment of need, often spoken under the most adverse conditions and with none of the aids which electrical amplification and broadcast give today. To be redundant and bombastic in such circumstances would seem inevitable. It is re-markable that the quality of Wilson's style manages not only to survive but actually to find itself and to reach heights which scholarly pre-meditation could not assure.

Style in oratory is of a special kind. Lucidity is only a part of it, for the ultimate aim must be not so much to instruct the mind as to transform and renew it. It is to create, however transiently, a mood in which action of a certain kind becomes possible. Wilson's speaking, as we can judge it on the printed page after all these years, had this essential quality. He spoke quietly, in a voice seeming to address each individual in the largest hall. One still feels the intensity, the directness of communication, the action of mind upon mind. Perry Miller, writ-ing about Jonathan Edwards, has described this kind of oratory as "a consuming effort to make sounds become objects, to control and discipline the utterance so that words would immediately be registered not as noises but as ideas." Jonathan Edwards had said of his own preaching that "the main benefit is to be by the impression made on the mind in the time of it, and not by the effect that may arise after-wards as a remembrance."

To make such an impression on the mind "in the time of it" was vital to Wilson's statesmanship. For it was the essence of his appeal that he could stir men to do things which had appeared beyond their reach, to see visions which had hitherto lain clouded in self-interest. His educa-tional philosophy had demanded of young men what he called a period of withdrawal from the world; he feared that unless they were granted this boon in youth they might not afterward be able to keep them-selves whole amid the partial associations and narrow loyalties which the life of action required. Later he sought deliberately to make men transcend expediency and attain to the realm of duty. When he first entered public life his leadership had just this effect. Men and women felt that they moved in a purer air; the New Freedom, at least in its moral aspect, was the freedom to be one's best self. But it was at the climax of his career, when the problems of a new international order had become central, that Wilson came nearest to achieving the perfec-tion of his art. Under his spell, for an unforgettable moment, the image of a united mankind glimmered before men's minds. The League of Nations was at best an inadequate instrument. But in focusing men's thoughts upon it Wilson hoped that he could make them different from what they had been, that he could push back the frontiers of selfishness and radically enlarge the domain of the possible.

Style, of course, cannot do everything. Wilson's error was perhaps to have expected too much of the power which he felt within himself. Even the greatest of words leave the old and weatherbeaten world pretty much as it has always been—the prey of men's passions, of their rooted interests and unreasoning loyalties. The nationalism of centuries could not be dissipated, even though for a season men and women seemed earnestly to desire that it should be. Wilson's tragedy was that the effect of his preaching, so powerful "in the time of it," did not sufficiently persist afterward as a remembrance. All this must be admitted if we are to understand the meaning of his career. But in seeing how he fell short of the goal, let us not forget that he brought something to statesmanship which was not only infinitely exciting while he lived and fought but which has lessons for the future of free government. The heights which men have glimpsed they will sooner or later attain to. The resources which Wilson effectively tapped still lie below the surface, waiting for the man who shall once again call them to life.

I return now to the problem of Woodrow Wilson as a moralist. If it is difficult for us to understand the stylist, the moralist seems even more remote from our experience and comprehension. Yet here, too, we are dealing with something fundamental to Wilson's politics—not an ornamentation, not a pious gloss, not a mere invocation of the diety in the peroration. Religion was for him at the heart of politics because politics concerned itself with man's freedom. The battles he engaged in could all be seen in terms of the affirmation of the essential self, the transcendence of the attachments which narrowed and circumscribed the soul. At Princeton he had fought against the clubs primarily because the clubs took men out of the free air which he believed the student should breathe, plunging them into worldly values. In New Jersey he fought against the bosses. But it was no ordinary fight, because in his imagination he had elevated the bosses to representatives of an age-old tyranny.

The New Freedom, I have already suggested, was the freedom of a man to be his best self. Wilson saw the humanity of his day distorted by hidden power in both the political and economic spheres—by the bosses and by the trusts. Through the prevalence of association, he feared, men's consciences were being subdivided and parceled out. The individual was getting lost in the group—the lawyer in the great law office, the doctor in the large hospital, the entrepreneur within the folds of the corporation. To get the individual disengaged was the Wilsonian objective. On a far larger scale, when the issues of the World War had become clear in his mind, the same objective ruled his foreign policy. Wilson wanted to free men, once and for all, not only from such palpable tyranny as the Kaiser represented, but from the more subtle and more pervasive tyranny of nationalism.

Such freedom may be seen as part of the age-old political struggle. But with Wilson it was given an added dimension by his religious faith, by his concept of the individual and of his relationship to the Creator. Why did he want the individual to be free? So that he could do as he pleased? So that he could have leisure and devote himself to what the advertising writers like to call "gracious living"? Nothing of this sort. Wilson passionately desired freedom because he believed that only when men had achieved this state could they know God. Once the ties of worldly association had been duly subordinated, a man stood where he had always been meant to be: under the eye of the Creator, in a direct relationship with the source of all being. The individual walked a perilous path and faced in the end a fearful predicament. For in proportion as he was free he was his own, challenged to act yet doomed to fall short; alone, yet under the judgment of an implacable deity. Freedom was a challenge to duty and honor in a world where no man could be sure what duty was, or where the path of honor might lead.

History, as Wilson saw it, was full of the ambiguities of man's mortal lot. In one of his speeches he speaks of King David in the Old Testament. David, he says, was one of those men marked "in the history of mankind as the chosen instrument of God to do justice." Yet David himself was far from a perfect instrument. He was "a selfish and sinful man who one day must stand naked before the judgment of God." So, in the final test, Wilson must have seen himself: an instrument for good, but doomed to fall short of the goal. In a radio interview where I recently appeared with Wilson's daughter, Mrs. Eleanor Wilson McAdoo, the interviewer asked at one point whether it was true that Wilson had died after his defeat of a "broken heart."

The daughter paused for a moment. "No," she said proudly. "My father was a Christian. Christians don't die of a broken heart. Only egotists do that." The Christian, it may be said, sees himself as clay in the potter's hand; and it is not for the clay to bemoan the proportions of a vessel of which it cannot know the final outlines.

To enter public life with convictions of this sort is a dangerous thing; and Woodrow Wilson did not always escape the pitfalls in his way. The line between righteousness and self-righteousness is razor-thin. Wilson crossed over it on many occasions. He could be proud and wilful. He could be intolerant, not only of fools, but of wise men who disagreed with him. His enemies saw these shortcomings and did not forgive him for them. But the essence of Wilson was something very different: it was a noble ethical feeling which gave zest to battle, lifting men to a realization that great issues were at stake and that the outcome was meaningful to themselves and to history. To act was to take great risks; but not to act, where a good cause was involved, was cowardice and sin.

The coming of World War I put Wilson's faith to its severest test. He was personally handicapped, not having devoted to foreign affairs anything like the study which since youth he had been giving to con-stitutional and domestic issues. Moreover, his type of leadership, the direct persuasion of the citizenry, was not applicable to the concealed and tortuous processes of diplomacy. Worse than these factors was the nature of the crisis itself. As a moralist and philosopher Wilson could not but see the ambiguity of the motives animating the peoples on both sides; he could not but discern the shadowed and controversial back-ground of the struggle. The simple patriot viewed the grim picture in black and white. Wilson was on the outside, and he saw the tints and gradations. Speaking to a group in the White House early in the war, he remarked that "It would be impossible for men to go through the dark night of this terrible struggle if it were not that they believed they were standing, each on his own side, for some eternal principles of right." It was a reflection worthy of Lincoln, brooding with compas-sion upon the dilemmas of the Civil War. That it was infuriating to the Allies need hardly be stressed.

In the end, of course, Wilson was driven to the point where the German leaders—though not the German people—seemed the embodi-ment of wickedness; and he invoked force—"force to the uttermost, force without stint or limit"—as the only arbiter in the struggle. Yet I think it can be said in fairness that he never lost the sense that force by itself could settle nothing. Certainly he saw that victory would be a snare, if it involved terms imposed by arms and without roots in the age-old concepts of right and justice. Through the worst of the carnage he retained the sense of a truth higher than that which national self-interest and security sanction—a realization (again worthy of Lincoln's) that men's ways are not God's and that God's are not always discernible on this earth.

The postwar chapters are those which make Wilson seem most vulnerable today. The evangelical tone of his speeches abroad, his insistence on a mission which America was destined to fulfil, fall strangely in a generation where we have been taught that limited commitments and localized aims are the measure of a sound foreign policy. It should be noted in Wilson's defense that the Old World was longing ardently to hear just such a voice as his. Worn with internal strife, it waited for an influence from the outside which could heal and restore it. Wilson's appeal, moreover, was free of those overtones of complacency which have seemed so distasteful to many of us. He came to the issues of foreign policy refreshed and fortified by victories for a wider justice at home. He honestly believed that America, purified by reform and united by common discipline, was prepared to take leadership on the world stage. He spoke in terms of faith, not slogans; and he sought to establish the standards toward which we were moving as a nation, not to impose the precise forms of an economic or political status quo.

The reaction against Wilson in the years following World War II came largely from men who had grown disillusioned with a weak and confused universalism in foreign policy. They disliked the veneer of propaganda which was so frequently substituted for rational foresight and disciplined effort. To take one step at a time, to balance one's commitments against one's resources, to be prudent and practical—these seemed the criteria of sound policy. They were the criteria, moreover, which made it possible for a newly trained group of professional diplomats to play their role with efficacy. Granting everything in the way of healthy criticism which these men were able to contribute, it may still be pointed out that the example and tradition of Wilsonism are precious ingredients of America's claim to leadership.

The country's strength can seem diminished for lack of a clear sense of purpose, for lack of faith and a willingness to engage in large designs. The crusading spirit, just now in disrepute, may serve for other ends than the imposition of America's terms upon nations that are at odds with us. It may serve, as well, for an insistence upon justice, for an attack on racial bias and outmoded colonial systems. There are many reasons for saying, even in this sophisticated and realistic age, that the American experience is unique and that we must stand before the world for something more than our own self-interest, narrowly conceived. The adventure in freedom undertaken on this virgin continent, the welcome extended to men of all nations and creeds, have made us in fact a composite people, representative of some of mankind's best hopes. We are called to a large destiny. We are involved in more than our own national fate. It is when the knowledge of these things grows dim that we can return with profit to Wilson's example. With his moral commitment he points the way to a side of American policy which we forget or ignore at the cost of being something less than it is in our nature to be.

For my last point I would like to look at Wilson as a liberal leader. Here again he has been misunderstood and misjudged. We all know that Burke was his first hero; that he excluded Jefferson from his "Calendar of Great Americans" on the grounds that his thought had been weakened by a strain of alien philosophy; that he was once so politically imprudent as to express the wish that some way might be found of knocking Bryan, once and for all, into a cocked hat. Such evidence of Wilson's conservative tendencies cannot be discounted. Nor need we ignore the fact that as the president of an educational institution he did not invariably spurn the opportunity to placate the less enlightened members of the alumni body. Yet to stop here, and to argue that Wilson's leadership of the liberal Democratic forces was a maneuver designed to satisfy his ambitions, is to miss the whole point of the man. He had been a reformer from the start. From the days when as a boy he had begun tinkering with constitutions he had been out to change the established arrangements of things.

Wilson's first book, *Congressional Government*, can be read as an attempt to pierce the literary tradition which surrounded the Constitution. That was in itself a daring enough enterprise. Chesterton speaks somewhere of that dazzling type of imagination which sees what actually exists, instead of seeing what everyone says exists. But Wilson had more than imagination; he had reforming zeal. He wanted to transform the American system so as to centralize responsibility, focus power, reveal to the people what actually was being done and why. He wanted to get affairs out of the fog of the committee room into the light of the legislative chamber. Such a change is not a matter of organization

255

merely; it is bound to affect the spirit and scope of government. The young Wilson was much too astute an observer of history to suppose that responsible men, with legitimate power in their hands and the light of publicity upon them, would sit still and do nothing. He knew they would act; and he knew action was the chief end, not alone of life, but of government.

Wilson's urge for reconstruction of the governmental system was reinforced by his reading of American history. He saw clearly that with the closing of the frontier in 1890 something revolutionary had happened to our society. We had entered upon a new phase, when it was no longer possible to escape our problems by moving into unpeopled territories. We had to turn about and live with ourselves. We had to find ways to compromise and adjust the sectional claims which the post–Civil War growth had brought to the fore. A southerner, Wilson never viewed the country as a southerner, nor did he as an easterner. His eye ran across the whole continental expanse, seeing it in the richness and diversity of its life, the separate parts alive with expectations needing to be met if the health and vitality of the whole was to be assured. The old forms of government were not adequate to meet the challenge; Wilson asked consistently and eloquently for the kind of government which measured up to the needs of a new age.

His basic liberalism had roots, too, in his theory of the Constitution. When others were still seeing the Constitution as something which had been written once and for all, its content settled and defined by the founding fathers, the young scholar at Princeton was preaching a very different doctrine. He taught, rather, that the Constitution was a changing thing, a skeleton waiting to be given new flesh with each generation. The great judges were not men bound slavishly to precedent. They were statesmen; they were men with something of the quality of the prophet, something, even, of the poet. In due course Wilson was to find within the Constitution ample sanction for his own bold courses of action. In a man like Brandeis he was to find his ideal of what the good judge should be.

With all his inclinations thus bent to political action and to a kind of government capable of acting effectively, Wilson came into politics at a time when the trusts were preoccupying public attention. Had there been any doubt as to the side on which Wilson might find himself where other issues were concerned, there was none whatsoever in regard to the trusts. Wilson was on the side that wanted to check and control them. As I have already indicated, the trusts were for Wilson a moral problem before they were a political one. He saw them as a threat to man's freedom before he saw them as an incumbrance to the social order. It was in the conjunction of his moral and political sense that the fire was struck which permitted him to emerge as the crusading spokesman for the New Freedom.

Wilson's practical solution to the problem of the trusts was disappointing. A chasm separates the bold affirmations of the 1912 campaign speeches from the excessively prudent recommendations to the Congress after his election. Yet these practical solutions were, after all, for the day only. It was because he saw the moral problem so keenly that his thought endures with a genuine and continuing relevance. What was his real concern? The campaign speeches show the prescience with which he discerned the growing power of the group over the individual. Everywhere he found men losing the spirit of enterprise, the capacity to dare, the willingness to take risks which he deemed essential to the free life. Channels, formerly opened, were being closed; what he called "the man on the make" was losing ground to the man who was already made and secure in his protected position. There were bad trusts, of course, but these were not the heart of the matter. The heart of the matter was the trusts which hewed strictly to the law, which, more than that, were humane in their attitudes to the employees and enlightened in their sense of responsibility to the community. These, perhaps more than the others, were in danger of denying men their essential dignity.

For these good trusts Wilson used the phrase "philanthropic tyranny." He made it clear that he, for one, did not want to live under kind masters any more than under masters of a different stripe. To be sure, men might find satisfactions through participation in the group. They might even find happiness. But "I am not sure," Wilson had characteristically told the undergraduates at Princeton, "that it is of the first importance that you should be happy."

The tendencies which Wilson discerned in 1912 have been raveled out for all to see and face up to. Today the trusts are virtually all good trusts. The modern corporation is almost frighteningly enlightened. It has a soul—so much so that some observers are beginning to ask whether the soulless corporation, the butt of earlier reformers, was perhaps not preferable to this subtle and pervasive influence which tempts men without compelling them and ensnares them without making them conscious of their subjection. The company country club, the company athletic teams, the company psychiatrists are all signs of the new benevolence. Nor can we persuade ourselves that the young people fail to sense the attraction. It is hard to deny that a kind of happiness lies in the prestige, in the leisure, in the life-long security which the great corporations promise. That is not the question. The question, as Wilson put it, is whether it is of first importance that men should have happiness of this particular kind.

It is the great unanswered question of our generation. I do not know how the answer will finally be determined. But at least it should be clear that Wilson has something to say to us on this point—perhaps not the least important of all the insights which his life leaves to us.

I said at the beginning that many of Wilson's recent biographers miss the scale of the man and the dimensions of the stage on which he played his part. We shall not understand him in any of his roles—as not in the three which I have discussed: stylist, moralist, liberal—unless we can stand back and see the man whole. It was the peculiar mark of his leadership to give all he touched an aspect larger than life, to transform the fracases of education or politics into battles in which man's soul seemed to be at stake. He saved trivial things from seeming trivial; and in the greatest matters (to borrow a phrase which he used in a different connection) the sword he wielded seemed to carry the light of heaven upon its blade. Thus must we explain the excitement he brought to affairs; thus, too, the indignation of men opposing him, who found their ways judged by standards which they had not met before in the political arena. In the end Wilson was caught in the whirlwind he had loosed. He who had set forces in motion found himself, at the climax of his career, borne along by storms over which he could exert no control.

The frail mortal, the leader who had challenged the old Adam that is in all men, became a puppet in conflicts where the gods themselves seemed to be engaged. He went down, a broken man. But the gods are not done, and the great issues—war or peace, life or death—continue to be the stakes for which they play. Such is the theme of the drama in which this man played his part. Seeing it thus we can judge his shortcomings for what they were and see his character and example as history will see them—no mean character surely, no inconsiderable example:

> So huge the all-mastering thought that drove—
> So brief the time allowed—
> Nations, not words, he linked to prove
> His faith before the crowd.

INDEX

Index

Index

Index

Date Due

MAR 2 1 '61		
APR 1 0 '63		
APR 1 APR 15 '64		
APR 28 '64		
MAY 10 '65 APR 7 '66		
MAY 3 '67		
MAY 6 '68 MAY 4 7 MAY 4 7U		
MAR 16 '72		
MAR 31 72		
NOV 1 5 78		
AP 1 0 '79		
MR 23 '81		
AP 1 3 '81		
🄶🄱	PRINTED	IN U. S. A.	